# The Road to the
# National Assembly for Wales

edited by

J. BARRY JONES and DENIS BALSOM

UNIVERSITY OF WALES PRESS
CARDIFF
2000

British Library Cataloguing-in-Publication Data.
A catalogue record for this book is available from the British Library.

ISBN 0–7083–1483–X paperback
      0–7083–1492–9 hardback

Typeset at University of Wales Press
Printed in Great Britain by Dinefwr Press, Llandybïe

THE ROAD TO THE NATIONAL ASSEMBLY FOR WALES

# Contents

List of Maps, Charts and Tables                                    vii

Preface                                                             ix

Notes on Contributors                                               xi

Introduction
J. BARRY JONES                                                       1

1  Political Developments in Wales 1979–1997
   DENIS BALSOM                                                      5

2  Changes to the Government of Wales 1979–1997
   J. BARRY JONES                                                   15

3  Unfinished Business: Labour's Devolution Policy
   KEVIN MORGAN and GEOFF MUNGHAM                                   28

4  Too Important to be Left to the Politicians: The 'Yes' for
   Wales Story
   LEIGHTON ANDREWS                                                 50

5  The 'No' Campaign: Division and Diversity
   J. BARRY JONES (ed.)                                             70

6  No Dreads, only Some Doubts: The Press and the
   Referendum Campaign
   KEVIN WILLIAMS                                                   96

7 Television and the Referendum
  IOAN BELLIN                                                    123

8 The Referendum: A Flawed Instrument
  J. BARRY JONES (ed.)                                           133

9 The Referendum Result
  DENIS BALSOM                                                   151

10 Voting Patterns in the Referendum
   RICHARD WYN JONES, DAFYDD TRYSTAN and
   BRIDGET TAYLOR                                                161

11 Post-Referendum Politics
   J. BARRY JONES                                                176

12 Labour Pains
   J. BARRY JONES                                                194

13 The First Welsh General Election
   DENIS BALSOM                                                  212

14 The New Welsh Constitution: The Government of Wales
   Act 1998
   KEITH PATCHETT                                                229

15 Aftershock
   J. BARRY JONES and DENIS BALSOM                               265

   Conclusion
   J. BARRY JONES and DENIS BALSOM                               275

   Index                                                         284

# List of Maps, Charts and Tables

*Maps*
9.1  Voting in the 1997 devolution referendum                          158
10.1 Turnout in the 1997 devolution referendum                         163
10.2 Deviation in vote in the 1997 devolution referendum               165
13.1 The 1997 general election in Wales                                220
13.2 The 1999 National Assembly election                               221

*Charts*
9.1  Unemployment by referendum ranking                                155
9.2  National identity by referendum ranking                           157
13.1 General election tomorrow, May 1999                               223
13.2 Differential turnout                                              223
13.3 Vote switchers (profile of Plaid Cymru vote May 1999)            223
13.4 Vote switchers (defections to Plaid Cymru vote May 1999)         223
13.5 Vote switchers (why Labour voters switched to Plaid Cymru
     May 1999)                                                         224
13.6 Labour's 1997 vote (by 1999 behaviour)                            224

*Tables*
1.1  Changes in distribution of labour in the Welsh economy,
     1971–1991                                                           7
1.2  Parliamentary representation from Wales 1979–1997                  10
1.3  Shifts in public attitudes to devolution                          13
6.1  Circulation of English-language morning and evening daily
     press in Wales                                                     99
7.1  Network news coverage of the referendum campaign                 131
9.1  Results of the 1997 devolution referendum                        153
9.2  Change in support for devolution 1979–1997                        159
10.1 1997 Welsh referendum result                                     162

10.2 Age and referendum vote 1997   166
10.3 Age and referendum turnout 1997   167
10.4 Age and referendum vote 1979   168
10.5 Age and referendum turnout 1979   168
10.6 Party identification and referendum vote 1979 and 1997   169
10.7 Party identification and referendum turnout 1979 and 1997   169
10.8 Country of birth and referendum vote 1997   170
10.9 Ability to speak Welsh and referendum vote 1997   170
10.10 Ability to speak Welsh and referendum turnout 1997   171
10.11 Self-ascribed national identity 1997   172
10.12 Television viewing and referendum vote 1997   173
12.1 Welsh Labour leadership election result 1998   203
12.2 Welsh Labour leadership election result 1999   210
13.1 Result of the first elections to the National Assembly for Wales May 1999   222

# *Preface*

The establishment of the National Assembly for Wales, arguably the first all-Wales political forum, is an event of great significance. Together with the new Scottish Parliament, the National Assembly will transform the character and shape of British politics. In a more profound fashion, it will change the face of Welsh politics, the policy process, administrative system and political culture. Clearly, the events that have brought this about merit careful consideration.

This book considers those events – the referendum in September 1997 and the first Welsh general election in May 1999 – and places them in context; the overwhelming rejection of devolution in the 1979 referendum, the eighteen years of continuous Conservative government and the development of a Welsh 'quangocracy', and the Labour Party's hesitant decision to renew its commitment to devolution. Against this background, the circumstances of the referendum and the general election are tracked and evaluated.

Although the book has an academic framework and an objective analysis, much of its contents present an insider's view of, for example, the erratic development of Labour's devolution policy, the 'Yes' campaign's attempt to dominate the agenda during the referendum campaign, and the 'No' campaign's largely successful ploy to isolate itself from the Conservative Party and frustrate Labour's intention of fighting the referendum on a Labour v. Conservative battleground. Consequently, the book gives a flavour of what the political organizers and activists were trying and, in many cases, failing to do. The book also recognizes the importance of post-referendum politics, which not only revealed tensions within parties but laid the foundations for a devolved party political system to parallel the devolution of executive functions to the National Assembly.

In the course of almost fifteen months the editors organized two conferences with the authors of chapters and met with several on an individual basis to discuss the appropriateness of this or that approach. The book was also the first joint project of the Welsh Governance Centre in Cardiff University and brought together academics from diverse disciplines with a common interest in Wales and its future development. At the end of the day we believe we have a unique record and evaluation of the most significant events of Welsh politics in the twentieth century.

J. B. J. and D. B.
Welsh Governance Centre
Cardiff University
March 2000

# Notes on Contributors

**J. Barry Jones**, Director, Welsh Governance Centre, Cardiff University.

**Denis Balsom**, Honorary Research Fellow, Welsh Governance Centre, Cardiff University.

**Leighton Andrews**, Director, Welsh Context.

**Ioan Bellin**, Researcher, HTV Political Unit.

**Richard Wyn Jones**, Director, Institute of Welsh Politics, University of Wales, Aberystwyth.

**Kevin Morgan**, Professor of European Regional Development, Welsh Governance Centre, Department of City and Regional Planning, Cardiff University.

**Geoff Mungham**, Senior Lecturer in Journalism, Welsh Governance Centre, School of Journalism, Media and Cultural Studies, Cardiff University.

**Keith Patchett**, Emeritus Professor of Public Law, University of Wales, and constitutional adviser.

**Bridget Taylor**, Academic Administrator in the Social Studies Faculty, University of Oxford.

**Dafydd Trystan**, Lecturer in Politics, Department of International Politics, University of Wales, Aberystwyth.

**Kevin Williams**, Senior Lecturer in Journalism, Welsh Governance Centre, School of Journalism, Media and Cultural Studies, Cardiff University.

# Introduction

J. BARRY JONES

Devolution to Scotland and Wales is arguably the most significant change to the constitution of the United Kingdom in the twentieth century. The establishment of the Irish Free State in 1922 redrew the boundaries of the United Kingdom but left its constitutional structures intact. By contrast, devolution has profound implications for the governmental process and the role of the Westminster Parliament. Furthermore, unlike 1979, Labour's plans to decentralize political power to Scotland and Wales in 1997 did not stand alone, but were part of a constitutional reform package agreed with the Liberal Democrats in the run-up to the general election. The package included the reform of the House of Lords, a commitment to consolidate London's government under an elected mayor and assembly and a rolling programme of devolution to the English regions. The significance which the Labour Party attached to the constitutional reform programmes can be gauged by its manifesto commitment. Devolution, which had consigned Labour to eighteen years in the political wilderness, was the first item on the legislative agenda of the new Labour government.

Against this background, it is surprising that the policy for Welsh devolution was approached with such exaggerated stealth. In mitigation one can understand a certain amount of caution. The Welsh Labour Party had been deeply divided by devolution and traumatized by the scale of its rejection in the 1979 referendum which appeared to leave no margin for doubt. Nevertheless, there were doubts. The executive devolution proposed for Wales in 1979 was, according to polls, the least likely to engender enthusiastic support; the referendum vote was as much a judgement on the Callaghan government as a rejection of devolution.[1] Those doubts increased during eighteen years of Conservative government, whose pursuit of vigorous monetarist polices radically restructured the Welsh economy. Yet despite the consequent shift of public opinion in favour of devolution (see chapter 1), Welsh Labour's leadership was more concerned with placating anti-devolutionists within the party than with developing a policy to enthuse the Welsh electorate. It was argued that as devolution was party policy, and fully approved by conference, winning the general election would be sufficient to ensure its introduction.

However, all this was set aside shortly before the start of the election campaign. 'New Labour' was determined to shed its reputation of a 'high tax' party, but the proposed Scottish Parliament was to have limited tax-raising powers. Scottish Conservatives identified the powers as a chink in Labour's armour and claimed the 'tartan tax' would impose additional burdens on Scottish taxpayers. The charge touched a raw nerve in New Labour. With very little, if any, consultation with his Scottish and Welsh Shadow Secretaries, Tony Blair announced that the devolution proposals would have to be approved by referendums in Scotland and Wales before the legislation could be introduced. The intention was to remove Scottish taxation as an issue. The Scottish electorate was to be asked two questions; one on devolution and the other on tax. They could vote either in favour of the tax-varying powers or to reject them. In both cases Labour would be absolved of responsibility and the Tories' 'tartan tax' jibe thus invalidated.

The referendum decision was driven solely by the Scottish tax issue, which was irrelevant to Wales, but Wales was dragged along on Scotland's coat tails much as it had been in 1979. Furthermore, Labour's Welsh devolution proposals, developed to resolve internal party tensions, were now obliged to gain popular approval. As in 1979, Welsh Labour found itself fighting a referendum for which it was not prepared, and in support of devolution proposals which it recognized were less than perfect. At this stage Ron Davies's expressed view, 'Devolution is a process not an event', acquired the status of a mantra, to be endlessly repeated as a statement of political faith and a tacit admission that the government's Welsh devolution proposals were inadequate.

Welsh Labour's 'local difficulties' with devolution clearly affected the general election campaign which overwhelmingly reflected British issues. The only slight deviation from the British norm was whether the Conservatives might lose all their Welsh seats and Wales would become a 'Tory-free' zone. The UK electoral outcome was regarded as such a foregone conclusion, that *The Western Mail* frequently demoted election stories from its front page and ran articles anticipating a Conservative defeat. Similarly, the publication of the four Welsh party manifestos made little impact. John Prescott (Labour's Welsh-born deputy leader) launched his party's Welsh manifesto with five pledges on policy, including devolution, a commitment also made in the Plaid Cymru and Liberal Democrat manifestos a week later. Only the Welsh Conservatives declared their support for the constitutional status quo, but their opposition to devolution was well known and made barely a ripple on the electoral scene.

Some devolution issues did emerge during the campaign, but more by accident than design. They reflected differences within the Labour Party and illustrated the difficulties of promoting two contrasting devolution policies (one for Scotland and the other for Wales) in the same electoral campaign. The Conservative Welsh Secretary, William Hague, accused his Labour counterpart, Ron Davies, of a secret deal with the Liberal Democrats to increase the number of seats in the Welsh Assembly from sixty to eighty, by doubling the proportional element. Welsh Labour's executive had reluctantly accepted a minimalist PR element in the Assembly elections at Tony Blair's request. To be told that this was to be changed as a result of a secret deal with Paddy Ashdown provoked consternation amongst Welsh Labour back-benchers. Denzil Davies, a Treasury minister in a previous Labour government, declared his outright opposition to any element of PR in the Welsh Assembly and indicated he was prepared to take an anti-devolution position.[2]

Later, while campaigning in Scotland, Tony Blair compared the powers of the proposed Scottish Parliament with those of an English parish council. Understandably, this made a considerable impact in Scotland. In Wales, however, it cut the ground from beneath Ron Davies; the Welsh Assembly would possess neither the revenue-raising powers nor the legislative functions of a Scottish Parliament. The issue appeared to vindicate the position of some Labour MPs in the south Wales Valleys who had made little attempt to disguise their scepticism for devolution. Two weeks later, in the immediate run-up to the election, another crack appeared in Labour's devolution policy. Ron Davies was subjected to aggressive interrogation on the limited powers of the Welsh Assembly, and responded by asserting that to give it tax-raising powers was 'economic illiteracy' and 'a blue-print for a fool's paradise'.[3] In attempting to defend the party's Welsh devolution policy he had, in effect, trashed the proposals for Scotland.

Despite the constitutional significance of devolution, the vast majority of Labour candidates ignored it, some not even mentioning it in their campaign material. The only parties which seriously debated the issue were Plaid Cymru, who condemned Labour's Welsh Assembly as a talking shop when what was needed was a power house; and the Conservatives, who reiterated the argument that any form of devolution would endanger the Union. Both failed to produce any response. In truth, devolution was not an issue during the campaign. It had hardly been a subject of debate amongst the general public, and polls showed that support for devolution actually dropped during the campaign. All the indications were that the debate proper would start after the election, not so much between the Welsh parties but within the ranks of the Labour government and the Welsh Labour Party.

Between 1979 and 1997 there were dramatic and far-reaching changes in the Welsh economy and Welsh society. Eighteen years of Conservative one-party government left an indelible impact on the Welsh political culture. Clearly things had changed since 1979. But some things stayed the same; the Welsh Parliamentary Labour Party was divided on the devolution issue as it had been in 1979, but it lacked a Neil Kinnock or a Leo Abse around whom anti-devolution sentiments could consolidate. The question that was to remain unanswered until the referendum was whether the undoubted changes in Wales were sufficient to overcome powerful, traditional forces of Welsh political life.

## Notes

1. J. Barry Jones and R. A. Wilford, 'Implications: two salient issues', in D. Foulkes et al. (eds.), *The Welsh Veto* (Cardiff: University of Wales Press, 1983).

2. J. Barry Jones, 'The 1997 general election in Wales', *Regional and Federal Studies* 7, 3 (1997), 173–6.

3. *Western Mail*, 22 April 1997.

# 1  Political Developments in Wales 1979–1997

DENIS BALSOM

Immediately following the rejection of the devolution proposals at the 1979 referendum, Mr Callaghan's Labour government was defeated on the floor of the House of Commons. In being forced to go to the country in this way, Mr Callaghan became the first Prime Minister in more than a century effectively to be removed from office by losing a vote of confidence. The election that followed saw the election of the Conservatives under Mrs Thatcher. In electing the first woman Prime Minister, Britain was taking a historic decision. Mrs Thatcher was to remain in office for the following eleven years, by which time Britain would have undergone fundamental change. In Wales this process of change was particularly acute; yet, without having been through this cathartic experience, it is doubtful that Wales would have seized the opportunity for devolution in 1997.

## Thatcherism and Wales

In retrospect, the election of Mrs Thatcher in 1979 is now recognized as a watershed event which heralded an era of major social and attitudinal change throughout Britain. From the outset, the new Conservative government's radical agenda was committed to reduce substantially the public sector in Britain and to redefine the balance of the mixed economy. It appeared as if the post-war consensus was perceived as a temporary aberration that could be undone by the time of the next general election, and Britain made 'Great' once more.

Mr Callaghan's successor as leader of the Labour Party was another Welsh MP, Michael Foot. Although he was a distinguished scholar and parliamentarian, this was undoubtedly a stop-gap appointment. Labour needed time to address its key values and relationships with fraternal organizations such as the trade union movement. Given the scale of the transformation to come, the outcome of the 1979 election in Wales showed little change. The Conservative government held eleven seats in Wales, the Labour Party twenty-one, with the Speaker, George Thomas, now occupying a non-party role. The Liberals retained two seats and Plaid Cymru also returned two MPs. The loss of two Labour seats to the Conservatives, whilst unusual, was explained as further evidence of Anglicization. Areas of the country, such as Anglesey and Brecon and Radnor, were thought to be losing their 'Welshness' and were thus much more likely to conform to the patterns of political behaviour found in communities of a similar nature elsewhere in Britain. The Conservative gain of Montgomery challenged a Liberal dominance of nearly a century and also seemed to spell out the same message of an increasing homo-geneity in rural Wales. In recapturing Carmarthen from Plaid Cymru, however, Labour may well have felt they had righted a previous aberration in the seat where Plaid Cymru had won their first parliamentary election at a by-election in 1966.

The real impact of the Thatcher revolution, however, was to be felt in the Welsh economy. A government committed to reducing the size and scale of the public sector was bound to have a disproportionate effect in Wales. It used to be said that Wales had the largest public sector west of the Iron Curtain. Within a few years, however, major structural adjustments had produced a massive decline in employment in the coal and steel industries, and the various public utilities had been privatized. Furthermore, radical changes were under way in the remaining public services with many tasks and functions, previously undertaken internally, now being put out to competitive tender or governed by market testing. Table 1.1 charts the shift in manpower between the various sectors of the Welsh economy over twenty years and demonstrates the scale of this restructuring. In addition to the aggregate impact of change, the high cost of unemployment and social dislocation that accompanied this change must also be taken into account.

The most dramatic manifestation of this trend of social change was the miners' strike of 1984–5. Whilst the south Wales miners were not in the vanguard of those in the National Union of

Table 1.1: Changes in the distribution of labour in the Welsh economy

|                         | 1971 % | 1981 % | 1991 % |
| ----------------------- | ------ | ------ | ------ |
| Agriculture and forestry | 2.9    | 2.4    | 2.0    |
| Energy and water        | 7.7    | 6.5    | 2.5    |
| Manufacturing           | 33.7   | 25.6   | 22.6   |
| Construction            | 6.7    | 5.8    | 4.4    |
| Services                | 49.1   | 59.9   | 68.5   |

Mineworkers wishing to challenge the government policy for the coal industry, once the strike was called, south Wales displayed its traditional solidarity. The inevitability of social change was confronted by an anachronistic demonstration of raw industrial power. Eventually the miners were forced back defeated, but tried to retain their dignity with bands playing and flags held aloft. In reality however, an age had passed, and Wales was finally coming to terms with the industrial consequences of the late twentieth century.

## Political realignment

The political realignment inherent in the new circumstances appeared to pre-date, slightly, the miners' strike. Mrs Thatcher enjoyed a landslide victory at the 1983 election, being returned to government with a majority of 144. Although an ideological revolution was under way, this triumph was largely credited to Mrs Thatcher's leadership during the armed conflict with Argentina over the Falkland Islands. The widespread jingoism exhibited in the tabloid press was not uniformly echoed in Wales. Welsh troops suffered heavy losses during the conflict, whilst others recalled traditional Welsh links with Argentina and the past colonization of Patagonia. The more romantic claimed that Welsh soldiers should not be forced to engage with those to whom they might conceivably be related.

The Boundary Commission report of 1983 fundamentally redrew the electoral map of Britain. The review also increased the number of parliamentary seats for Wales from thirty-six to thirty-eight. Whilst the traditional Valleys seats were largely retained, elsewhere the commissioners attempted to align political boundaries with those of local government. These new seats recognized the rapid growth in the population of the border areas of Wales and the depopulation of some of the older industrial communities. The net impact of the boundary revision was assumed to work against the interests of the Labour Party in Wales, but it was not remotely expected that the Conservative Party in Wales would consequently elect fourteen MPs. Labour's crisis was further compounded by the electoral appeal of the new Alliance (between the Liberal Party and Social Democratic Party). The Alliance secured a quarter of the vote across Britain as a whole, and almost as much in Wales. The Alliance not only retained the traditional Liberal seat of Cardigan, but recaptured, against the Tory tide, Montgomery. Such was the appeal of the Alliance that, even in south Wales, many of Labour's safest seats had their majorities substantially reduced.

Following the election, Michael Foot resigned as Labour leader, only to be replaced by yet another Welsh MP, Neil Kinnock. The new leader was known across Britain as a left-winger, but in Wales he was more renowned as the arch-opponent of devolution. Together with Leo Abse, Neil Kinnock had led the referendum campaign to defeat the 1979 proposals for a Welsh Assembly. His election to the Labour leadership seemed to deny any opportunity for further progress towards the goal of greater autonomy for Wales. For most of Mr Kinnock's period of leadership, however, devolution to Wales was not so much denied as irrelevant. The trauma of two successive election defeats, the defection from the party of the 'Gang of Four' to form the SDP and the new danger posed by the Alliance all meant that the Labour Party's highest priority was to concentrate on internal reform and retrenchment. The process of modernization of the party, that was eventually to bring Mr Blair to power in 1997, had its origins during the Kinnock era. Labour's prime objective in fighting the 1987 election was to reaffirm its position as the second party of Britain. Overturning the 1983 Conservative landslide was never a realistic target, but reasserting the party as the only alternative government and checking the rise of the Alliance was imperative. The election result showed a swing to Labour from the Alliance of some 3 per cent with the Conservative share of the vote remaining largely static.

Overall, Labour gained twenty seats, but, most importantly, it denied the Alliance any additional seats.

In Wales, the record Conservative haul of fourteen seats in 1983 was reduced to eight. The Labour Party gained Bridgend, Cardiff West, Clwyd South West and Newport West. The Liberals, fighting as part of the Alliance, retained their mid-term by-election success in Brecon and Radnor. The Conservative Party paid the price of Thatcherism in Anglesey where Keith Best, the popular Tory MP, was forced to stand down following irregularities in the purchase of privatization shares. The newly drafted Conservative candidate for Ynys Môn (Anglesey), Roger Evans, was defeated by Plaid Cymru's Ieuan Wyn Jones. Nicholas Edwards, who had served as Secretary of State for Wales since 1979, also retired in 1987. He was succeeded as MP for Pembroke by Nicholas Bennett, but more importantly, as Secretary of State by Peter Walker, the MP for Worcester. Mr Walker, a senior politician with formidable Cabinet experience, had been at odds with Mrs Thatcher and, it was widely rumoured, was offered the post at the Welsh Office in a gesture designed to humiliate him. Mr Walker however, was able to manipulate the broad-ranging Welsh Office portfolio to his own advantage, whilst Wales undoubtedly gained from his adept management and political skills. Mr Walker's appointment, however, set a further precedent: he was the first Secretary of State who was neither a Welsh MP nor a Welshman. His Conservative predecessor, Peter Thomas, had sat for Hendon South whilst he was Secretary of State 1970–4, but had formerly been MP for Conwy and had an impeccable Welsh pedigree. The succession of non-Welsh Secretaries of State that followed Mr Walker provided a telling indictment of the Conservative Party in Wales. Together with the growth of the quango state, the apparent 'colonial' presence of an English-based Cabinet minister to rule Wales provided a potent symbol for those who wished to revive the arguments for devolution.

Mrs Thatcher resigned as Prime Minister in 1990 and was succeeded by John Major. A strident ideologue appeared to have been replaced by a passive, nondescript party manager, and Labour's hopes for success at the next election rose accordingly. The opinion polls suggested a likely Labour win in 1992, but were eclipsed by the fourth successive Conservative victory. In Wales, Labour returned twenty-seven MPs, the Conservatives six, Plaid

Table 1.2: Parliamentary representation from Wales 1979–1997

| | Labour | Conservative | Liberal/Alliance | Plaid Cymru | Others | Total |
|---|---|---|---|---|---|---|
| 1979 | 21 | 11 | 1 | 2 | 1* | 36 |
| 1983 | 20 | 14 | 2 | 2 | 0 | 38 |
| 1987 | 24 | 8 | 3 | 3 | 0 | 38 |
| 1992 | 27 | 6 | 1 | 4 | 0 | 38 |
| 1997 | 34 | 0 | 2 | 4 | 0 | 40 |

* The Speaker, George Thomas.

Cymru four and the new Liberal Democrats only one. The Conservatives lost three seats to Labour, Delyn, Cardiff Central and Pembroke, but had the satisfaction of regaining Brecon and Radnor from the Liberal Democrats and reinstating more recent by-election losses in Monmouth and the Vale of Glamorgan. Plaid Cymru made a further gain when Cynog Dafis captured Ceredigion and Pembroke North, leaping from fourth place at the previous election. Following the election, Mr Kinnock resigned as leader of the Labour Party to be replaced by John Smith. Mr Smith had previously served in the Callaghan government and had been the minister responsible for the devolution legislation in 1977–8. The issue of devolution remained critical in Scotland and, following a further electoral defeat, the Labour Party accepted that it could no longer be ignored. Mr Smith, however, would have been acutely aware that, irrespective of the referendum defeat in Wales in 1979, devolution to Scotland could not proceed alone. Unless Wales, too, formed part of a wider package of constitutional reform, any proposals for Scotland would be deemed a threat to the unity of the United Kingdom. Suddenly, the Labour Party in Wales had to rediscover devolution.

The political complexion of Wales in 1992, however, was very different from that of 1979. A new cohort of MPs had replaced many of those who had held seats since the 1940s and 1950s. Leo Abse had retired, as had Fred Evans. Ifor Davies and Ioan Evans had died, George Thomas had left the Speaker's chair for a peerage, Jim Callaghan and Michael Foot had also left the House of Commons. Wales now had four Plaid Cymru MPs, and a former Plaid Cymru MP had also become a member of the House of Lords. Whilst the new generation of Labour MPs had not been elected on a specific commitment to devolution, the most effective critique of Conservative government in Wales and the need to address the 'democratic deficit' pushed the policy debate in this direction.

The tragic early death of John Smith in 1994 denied full elaboration of his proposals for devolution to Wales and Scotland and plans for the English regions. The imminence of the elections to the European Parliament meant that Labour deferred their leadership election and fought the campaign under the temporary leadership of Margaret Beckett. The European elections, however, gave perhaps the strongest indication of the magnitude of the political change overtaking Britain. The Labour Party, although by no means unanimous in its attitude to Europe, secured a huge success. In Wales, all five European seats were won by Labour, whilst the Conservatives slipped to third place overall with less than 15 per cent of the votes cast. Plaid Cymru, with 17 per cent of the votes, made much of their new status as the second party of Welsh politics. The subsequent election of Tony Blair as Labour leader took the party into the 1997 election with a strong lead in the polls and every expectation of success. In the event, Labour secured a landslide victory and the biggest majority in its history.

In Wales, Labour's success showed itself most clearly in the total rout of the Conservative Party. The Tories' share of the vote slumped to less than 20 per cent for the first time in over a hundred years, and the party failed to win a single parliamentary seat. Three elections on from having returned fourteen MPs, the Conservatives were virtually extinct. Following a further Boundary Commission review, Wales now returned forty MPs to Parliament and the Welsh Parliamentary group consisted of thirty-four Labour members, four from Plaid Cymru and two Liberal Democrats. The new government had been elected on a manifesto commitment to proceed with devolution to Scotland and Wales, and the new Secretary of State for Wales, Ron Davies, the principal architect of the Welsh proposals, proceeded quickly to ensure implementation.

It is worth noting, however, the very different political climate of Wales in 1997 compared with that of 1979. In particular, a consensus had largely been achieved concerning the potentially divisive issue of the Welsh language. With the launch of S4C, the Welsh-language fourth television channel, in 1982, a major issue of contention between linguistic activists and the government appeared to have been settled. The Conservative administration went on to establish the Welsh Language Board in 1988. Initially acting in an advisory capacity, after the passage of the Welsh Language Act in 1993 the Board became a statutory body. The new language legislation required all parts of the public sector to adopt policies that recognized the place of both languages in their work. There was a commitment not to a common standard of bilingualism but to a scheme which recognized a level of bilingual provision that was appropriate to the circumstances. Thus a language policy adopted for Gwynedd would differ from that for Torfaen, but the strength of the Act was to require all public bodies to adopt such an approach. During the years of Conservative government, the teaching of the Welsh language in schools had also been greatly strengthened. With the creation of the National Curriculum in the Education Act of 1984, Welsh had become a compulsory subject for all children up to the age of fourteen and for most until sixteen years of age. Whilst the linguistic zealots might have wished to see these reforms go further, the tension previously associated with the language had been resolved. More importantly, a Wales was being created where the place of language was defined in law and therefore could no longer be used to scaremonger or as an intimidatory issue. The debate concerning devolution could now take place around the re-spective political merits of any scheme and its impact upon the quality of democracy in Wales. In this sense, a huge change in the wider political circumstances surrounding the decision-making processes of Wales had been achieved since the débâcle of the 1979 devolution referendum.

## Public support for devolution

It remains one of the great ironies of recent Welsh political history that, whilst abstract, theoretical support for devolution has remained buoyant, when the electorate has been confronted with the opportunity to take an actual decision to further this aim, public endorsement has evaporated. The public would appear to accept the idea of devolution in theory, but reject the concept in practice. In part, this is an issue of salience. Successive polls in Wales have also shown that, although devolution can attract public support, it is invariably of a lower priority than many other issues

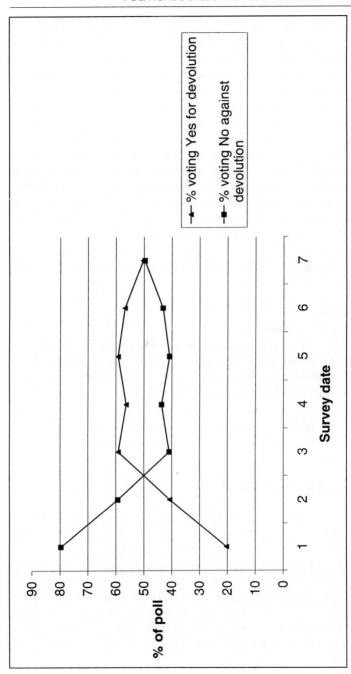

Table 1.3: Shifts in public attitudes to devolution

of the day, especially those concerned with the economy. The primary issues of employment and inflation, and the social agenda of education and health, have always ranked far higher than constitutional change and the creation of an Assembly for Wales in the priorities of the Welsh electorate.

Within a relatively short period following the 1979 referendum, opinion polls showed that substantially larger numbers than voted 'Yes' at the referendum appeared now to be in favour of devolution. The data charted in table 1.3 are drawn from a variety of survey evidence; a common pattern is evident. Support for devolution, expressed here in terms of a reiteration of the referendum question, continued at, or about, the 50 per cent level until the precise nature of the Labour Party proposals became clear in 1997 and the commitment to a further referendum was made. Polls taken during the referendum campaign show a growth in the 'No' vote, culminating in the effective tie that the referendum produced in September 1997.


## Conclusion

The advocates of devolution never successfully persuaded the public to accept that, through control of the domestic policy agenda coming to an Assembly, the important issues of everyday life in Wales could be addressed. It was only against the background of four successive electoral defeats that the Labour Party eventually endorsed a proposal for devolution in its 1997 manifesto, and it was only following the cumulative impact of eighteen years of Conservative government that the Welsh public could be persuaded to support such proposals. Even so, following the election of Mr Blair and Labour in May 1997 there was also, for many, a sense that, with a Labour government returned to pursue a positive, progressive social agenda, devolution to Wales might be unnecessary. Such conflicting sentiments clearly affected the low turnout at the referendum, the narrowness of victory and the poor level of participation at the first Assembly elections in May 1999.

# 2   Changes to the Government of Wales 1979–1997

## J. BARRY JONES

The 1979 referendum represented a massive rejection of constitutional change by the Welsh electorate. Although the dimensions of
the 'No' vote varied, the Labour government's devolution
proposals were defeated in all parts of Wales, from the Welsh-
language heartland of Gwynedd in the north-west to the heavily
anglicized areas of Gwent and South Glamorgan in the south-east.
The Conservative Party could claim, as it did, that it had more
accurately represented Welsh public opinion than had Labour,
Liberal and Plaid Cymru.[1] In the subsequent general election,
Conservative successes in Wales – the party won eleven seats with
32.3 per cent of the vote – appeared to vindicate its judgement.
Some observers of Welsh politics suggested that a process of accul-
turation was taking place, implying the acquisition by the Welsh
population of politico-cultural characteristics of the wider Anglo-
political and social system.[2] This perception was implicit in the
Conservative anti-devolution campaign, and in the claim that
devolution was the first step on a slippery slope to separatism and
that Wales's social and economic problems were solvable within
the Westminster parliamentary process.

Given this background, one would have expected the Conservative governments, which exercised political power between 1979 and
1997, to have consolidated Wales increasingly within the United
Kingdom state, and to have eschewed any tinkering with Wales's
constitutional position. Far from adopting this approach, however,
successive Conservative governments continued to treat Wales
differently from England. Additional powers were delegated to
the Welsh Office. Wales was not subjected to the 'culling of the
quangos' policy which was imposed on England. On the contrary,

Conservative governments presided over an extension of the quango state in Wales throughout the 1980s. The reform of local government in the early 1990s followed a quite different process in Wales from that in England, and the manner of that reform and its eventual outcome actually enhanced, rather than weakened, the case for political devolution. It is difficult to avoid the conclusion that the dramatic swing in favour of devolution between 1979 and 1997 owed much to the constitutional tinkering of Conservative governments headed by Mrs Thatcher and John Major.

While it is relatively straightforward to trace the various Welsh administrative and constitutional initiatives undertaken by the Conservatives, it is more difficult to explain why they happened. Part of the answer is administrative: the Welsh Office existed, and therefore it was convenient to make it responsible for the application of new policies as they emerged. Political will could have inhibited this process of 'administrative creep' but there is no evidence that any such political will existed. No attempt was made either to run down the Welsh Office, arguably a constitutional aberration in a unitary state, or to reintegrate Wales administratively with England. Mrs Thatcher came to power with a radical political agenda: to roll back the frontiers of the political state and to reduce the responsibilities of government, particularly in economic affairs, through a policy of privatization. With such a far-reaching agenda, Wales was a minor complication. Despite Conservative successes in the 1979 general election, there were very few Welsh votes to be gained or lost which might encourage a more interventionist role by the government. In short, the 1979 referendum revealed that Wales did not pose a threat to the UK state, and while it would be wrong to assume that Conservative governments took Wales for granted, there were more pressing territorial problems: specifically Northern Ireland, to a lesser extent Scotland and, for a brief period, the Falklands.

## The Select Committee for Welsh Affairs

During the course of the 1979 referendum campaign, one of the few points of agreement to emerge was the desirability of establishing a framework of democratic accountability for the various nominated and *ad hoc* bodies in Wales. The pro-devolutionists had regarded the proposed Assembly as capable of fulfilling this role, whilst their opponents, particularly the Conservatives, had argued that the task would be more efficiently discharged by a House of Commons Select Committee. It was, therefore, not wholly un-expected that the new Conservative government used the occasion for the repeal of the Wales Act to announce the establishment of a Select Committee for Welsh Affairs. It was a centralist alternative to the policy of devolution; one which, although betokening a recognition of a distinctively Welsh dimension to British politics, also ensured the reassertion of the primacy of Parliament at Westminster. The committee's Conservative architects perceived it as a more efficient means of securing executive accountability; this view was shared by the committee's Labour membership, three of whom (including its first chairman, Leo Abse) had constituted half of the renegade 'gang of six', who had fought vigorously against the Labour government's proposals. Thus both Conservatives and Labour anti-devolutionists on the committee had a vested interest in demonstrating that Welsh interests could be properly safe-guarded through this reform of the Westminster committee system.[3]

In the later stages of the referendum campaign the anti-devolu-tionists had assiduously calculated Wales's heavy dependence upon central-government subsidies. The election of a Conservative government committed to a monetarist strategy, the imposition of stringent cash limits and cuts in public expenditure thus had a disproportionately negative impact upon Wales. Within twelve months of the referendum the Welsh economy was embarked upon a serious downward spiral. This was exacerbated by a series of government decisions, including the ending of steel production at Shotton, the rundown to half capacity of the Llanwern and Port Talbot works with disastrous implications for the Welsh coal industry, and the substantial cutback in government support of regional development policies. Against this back-ground, the Select Committee predictably chose unemployment and the condition of the Welsh economy as its first subject for investigation.

The committee's first report, published on 31 July 1980[4] when unemployment in Wales was higher than in any other area of the UK with the exception of Northern Ireland, unanimously recom-mended a vastly expanded regional-aid programme for Wales, coupled with the warning of 'risks of serious social disorder if there were to be very high and chronic unemployment, particularly among the young'. The government, in a considered response published in December 1980, rejected both the committee's diagnosis and its prescriptions; only two of the committee's thirty-eight recommendations proved generally acceptable to the Welsh Office.[5]

The unanimity of the report suggested that Welsh interests could still win preference over partisanship. But the government's near-total rejection of the committee's recommendations revealed the stark realities of the political power structure in Westminster; it raised doubts as to the political viability of the Select Committee, its ability to present itself as a significant medium for representing and transmitting Welsh interests, and as a substitute for the proposed Welsh Assembly.

Doubts concerning the political efficacy of the Welsh Affairs Committee were reinforced during the 1980s and 1990s. The retirement from politics of Leo Abse, the committee's first chairman, deprived it of a high-profile back-bencher well versed in manipulating the media. It was a loss from which the committee never recovered. Furthermore, it was unable to repeat the relative success of its first report, which had gained extensive and favourable press coverage throughout Britain. Subsequently, the topics chosen for its investigations tended to produce either background research, or short-term, superficial, parochial reports. As the committee lost its newsworthiness, its political legitimacy declined. There had always been an inherent anomaly in the committee's composition, which was required to reflect the Conservative majority in the Commons while disregarding that party's minority position in Wales. As the Conservatives progressively lost their remaining seats in Wales (in the 1983, 1987 and 1992 general elections), the number of Conservative Welsh MPs was so reduced that the party's majority in the committee could only be sustained by drafting in Conservative MPs from English constituencies. By 1997 the argument that the Welsh Affairs Committee was an appropriate alternative to an elected Welsh Assembly no longer carried conviction.

## The Welsh Office

The Welsh Office had been established by the Labour government in 1965 in the teeth of Conservative opposition. In 1975 it acquired significant economic powers of intervention arising from section 7 of the Industry Act which, operating through the Welsh Development Agency (WDA), enabled it to develop a coherent programme aimed at attracting inward investment. The new Conservative government in 1979 conspicuously failed to limit the role of the Welsh Office but actually added to its powers. In 1980 the Welsh Office assumed responsibility for negotiating with the Treasury the level of central-government support for the council tax. Subsequently, under the Thatcher and Major administrations, it gained administrative responsibility for the health service, agriculture, secondary and further education, and finally the university sector in Wales. For most domestic purposes the Welsh Office had, by 1995, become the expression and means of government in Wales.[6]

The growth of Welsh Office responsibilities was reflected in the increased numbers of civil servants employed in the Welsh Office. When first established, it had slightly more than 200 civil servants, with a total expenditure somewhat less than £250 million a year. In 1995 that expenditure had reached £7 billion representing 70 per cent of public expenditure in Wales. However, while the Welsh Office grew in financial importance and administrative responsibilities, it did not grow in democratic accountability. The office's political leadership, a Secretary of State and two junior ministers, were all Conservative and thus representative of a minority political opinion in Wales. The four Secretaries of State between 1983 and 1997, Peter Walker, David Hunt, John Redwood and William Hague, were English MPs representing English constituencies. Nor was the Welsh Office's discharge of its duties beyond reproach. In December 1993 the auditor general published a damning report on the Welsh Office's sloppy accounting which revealed that approximately £100 million of public expenditure was unaccounted for.[7] The opposition parties in Wales concluded that a proper degree of public accountability could only be obtained by an elected Welsh Assembly.

## The Welsh quango state

Mrs Thatcher had won power in 1979 committed to rolling back the frontiers of the state and, in particular, to the culling of the quangos which she identified with the Labour inheritance of state intervention and corporatism. Immediately after coming into office she asked Sir Leo Pliatzky, a retired Permanent Secretary, to review the nature and extent of the quangos with a view to reducing their number and influence. This proved to be more difficult than the new government had anticipated. The evidence indicates that while there had been a slight reduction in the number of quangos, their expenditure had increased in real terms. By 1993 a new political élite was running many of Britain's public services, an élite which tended to be male, with a public-school background, a career in business and Conservative Party leanings. This raised serious questions about the application of public policy in Britain as a whole.

In Wales the situation raised sharper questions. Since the Second World War the Conservatives had been the natural minority party in Wales, consistently polling less than a third of the vote in parliamentary elections, and even less at the local government level. This did not matter very much until the development of quangos in Wales reached a level at which a significant proportion of public services were delivered by quangos and not by local elected authorities.[8]

In no small degree the emergence of a Welsh administrative identity has been based upon distinctly Welsh quangos starting with the Central Welsh Examination Board in 1890 and followed by the Welsh Health Insurance Commission in 1907. After the creation of the Welsh Office in 1964 the momentum increased and new quangos came into existence covering most aspects of Welsh life: the arts, sport, health and the countryside; tourism, inward investment, land, housing and economic development; and most recently higher and further education. The development was so considerable that one political journalist referred to Wales as 'Quangoland'.[9] By 1993 the Welsh quangos were responsible for an expenditure of over £1.6 billion a year; two of the quangos, the Welsh Development Agency (WDA) and Housing for Wales/Tai Cymru, were amongst the top forty quangos in the United Kingdom.

However, these developments led to concerns being expressed about the extent and influence of Welsh quangos and how their membership should be constituted. In January 1993 the Wales Labour Party held a press conference to launch a paper on 'Quangos in Wales' in which it accused the government of 'stuffing public bodies in Wales with Tory placemen'.[10] In particular, Labour condemned the practice of Conservative representatives, rejected by their electorate, subsequently being appointed by the Welsh Secretary to chair quangos: specifically Beata Brookes, defeated in the 1987 European elections prior to her appointment on the Welsh Consumer Council, and Ian Grist, who lost his Cardiff Central seat in the 1992 general election but was appointed within weeks to the South Glamorgan Health Authority. Labour was also concerned with multiple appointments to quangos: for example people like Sir Geoffrey Inkin and Dr Gwyn Jones. The clear implication behind these criticisms was that the Welsh Secretary of State should appoint more representative persons to the quangos: more women, fewer Conservatives and more Labour sympathizers.

Another concern was that Welsh quangos were not properly accountable to the electorate but lodged in the semi-secret world of the executive branch of government. Rhodri Morgan MP had been engaged in guerrilla warfare against the WDA for several years, criticizing and highlighting its alleged financial improprieties. Earlier in 1993 the WDA was subjected to the ordeal of examination by the respected and feared Public Accounts Committee. Various 'skeletons' were discovered and warnings were issued. But it is rare for public bodies in Wales to be subject to the attention of the Public Accounts Committee; there are bigger, more expensive fish to fry in Westminster. Nor could the Welsh Affairs Committee have acted as a substitute. It was not a specialist committee, but possessed the widest possible remit (public policy in Wales) and by 1993 had lost much of its credibility. Thus the issue of the public accountability of Welsh quangos was not resolved but allowed to fester on until the general election in 1997, when it provided one of the strongest arguments for political devolution and an elected Assembly.

## Local government reform

The democratic deficit in Wales was well illustrated by the case of local government reform. Unlike England, where an independent commission was appointed to make recommendations, the Welsh Office decided in 1991 to run its own consultative process. Welsh local authorities, particularly members of the Assembly of Welsh Counties (AWC), became increasingly disillusioned with the consultation process, feeling that their views were not being taken into account. The counties had always argued that the county system should be largely retained because it was more economic and efficient.[11] However, in July 1993 the Welsh Secretary announced that the thirty-seven districts and eight counties were to be replaced by twenty-one (later twenty-two) new unitary authorities.

The AWC was incensed by the announcement and immediately called for the appointment of an independent commission to produce proposals, an elected assembly to bring quangos within a framework of democratic accountability and, if the government failed to withdraw its proposals, to initiate a policy of non-cooperation. In August 1993 the AWC met with the Convention of Scottish Local Authorities (COSLA) and agreed a joint plan of non-cooperation with the government in both Wales and Scotland. The Welsh Secretary was left with the dilemma of pushing ahead with the reform proposals despite the opposition of the Welsh county councils, or of abandoning them. In July of that year the new Welsh Secretary, John Redwood, appeared to indicate that his mind was not closed when he suggested that, in some parts of Wales, a modified two-tier system might be implemented. But the government's proposals, as presented in the Queen's Speech in November 1993, returned to the original Welsh Office scheme.

Opposition within Wales was considerable. In what appeared to be an embarrassing climb-down, Redwood announced that the Welsh local government reforms would be delayed by twelve months, a decision which encouraged opponents in the hope that further concessions might be extracted from the Welsh Office. However, the decision to introduce the proposals first to the House of Lords rather than the House of Commons relieved the parliamentary timetable in the Commons and overcame the anticipated twelve-month delay. The government then used its majority to push the legislation through Parliament.[12]

The whole question of local government reform raised the question of the extent to which the Welsh interest could be accommodated with Westminster. During the passage of the Local Government bill the Conservative government suspended standing order 86, which stated that any bill relating exclusively to Wales should in its committee stage be considered by all the Welsh MPs. The government realized that a committee so constituted would defeat the bill. It therefore suspended the standing order and drafted in nine Conservative MPs from English constituencies to ensure a government majority. Although this was not unconstitutional, the government's action graphically illustrated the ease with which Welsh interests, as defined and supported by the overwhelming majority of Welsh MPs, could be overridden by a government whose parliamentary majority was based upon its electoral support in south-east England.

## Parliamentary Unionism

The area in which Conservative governments showed their least sure touch was in seeking to resolve the problems of the territorial management of Wales through the parliamentary process.[13] In this context the approach adopted by Mrs Thatcher was distinct from that attempted by John Major, but each was unsuccessful, and in the 1997 general election the Conservatives suffered the indignity of losing all their seats in Wales.

The Conservative Party has always prided itself as the 'Unionist' party, distinguishing itself from all other parties which it has historically regarded as less committed or less able to protect the Union of Great Britain and Northern Ireland.[14] This view is debatable. It is at least arguable that Conservative intransigence contributed to the partition of Ireland and the secession of the Irish Republic. Furthermore, Labour's electoral strength in Scotland and Wales and that party's belief in a united working class have done more to maintain the unity of Britain than Conservative Unionist ideology and rhetoric. However, Mrs Thatcher did not fit perfectly into the traditional mould of Conservative Unionism. In many policy areas she was more a radical than a traditional Conservative. She was undoubtedly a staunch supporter of the Union, but where traditional Conservative Unionism was flexible and innovative, Mrs Thatcher's Unionism was unyielding.[15] The evidence suggests that she had little knowledge of, or interest in, Wales or Scotland and that her notion of Unionism was one in which both Celtic peripheries would be progressively integrated into the British (largely English) pattern. James Mitchell,[16] a Scottish academic, argues that this attitude revealed Mrs Thatcher not as a traditional Unionist but as an assimilationist. This could explain her attitude to the Welsh Affairs Committee, whose activities she tolerated and whose recommendations she mostly ignored. It also explains her disregard for Welsh sensitivities, her appointment of an English MP, Peter Walker, as Welsh Secretary of State, in 1983 and the drafting in of English MPs to safeguard the Conservative majority in the Welsh Affairs Committee after 1987. Both moves could be said to have been forced on Mrs Thatcher because of the chronic weakness of the Conservatives in Wales. But that merely highlighted the profound difficulties of accommodating the Welsh territorial interest within the conventions and procedures of the Westminster parliamentary process.

John Major's Unionism was much more in the traditional mould, recognizing that Wales was different from England and willing to countenance reforms, provided they did not infringe the constitutional principle of parliamentary supremacy. In 1993 a Welsh Language Act was passed into law extending the legitimate use of the Welsh language by public and private bodies. A Welsh Language Board (another quango) was set up to supervise the application of the Act and to encourage the private sector to adopt bilingualism wherever sensible and appropriate. This was precisely the form of territorial management of the United Kingdom which Major could apply without qualms, coinciding as it did with the Conservative Party's constitutional principles and political interests.

In March 1993, Major's predisposition to a more sensitive and positive form of Unionism led to the 'Grand Committee strategy'. This involved the Scottish and Welsh Grand Committees, consisting respectively of all Scottish and Welsh MPs, being granted extra powers and duties. The justification for this move was the time constraints in Westminster in the handling of the Scottish parliamentary business. But the reforms totally ignored a political fact: the Scottish and Welsh Grand Committees were dominated by Labour MPs hostile to the Conservative government's legislative programme. The Welsh plans leaned heavily on the Scottish proposals, but in the absence of specifically Welsh legislation in Westminster, they were even more dubious. Their significance can be gauged by the fact that, following the promotion of David Hunt from the Welsh Office to Employment in May 1993, the Welsh Grand Committee plans were conveniently forgotten until November 1995, when the new Welsh Secretary William Hague reintroduced them in a slightly modified form. The Welsh Grand Committee would meet more frequently and in various parts of Wales (not just Cardiff), would debate government business as it affected Wales, receive ministerial statements and question ministers. But to what effect? The role envisaged for the committee hardly merited the government's intention that it should meet up to seven times a year. Its composition (four Tory MPs out of thirty-eight) and the requirement that it meet in different parts of Wales led the political correspondent of *The Western Mail* to assert that it would be a 'mobile talking shop'.[17]

The derision with which the reform was received suggested that the Conservatives ..L.. incapable of producing an effective arrangement for the territorial management of Wales. Opposition parties in Wales concluded that a limited reform of parliamentary procedures was inadequate and that the Welsh interest could only be properly satisfied with a more radical constitutional change.

## Conclusion

Developments in the government of Wales between 1979 and 1997 changed political attitudes. The loss of a fourth successive general election in 1992 persuaded the Welsh Labour parliamentary group to question whether a government whose majority was based upon votes in the south-east of England could legitimately claim a mandate in Wales. Similar doubts as to the legitimacy of Conservative authority in Wales had always been promoted by Plaid Cymru; and the Liberal Democrats, strong federalists in the context of Welsh devolution and the European Union, were traditionally disinclined to regard the British Parliament as an absolute authority. After 1992, this view found increasing support among Welsh local authorities, who felt the full impact of a centralist and centralizing government exploiting the constitutional principle of parliamentary supremacy to undermine and downgrade local autonomy. Thus, across the political spectrum in Wales, the principle of parliamentary supremacy became subject to sceptical reappraisal.

The shift in political attitudes in Wales was not the product of nationalist aspirations; Plaid Cymru's vote remained stuck below the 10 per cent ceiling throughout the eighteen years of Conservative government. The post-1979 changes were the product of a sense of grievance against a Conservative government which controlled the Westminster Parliament, and which had failed to take sufficient account of the Welsh 'interest' or, to be more precise, a range of Welsh interests. This had for long been the case in the heartland of the Welsh language (*Y Fro Cymraeg*). Between 1979 and 1997 these sentiments became increasingly common in the anglicized, industrialized parts of south-east Wales. Whether this shift in attitudes was sufficient to produce a majority for the 'Yes' campaigners in the referendum was to remain an open question until the early hours of 19 September 1997.

## Notes

1. B. Jones and R. A. Wilford, 'Implications: two salient issues?', in D. Foulkes, B. Jones and R. Wilford (eds.), *The Welsh Veto: The Wales Act 1978 and the Referendum* (Cardiff, University of Wales Press, 1983), p. 229.

2. Ibid., p. 225.

3. B. Jones, 'The Welsh Office: a political expedient, or an administrative innovation', *Transactions of the Honourable Society of Cymmrodorion* (1990), 281–92.

4. Welsh Affairs Committee, First Report: *The Role of the Welsh Office and Associated Bodies in Developing Employment Opportunities in Wales* vol.1, HC 731, 1979–80.

5. B. Jones, 'The Select Committee on Welsh Affairs', in G. Drewry (ed.), *The New Select Committees* (Oxford: Oxford University Press, 1985).

6. B. Jones, 'The Welsh Office: a political expedient, or an administrative innovation'.

7. Comptroller and Auditor General (1993), National Audit Office, *Welsh Office: Premises Management* (HCP 1992–3), 444.

8. B. Jones, 'Government by appointment: quangos and democracy in Wales', *Planet*, 101 (1993).

9. J. Osmond, *The Democratic Challenge* (Llandysul: Gomer Press, 1992).

10. Labour Party Wales, *Who Runs Wales? A Briefing Paper on Quangos in Wales* (Cardiff: Wales Labour Party, 1993).

11. G. A. Boyne, P. Griffiths, A. Lawton and J. Law (eds.), *Local Government in Wales* (York: Rowntree Trust, 1991).

12. B. Jones, 'Welsh politics and changing British and European contexts', in J. Bradbury and J. Mawson (eds.), *British Regionalism and Devolution* (London: Jessica Kingsley, 1997).

13. J. Bradbury, 'Conservative governments, Scotland and Wales: a perspective on territorial management', ibid.

14. B. Jones, 'Devout defender of the Union: John Major and devolution', in P. Dorey (ed.), *The Major Premiership* (London: Macmillan, 1999).

15. F. Mount, *The British Constitution Now* (London: Mandarin, 1992).

16. J. Mitchell, 'Unionism, assimilation and the Conservatives', in J. Lovenduski and J. Stanyer (eds.), *Contemporary Political Studies* (Oxford: PSA/Blackwell, 1995).

17. M. Settle, 'Major will have to face Welsh MPs, says Hague', *Western Mail*, 1 December 1995.

# 3 Unfinished Business: Labour's Devolution Policy[1]

KEVIN MORGAN and GEOFF MUNGHAM

## Introduction

The news was hardly encouraging. Having been dispatched to Wales to test public attitudes to devolution, Philip Gould felt obliged to send a sombre memo back to Millbank Tower, the Labour Party's London headquarters.[2] On the basis of focus group meetings which he had convened just four months ahead of the referendum, Gould, a shrewd polling expert, was disturbed by what he had found. For someone who knew little of Wales, Gould proved to be remarkably prescient in his assessment of the situation. The referendum, he wrote to his Millbank colleagues, was going to be problematical for a number of reasons:

> It could be close, and the no vote could win. The most recent poll shows a lead of 10% with a large number of undecideds. These focus groups show the yes vote only just ahead of the no vote (49% to 45%).
> Awareness is so low that the eventual vote is very hard to call.
> The arguments against are quite widely and deeply held. More no arguments were spontaneously listed in the groups than yes arguments.
> There is a lot of emotional resistance to the Assembly. People in Wales feel vulnerable and uncertain both on a personal and national level. They do not want things to start going wrong and are suspicious and nervous of change.
> I am not sure that I trust the polls. If anywhere was to suffer from a 'spiral of silence' it is Wales, which has an electorate that combines such a lack of confidence with a public desire to please and a subtle and convoluted approach to political issues. (Gould, 1997)

Why should the Assembly, a key part of Labour's programme of constitutional reform, elicit such 'emotional resistance' from some of the party's very own supporters? The answer to this question is to be found not so much in the cut and thrust of the referendum campaign as in the deeper structures of feeling, the political schizophrenia in particular, which pervaded the Wales Labour Party (WLP) for most of the post-war period. Indeed, in this chapter we shall argue that the trials and tribulations of Labour's devolution policy in Wales, both before and after the debacle of 1979, owed much to the unresolved schizophrenic tension between two political traditions – centralism and devolution – which had co-evolved in the Welsh Labour movement since Home Rule began to attract attention in the years immediately before and after the First World War.

In the next section we briefly explore these political traditions in the WLP because they continued to shape the debate about how to (and indeed whether to) construct a new devolution agenda after the ignominy of the 1979 referendum, when the issue had seemingly been settled in favour of the status quo. With the concept of devolution back on the political agenda, we then examine the debate within the WLP in the 1990s with respect to the scope and limits of the proposed Assembly. Heated and convoluted though it was, this debate begins to transcend the traditional script, with its crude polarization between centralism and devolution, and signals the possibility of a new, more judicious political settlement. What was also distinctive about this debate was the way in which the WLP, or at least the pro-devolution wing of it, engaged other parties in debate with the aim of building a broad coalition to advance the cause of the Assembly.[3] While this new cross-party dialogue was born of necessity, it nevertheless created the conditions for a less tribalistic, more inclusive form of politics to emerge in Wales. The key question here, of course, is whether the new politics of 'inclusivity' will come to be seen as a contingent and ephemeral feature of the referendum campaign or, more significantly, as a legacy which endured because it was valued and nurtured by the Assembly.

## One party, two traditions: the schizophrenia of Welsh Labourism

Though it is not sufficiently acknowledged, the Labour Party has made a significant contribution to the longevity of the British state by helping to preserve the latter's territorial integrity. The fact that this territorial integrity is so often taken for granted, that it should even appear 'natural' as it were, speaks volumes for what has been achieved. It could easily have been so different. On the face of it the territorial character of the British state would seem to be a precarious arrangement because, given its multinational character, it is not a conventional nation-state, and the twentieth century is littered with examples of multinational states breaking up in disunion (Rose, 1982; Keating and Loughlin, 1997). With hindsight this idiosyncratic state system has proved to be surprisingly robust; during the twentieth century, for example, it survived a whole series of potentially fatal crises, including two world wars, the inter-war depression and the accelerated closure of coal and steel, industries which were once considered to be virtually synonymous with Scotland and Wales. Clearly, some things work better in practice than in theory.

In territorial terms the distinguishing feature of the Labour Party is that it is the only party with a major presence in the 'periphery' which is committed to the maintenance of the British state, the issue which most conspicuously sets it apart from its nationalist rivals, the Scottish National Party in Scotland and Plaid Cymru in Wales. To the extent that it has championed the national claims of the Celtic periphery, as it did in a consistent and principled fashion up until the 1920s, the Labour Party has always sought to realize these claims in and through the British state, and the likes of Keir Hardie saw no inherent contradiction between Home Rule on the one hand and the maintenance of a British state on the other (Griffiths, 1979). Such equanimity did not last, however, and in the course of the post-war period the conflict between centralism and devolution within the WLP became ever more acute, fuelled by centralist-minded MPs who claimed that devolution would inadvertently benefit Plaid Cymru and thereby threaten the integrity of the UK.

In the pantheon of Welsh Labourism the centralist tradition takes its inspiration from Bevan, even though his credentials render him a somewhat ambiguous role model in this respect. Even so, the conventional understanding of Bevan is that he was, first and foremost, a *British* socialist who had little or no time for so-called 'Welsh issues'.

Perhaps the main evidence for this interpretation of Bevan as an incorrigible centralist is the devastating attack he delivered on the institution of the Welsh Day debate in Parliament on 17 October 1944, when this institutional innovation was inaugurated. It is worth dwelling on this historic occasion because Bevan is often mis-quoted, thereby creating the impression that the speech was more centralist-minded than it actually was. At a key point Bevan says:

> My colleagues, all of them members of the Miners' Federation of Great Britain, have no special Welsh solution for the Welsh coal industry which is not a solution for the whole of the mining industry of Great Britain. There is no Welsh *coal* problem. (Bevan, 1944)

A number of leading writers on Welsh political history have seized on this passage as evidence of Bevan's centralism yet, for some obscure reason, they choose to omit the reference to 'coal' in the final sentence (Osmond, 1977; Smith, 1997). Far from being a pedantic textual point, the omission gives a different meaning to the speech, reducing both the complexity and the ambiguity of Bevan's position. Indeed, in the very same speech Bevan is at pains to emphasize the point that

> Wales has a special place, a special individuality, a special culture and special claims, and I do not think that this is the place where any of them can properly be considered. There may be an argument – I think there is an argument – for considerable devolution of government, but there is no need for a special day in Parliament and this Debate has demonstrated it completely. (Bevan, 1944)

To the extent that the speech was informed by a coherent philosophy, which is unlikely, it was a plea for 'things in their proper place', that is for centralism *and* devolution where they were appropriate. In other words, in industrial matters, like coal, steel and agriculture, he favoured a British approach; whereas in matters of language, art, culture and education he welcomed a distinctively Welsh approach. This philosophy was to be developed at greater length three years later when he argued that 'distinctive cultures, values and institutions should flourish, so as to counteract the appalling tendency of the times towards standardisation, regim-entation and universal greyness' (Bevan, 1947).

No one has done more to retrieve 'the other Aneurin Bevan' than Robert Griffiths, who arrives at the most sensible conclusion of all, namely that Bevan's Welshness was a phenomenon with which he 'never fully came to terms' (Griffiths, 1978). Other historians have also come round to the view that Bevan's 'antipathy to Welshness can be overdone' (K. O. Morgan, 1989). For all these reasons it is difficult to see how Bevan can be wholly appropriated by the centralist tradition in Welsh Labourism without a disservice being done to a complex legacy.

Just as Aneurin Bevan is believed to personify centralism, so James Griffiths, the first Secretary of State for Wales, is taken to be the champion of devolution within the ranks of Welsh Labourism. Tellingly, after Bevan had ridiculed the very idea of a Welsh Day debate in 1944, it was Griffiths who rose to speak, and he lost no time in defending the decision to create parliamentary space for Welsh affairs in words which resonate over fifty years later:

> The reason why my colleagues and I asked for this debate is because we have no place in Wales where we can discuss these questions, and I was very glad to hear the hon. Member for Ebbw Vale (Mr A. Bevan) expressing a view which I share completely: that is, that the time has come when the whole process of legislation and of administration in this country ought to be looked at, because I think devolution will be essential for the proper working of democracy in the future. (Griffiths, 1944)

Griffiths was well aware of Bevan's personal odyssey in search of power, a quest that had taken him out of the valley, beyond the county and on to the centre, where he believed the levers of power lay. It was this perspective, Griffiths later reflected, which inclined Bevan to the view that 'devolution of authority would divorce Welsh political activity from the mainstream of British politics' (Griffiths, 1969). Their differences finally came to a head in the run up to the 1959 election, after Bevan had consistently frustrated Griffiths's scheme for a Secretary of State for Wales at the head of a Welsh Office. After one meeting the argument continued into the corridor, at which point it was reported that: 'Bevan turned to Griffiths and asked: "How much do you really want this thing?" His compatriot and fellow-miners' MP stopped and answered "With all my heart and soul". Bevan simply replied "Oh, alright then, have it"' (R. Griffiths, 1978).

Without Bevan's gracious change of heart it is highly unlikely that Griffiths would have succeeded in getting the commitment to a Welsh Office, headed by a Secretary of State, inserted into Labour's 1959 election manifesto. Griffiths would face other battles before his vision of a Welsh Office was realized in 1964, but none was as crucial as this final encounter with Bevan. Looking back, what is perhaps most striking about the debate between Bevan and Griffiths – between socialism and nationalism, central- ism and devolution – was not that they epitomized different political traditions, but that they refused to be imprisoned within these traditions: they freely conceded that the other had something to offer and it was this, the capacity to empathize, which ensured that their differences did not degenerate into tribalism, where genuine dialogue is impossible.

In the debate between centralists and devolutionists in the 1970s and 1990s, however, this capacity to empathize was conspicuous by its absence; hence the tribal quality of many of the exchanges. Indeed, such was the bitterness of the 1979 referendum, particularly with respect to the 'gang of six' Labour MPs who opposed their own government, that it was something of an achievement for the WLP to have survived the campaign intact, an experience that party managers vowed never to repeat.

As a result of this chastening experience the maintenance of party unity acquired a totemic significance for these managers when they eventually began to reconstruct their devolution policy after 1979. At first there was little appetite to return to the issue in any shape or form, but this reluctance quickly evaporated in 1987, after the party's third successive election defeat. By now it was clear, even to those who had viscerally opposed devolution in the past, that the governance question was back on the agenda for a number of reasons, principally the overcentralization of power in Whitehall, the emasculation of local government, the burgeoning of unelected quangos and a Welsh Office which seemed imperious and unaccountable, all of which was part and parcel of the demo- cratic deficit in Wales (Morgan and Roberts, 1993; Morgan, 1994).

The executive of the WLP used the medium of local government reform to advance the cause of regional government because, as early as 1976, Conference had unanimously called for the merger of county and district councils into single-tier, multi-purpose authorities 'as a matter of urgency'. At its 1990 Conference the WLP received the results of a two-year consultation exercise, in which over eighty organizations had tendered their views on reforming the structures of local and regional government in Wales. Among other things Conference committed itself to the following proposals:

- a single-tier of most-purpose local authorities
- an elected body for Wales to deal with the functions of the Welsh Office and its nominated bodies
- there should be no referendum; instead a manifesto commitment should be given to local government reorganization
- the pace of reform in Wales should parallel progress towards regional government in England. (WLP, 1990)

A further sign of the new climate came early in 1990 when Neil Kinnock, the party leader and a noted opponent of devolution, said that 'in the decade ahead we are going to see the national boundaries of Europe diminish in importance while regional and local identities and decisions grow in significance' (Kinnock, 1990). By the time of the 1992 election Labour was once again formally committed to a directly elected Wales-wide body and some former opponents of devolution were reversing their position in the light of the centralization of power under Thatcherism (Anderson, 1992). Because the pace of reform in Wales was to be linked to progress in England, however, ardent supporters of devolution queried the WLP's commitment to regional government at a time when their counterparts in Scotland were building a pro-devolution coalition in the form of the Constitutional Convention.

## The internal battle for devolution

Labour fought the 1992 election on a 'nominal' commitment to devolution. The then leader of the party, Neil Kinnock, showed no real enthusiasm for the devolution project, a coolness said to be shared by Barry Jones, then Shadow Secretary of State for Wales. Indeed, according to one highly placed Labour source, while Jones dutifully did a tour of local Labour parties in Wales to explain the Party's devolution proposals, in doing so he managed subtly to undermine the whole idea.

This reluctance to promote the devolution issue is understandable to any student of Labour politics. The strong urge to maintain party unity, so easily dismissed by many outside the movement as a 'gag' on argument and debate, is deeply rooted in the Labour tradition of solidarity and collective action. Producing a policy for devolution that would command a workable consensus inside the party has always eluded the party leadership. Small wonder, then, that in the 1992 election there was no real appetite for campaigning on an issue that was likely to 'distract' the party from the 'real business' of winning the election and putting Labour back into power after thirteen long years in opposition.

But Labour's defeat in 1992 helped revive the devolution issue. Three events in that year combined to draw attention to Labour's 'unfinished business'. Firstly, shortly after the general election, the Wales TUC at its annual conference passed a resolution calling for the setting up of a 'Welsh Constitutional Convention' (along the lines of the one already operating in Scotland) and even drew up a framework document out of which such a convention might emerge. Secondly, this initiative trigged alarm inside the Wales Labour Party executive, reflecting what Osmond has termed 'its nervous attitude towards cross-party collaboration on any issue, and least of all Welsh devolution' (1996). The executive's response was immediately to establish its own Constitutional Policy Commission (in June 1992), charged with the task of updating key areas of party policy ready for the next general election and, in particular, 'to re-examine policy in relation to the creation of a directly elected Welsh Assembly'.

Thirdly, John Smith, the newly elected Labour leader, appointed Ron Davies as the new Shadow Secretary of State for Wales. When the post was offered, Smith spoke of the need to get on with completing Labour's 'unfinished business' and asked Davies to 'develop the same policies for Wales as we have for our planned Scottish Parliament'. Davies needed no persuading. He had talked earlier about how strongly he had been affected by Labour's defeat in June and of how 'any lingering doubts' he might have had about the need for a Welsh Assembly were 'dispelled' by the prospect of a largely Labour-voting Wales forced to face a further five years of Tory rule from Westminster. Nor could anyone else doubt the strength of Davies's conviction following a speech he made in Treorchy in November 1992, when he argued for an elected Welsh Parliament and more powerful local government in Wales. This speech was described by one commentator as 'the most radical

speech about Wales by a Labour politician for a generation'
(Osmond, 1996).

The future for devolution policy was never going to be smooth.
Ron Davies had to produce proposals that would keep both local
government *and* the PLP (Parliamentary Labour Party) happy. The
concerns of the former were fuelled by impending government
plans to introduce unitary authorities in Wales, while the latter was
determined not to let the Assembly undermine party unity. Davies
began to try to build consensus by releasing a paper, *No
Devolution – No Deal,* to which he succeeded in getting all sections
of the party to subscribe.

As Davies took his first steps towards trying to build a coalition
of support for the Assembly in Wales, Labour's Policy Commission
submitted an interim report, *The Welsh Assembly: The Way
Forward,* to the Wales Labour Party Conference in 1993. It was
clear that the commission was proceeding cautiously. Conference
called for further detailed examination of the structures and
powers of an Assembly and committed the party to a 'wide-
ranging consultation process' on the issues involved. The commission's caution was understandable in the context of Labour
Party politics in Wales. There was no real support either inside the
Wales Labour Party or the party's executive for a constitutional
convention. A convention would have meant Labour, in the words
of one source, 'having to bring in Plaid and this would have caused
mayhem in the Valleys'. And a convention – which would almost
certainly have raised the issue of electoral reform – 'would only
have pushed the Party in Wales close to civil war'. While this claim
may have been exaggerated, it did serve to underline the problems
Ron Davies faced in carrying his party with him on devolution.

The following year (1994) saw a number of significant
developments. In March, the Parliament for Wales Campaign held
a conference attended by, among others, three Labour MPs.[4]
Although the event could scarcely count as seismic, it is of interest
because of the reaction it provoked from the Wales Labour Party
executive. Viewing the campaign as being too closely aligned to the
nationalist position, it severely reprimanded the MPs. The incident
was yet another indication of how potentially divisive devolution
was seen by the party leadership.

In May, the sudden death of John Smith inevitably raised the
question of how enthusiastic his successor might be for the

devolution project in Wales. When Tony Blair sought Ron Davies's support in his leadership bid, Davies offered it on two conditions: that Blair would, first, support devolution, and second, continue with Smith's commitment to the principle of 'inclusiveness' as a building block for constitutional reform (the 'I' word, as we shall see later, was to be the code for some form of proportional representation in elections to the Assembly). Although Davies got the reassurances he wanted, one of Blair's first acts on becoming leader in July, was to appoint Dr Kim Howells to Jack Straw's new shadow Home Office team, with special responsibility for 'constitutional reform'. At that time Dr Howells was a known anti-devolutionist, and Davies was later to record that he saw the posting as an attempt by Blair to 'rein back' on the devolution commitment.

The emergence of the new Labour leader coincided with the Policy Commission's issuing a consultation paper, *Shaping the Vision,* which tentatively raised three questions: on tax-varying powers, the power of primary legislation and the method of election. In the autumn the commission organized six 'public consultation meetings' around Wales. These sessions were, according to one observer, 'little advertised . . . low-key affairs . . . held on weekdays rather than during the evenings or weekends – times which minimized participation' (Osmond, 1996).

During the same period when the commission was touring Wales, Davies tried to push the Liberal Democrat notion of a *Senedd* as a device for building cross-party support for the devolution idea, and suggested that the body should have 'significant financial and legislative autonomy'. All this was carried in a front-page story in *The Western Mail* in November, on the eve of a visit by Tony Blair to Cardiff. The story implied that Blair was generally supportive, and the following day Davies issued a press release claiming that 'Tony Blair has put himself and the Party solidly behind a *Senedd* for Wales'. Unfortunately, a few days later, Davies was forced to backtrack after Blair's press officer (Alastair Campbell) wrote to *The Western Mail* denying Blair had made any such commitment.

In December there were further problems for Davies. Llew Smith – in a foretaste of things to come – published a 'personal manifesto' with the uncompromising title, *The Welsh Assembly: Why it has No Place in Wales,* which restated the familiar 'devo-sceptic' line. This was followed by the Wales TUC's submission to the Policy Commission, which counselled caution on devolution, seeing it as a troubling 'diversion' from the main project of returning a Labour government.

TUC fears about 'diversions' seemed confirmed when John Major, in a series of speeches and interviews given around the turn of the New Year, said he would be putting Labour's devolution plans at the top of the agenda for the next general election. This declaration threw the Labour leadership on the defensive (perhaps remembering the success Major had enjoyed late in the 1992 campaign when he played the 'Union card'). While there was little that could be done at this stage about Scotland – where commitments had already been made about tax and law-making powers and on PR (proportional representation) – there was pressure to soft-pedal on these matters in relation to Wales. It was as if Blair's team in London had started to view the devolution question more as a liability than an asset.

In Wales itself a difficult meeting of the Policy Commission took place in Transport House (Cardiff) in March 1995. Davies was surprised to find Dr Kim Howells present, and suspected he had either been put there by Blair or by some agreement between Anita Gale, the general secretary of the Wales Labour Party, and the leader's office. Davies challenged Howells's right to be in attendance but was overruled by Gale. His suspicion that Howells was there to play some kind of 'watchdog' role seemed confirmed when Howells lodged objections to any suggestion of the method of election containing a PR element. This took Davies by surprise, since shortly after Howells's appointment to Straw's team, Davies had outlined an Assembly proposal with a hundred members and full legislative powers, a proposal to which Davies later insisted Howells had agreed. Howells's change of tack appeared to suggest that the party leadership was seeking to dampen down expectations about the Welsh Assembly.

The commission next met at South Glamorgan County Hall in an atmosphere which several of those present described as 'bloody' and 'extremely unpleasant'. Much of the meeting saw Ron Davies and Rhodri Morgan ranged against Kim Howells, Terry Thomas and Wayne David MEP. Some time before the meeting Andrew Bold (the commission's secretary) had written a report for the commission which had been leaked to *The Western Mail*. Davies's account of what happened as soon as the meeting started makes interesting reading:

> When I arrived I found myself facing what was basically a kangaroo court. Ken accused me of leaking the report, which was not true, but caused a row. I had gone along with a series of amendments to put to the report, but found a majority – built around Ken Hopkins (the Commission Chair), Kim, Terry, Wayne and a couple of TU [Trade Union] representatives – stitched up against me. They successfully opposed all my amendments, and just wanted to endorse the document as it was, with no reference to electoral reform and no primary legislative powers.

What happened next, according to Davies, was to give him some room for manœuvre in subsequent negotiations:

> Over lunch – and by this time there were only 7 people left – I talked to Wayne and worked out a form of words acceptable to him along the lines of 'there might be a case for primary legislative powers in certain areas' and agreeing that the Executive should 'resolve the question of the electoral system'. As far as I was concerned this left the door open just far enough to allow me to come back to these issues later.

The 'open door' to which Davies referred proved difficult to pass through. A meeting of the executive, called to discuss a draft of *Shaping the Vision*, resulted in Davies losing the argument to Thomas and Hopkins, in what was said to be a 'very nasty' and 'ill-tempered' confrontation. Davies had made a particular point about the importance of the Assembly elections containing a PR element, arguing that the broader the political base of the Assembly, the greater its popular legitimacy, so making it harder for any Westminster government to try to weaken or scrap it. The argument was lost both inside the commission and inside the executive.

In May 1995 *Shaping the Vision* was approved at the Wales Labour Party conference with little debate. The report claimed the Assembly would 'assist the process of local government reorganization' (then taking place in Wales), rejected the case for 'general powers of primary legislation', said 'measures should be taken to ensure . . . gender balance' and, crucially, came down in favour of the first-past-the-post method of election. It now seemed that

Labour's internal debate on devolution had been settled in favour of the 'minimalists', but there were many in the party who saw that matter as being far from resolved.

The first reaction came with the formation of 'Wales Labour Action', a pressure group within the Labour Party, to campaign for a more radical and 'inclusive' approach to the business of Assembly-making. Chaired by Gareth Hughes (who was also a member of both the Policy Commission and the WLP executive), the group won the backing of several constituency Labour parties, some trade unions and prominent Labour figures like Rhodri Morgan and the MEPs Eluned Morgan and David Morris. Predictably, the group came under fierce attack from the party leadership in Wales, led by Anita Gale.

Davies, too, was unwilling to accept the verdict of conference. His tactic was to appeal directly to the trade-union leaders in Wales, telling them there was a need to reconvene the Policy Commission 'to move things on', and in this he got the key backing of George Wright, regional secretary of the TGWU (Transport and General Workers' Union) and Derek Gregory, regional secretary of Unison, the big public-sector employees' union.

Union support was crucial for Davies, since union representatives dominated the executive. At a September 1995 executive meeting it was agreed to reopen the issue of voting reform and to consider giving the Assembly 'additional power', specifically the power to reform the quangos. For Davies these were vital steps forward. Voting reform allowed him to return again to his central theme of making the Assembly 'inclusive'. The opportunity to revisit the issue of electoral reform was given to Davies by a clever piece of drafting in the final, approved version of *Shaping the Vision*. This referred to the first-past-the-post system as the 'preferred version' for electing Assembly members, giving Davies the opening he needed to return to the issue.

The Wales Labour Party conference in the following year was presented with a report which represented a major advance on *Shaping the Vision*. The report, *Preparing for a New Wales: A Report on the Structure and Workings of the Welsh Assembly*, included a call for an Assembly 'which will operate on a more consensual basis and whose workings will be more open and accessible'.

From this point on events began to move in Davies's favour. By this time, according to Davies, 'Blair was coming round to the idea of PR for the Assembly, to put us in line with Scotland', but he 'was also interested in greater Lib-Lab co-operation' for reasons that went beyond any calculations about the best way of garnering broad support for Labour's devolution plans for Wales. At the same time, by Davies's own reckoning, 'Ken [Hopkins] was becoming more amenable, realising that I was now likely to be Secretary of State in Blair's first government – and he also realised that Blair himself was now leaning towards PR' (at least for Wales and Scotland, if not for Westminster).

Blair's apparent new-found enthusiasm for PR found expression in a major speech he made in Wales on 28 June on Labour's devolution proposals, in which he said: 'It is vital that all of Wales feels included in the process of devolving power and feels represented in the Welsh Assembly.' More significantly, earlier that month Davies had organized a meeting in Blair's office where Ken Hopkins and Terry Thomas were told by Blair that he (Blair) wanted PR and won them over by asking for their help in delivering it.

One other important event took place in June – when Blair declared Labour's intention to legislate for devolution in Scotland and Wales through a referendum after the election (Blair's original position was that this measure was essential for Scotland, but not necessary in Wales, an approach Davies thought 'untenable'). The decision to opt for a referendum gave Davies the opportunity to link the Assembly with PR, thus making it easier to secure the backing of the other pro-devolution parties in Wales. At Davies's request, Blair then wrote formally to the Welsh executive asking them to reopen the PR issue. The executive agreed and the appropriate resolution, written by Davies, was moved by Terry Thomas on behalf of the GMB (General and Municipal Boilermakers Union).

On 15 July 1996 the WLP executive agreed to reconvene the Policy Commission, instructing it to report back in time to place a report before the 1997 Wales Labour Party conference. The commission set off on another round of consultations, taking in CBI (Confederation of British Industry) Wales, the Wales TUC, the Welsh Parliamentary Labour Party, the Welsh Local Government Association, other parties and meetings within the Labour Party in Wales. In the course of a series of commission meetings in September 1996, it was now proposed to slim down the Assembly to sixty members, based on the now familiar 40:20 formula. Davies asked Ken Hopkins to put this idea to Terry Thomas, which he did, with the result that Thomas took the lead on the issue on the commission. The gathering momentum in favour of electoral reform found expression in the commission's report, and its recommendation that the Assembly be elected according to 'an element of proportionality' – specifically, the AMS (additional member system) – was unanimously approved at the 1997 party conference. By endorsing the principle of PR, Labour was, said Ron Davies, reinforcing its 'commitment to a new, more open style of politics that will ensure that the Assembly enjoys the confidence of all the people it serves'. The extent to which these sentiments shaped Labour's preparations for the referendum campaign, which was to follow its election victory on 1 May 1997, is explored below.

## Labour's referendum campaign

During the summer of 1996 certain Labour circles were beginning to think ahead about how best to manage the referendum campaign should Labour win the next election. The first portents were not encouraging. In July 1996 Andrew Davies (a former member of the executive and a former party officer) was approached to take the post of special projects officer to do preparatory work for the campaign. There was widespread concern about the ability of the Wales Labour Party to do the job, and Davies was an experienced election campaigner. But, because of various internal problems, nearly ten months passed before Davies was finally confirmed in post, in April 1997.

The tension over Davies's position prefigured some of the wider problems that were later to weaken Labour's referendum campaign. In the first place, the ten-month delay meant that vital time was lost on doing the kind of preparatory work essential for effective campaigning. More important, perhaps, was the way in which the difficulties surrounding Davies's appointment revealed, right from the outset, some of the lines of conflict and division between many of those who were going to form the core of Labour's referendum campaign team. Even if these tensions had been absent, Labour still faced a formidable campaign task. Despite the heady rhetoric around the Assembly which came out of the 1997 Wales Labour Party Conference, the issue was not one which had enthused the wider party membership. For the most part, the often rancorous debate which locked together Ron Davies, the executive, the Policy Commission and Blair's office over the structure and functions of the Assembly had largely bypassed local Labour parties and the great majority of Labour's 25,000 members in Wales. Nor was it clear how actively Labour local authority leaders would work for a 'Yes' vote, and there was even less appreciation of public sentiment. As Andrew Davies, in looking back on the campaign, put it: 'We were all to some extent flying blind. We had no idea, at the start, of what real popular feeling was about the Assembly.' These problems might have partly been resolved had Ron Davies been supported in his bid to put devolution on Labour's agenda during the 1997 general election campaign in Wales. The proposal was 'totally opposed' by those in Millbank who, presumably, saw its inclusion as a 'diversion' from the 'real' issues they wanted to present to the electorate.

Shortly after the return of the new Labour government in May 1997 steps were taken to push forward Labour's campaign. Late in May there was a meeting, in Millbank, of Labour's 'National Referendum Co-ordinating Committee'. There was an inauspicious start, with some uncertainty in Millbank as to whether the referendum was to be held in 1997 or 1998 (in fairness, it must be remembered that Millbank's gaze had been totally focused for a long time on the 1997 general election).

It was eventually agreed to do focus-group research and in-depth polling to try to gauge the 'national mood' in Wales, though it was not possible to implement this idea immediately because of budget constraints. In the end Wales was awarded the bulk of Labour's referendum budget, over Scotland, after David Hill, then Labour's chief press officer, made the point that, in Labour election-speak, 'Scotland is the majority seat and Wales is the key marginal'. Hill also stressed that the referendum would be very different from the running of the recent general election campaign, using the analogy of the 1975 referendum campaign on Britain's entry into Europe, 'where Wilson needed to appeal for a "Yes" vote over the head of the Labour Party'. For this reason it was argued that it was vital that Blair be closely associated with the campaign in Wales. Finally, it was decided that Alan Barnard, a senior member of Labour's

Millbank team, would be the 'link' between Millbank and the campaign in Wales and would have responsibility for controlling the campaign budget.

In Wales the first meeting of a newly established 'Strategy Committee' took place at the end of May. The committee, chaired by Ron Davies, was to meet at least weekly throughout the campaign. Its membership included Peter Hain, Anita Gale, Andrew Davies, Nick Ainger (Ron Davies's parliamentary private secretary), John Adams (appointed secretary), Huw Roberts (Davies's special adviser), Terry Thomas (chair of the Welsh executive), Alun Williams (the Welsh executive's treasurer), Marlene Thomas (a former chair of the Welsh executive), Harry Jones (leader of the Welsh Local Government Association), Andrew Bold and Huw Lewis (Wales Labour Party officers), Jim Hancock (regional finance officer, TGWU) and Alan Barnard (since he came to exert a major influence, through his control of the campaign budget and because he was a Millbank 'import', he quickly earned the sobriquet of 'governor-general').

On paper it was a powerful team, but tensions became apparent from the start. Labour's general election campaign had been essentially a national strategy with a 'Welsh spin'. But the referendum was to be entirely a 'Welsh affair', and there was a feeling in some quarters that the Labour Party machine in Wales 'was not up to the job'. Just who was felt to be 'up to it' was a moot point. Relations between Ron Davies and Peter Hain were said to be strained. Although Davies chaired the 'Strategy Committee', Hain claimed a mandate from Blair to deliver a 'Yes' vote. Hain was known to have close links with Millbank. There was a feeling in some Labour circles that, while Millbank regarded Hain as 'one of us', they did not extend this trust to Davies (one telling example of the 'partisan' way in which Millbank distributed its favours came early in the campaign, when polling 'debriefs' were given to Hain, but without informing Davies's office).

Davies's uneasy relationship with Hain was further fuelled by impatience with what was seen as the latter's 'media-junkieism' – the tendency endlessly to give 'private' briefings to the press. To add to these fault lines within the campaign team, there were numerous other points of tension. Andrew Davies, as a consequence, became increasingly marginalized as the campaign unfolded. Within the committee Davies felt 'closest' to Ainger and

Roberts – especially the latter. There was also the problem of how to use Rhodri Morgan in the campaign. There had been widespread dismay in Welsh Labour circles at Blair's refusal to appoint him to Ron Davies's team at the Welsh Office. Morgan was a popular, high-profile figure in Wales, and it was believed that Davies wanted him to play a leading role in Labour's referendum campaign. Morgan, though, insists that he was never asked to play any formal part in Labour's campaign, but believed 'there was something of a row' in Blair's office when it was pointed out that there was no Welsh-speaker in the referendum team. This, according to one well-placed Labour source, got an 'abrupt response' from Alastair Campbell, who dismissed the point by saying Morgan had a 'moral obligation' to play a full part in securing a 'Yes' vote.

The size of the 'Strategy Committee' led to the setting-up of a smaller 'Task Force' to spearhead the campaign, comprising Ron Davies (as chair), Andrew Davies, Adams, Ainger, Barnard, Thomas and Gale. The move was not successful. Because Ron Davies was often unavoidably absent, the 'Force' was never taken seriously. There were also problems with those who felt the executive was being sidelined, and who resented Millbank's seeming attempts to 'take over' the campaign, feelings which led to several confrontations with Barnard over the funding of the campaign.

This antipathy to the 'Millbank Tendency' was shared by other Labour campaigners in Wales. There were complaints about Millbank's alleged 'lack of a grasp of politics in Wales'. Many were unhappy about what became dubbed the 'control-freak' aspect of the Millbank management style, based – it was said – on a 'mistrust of "outsiders"' and a 'dismissive' attitude towards ordinary party workers. Yet perhaps the biggest weakness evident in Labour's early campaign planning was, as one source put it, 'the failure to educate and enthuse our activists', something compounded by the lack of preparatory work and lack of time once the campaign had been launched. Time constraints meant that what emerged was very much a 'top-down' campaign, though there were those who believed that, had the political will existed to do so, it would have been possible to mobilize Labour's grass-roots workers.

The problem of trying to carve out a clear message for Labour's campaign was first approached by the use of focus groups. Four focus groups were arranged. Two (one male, one female) met in Maesteg on 11 June, the other two on the following day in Wrexham. The groups were drawn from Labour voters aged thirty or over, an age group thought to contain Labour's core vote. Gould came away from the Maesteg meetings extremely downcast. He was depressed by the groups' lack of basic knowledge about the Assembly and by the general absence of enthusiasm for the Assembly idea. The response in Wrexham, however, was more positive. In the memo which Gould sent to Barnard and Milbank reporting on his findings, he noted that 'awareness is so low that the eventual vote is very hard to call' and argued that, if things were to be turned Labour's way, they would need 'the endorsement of Tony Blair'. These findings came as no real surprise to those at the centre of Labour's campaign. But what did cause concern were the rumours that the issues around devolution for Wales had not been subjected to detailed scrutiny in Labour's policy review, with the clear implication that Blair was either 'lukewarm' about it, or gave the matter only low priority.

Any 'coolness' Blair may have felt towards the 'project' was replicated by other groups inside the Labour movement in Wales. Labour's devolutionists had particular problems with the local government sector and with some members of the Welsh Parliamentary Labour Group. Labour had strengthened its already formidable grip on local government in Wales under successive Conservative Party administrations since 1979. Every attempt by different Conservative governments to 'squeeze' local authorities in Wales (through a variety of fiscal measures and the stripping-away of core service functions) served only to increase the level of popular support for councils astute enough to present themselves as 'defenders of local communities' against the ravages of a Westminster government for which most people in Wales had never voted. In 1995 Welsh local government started on a difficult – and, for many, unwanted – process of reorganization into twenty-two unitary authorities. This 're-engineering' was taking place at the same time as Labour was wrestling with its plans for devolution. There were clearly some leaders of Labour-controlled local authorities in Wales who saw no advantage for them in devolution. For them, the prospect of an Assembly was more of a *threat* than an opportunity to redress the 'democratic deficit' in Wales. Their calculation was essentially self-interested: an Assembly would, so they argued (in private), inevitably want to encroach upon local government territory.

There was also another problem, namely the poor reputation of Labour local authorities in several parts of Wales, linked to notions of 'croneyism', 'inefficiency' and being resistant to new ideas. Andrew Davies was responsible for providing liaison between the campaign team and those local, Labour 'statelets'. Throughout, said Davies, 'the reputation of local government was a *big, big* problem for us'. Soon after the May election, Davies met Harry Jones, leader of both Newport Council and the Welsh Local Government Association. Jones gave Davies what help he could, though constrained by the fact that two of the most populous local authority areas in Wales (Cardiff and Rhondda Cynon Taff) had opted out of the association in a dispute over subscription fees. Davies himself produced a paper exploring ways in which local government could contribute to the campaign, via – for example – newsletters and endorsements. In the event, only Newport came out with a newsletter (and was promptly complained about to the district auditor over the alleged 'misuse' of public funds) and only a handful of Labour local parties mobilized their electoral machinery on behalf of the campaign.

Ron Davies was acutely aware of the significance of the local government sector. Along with Don Touhig, Davies worked hard to get every Labour group to come out publicly to support the Assembly. While they were successful, much of the support so publicly given was largely token. Perhaps this was all Davies and Touhig could have hoped for. This much seems to have been hinted in Andrew Davies's comment: 'In some respects the strategy was to "neutralise" them, rather than get their active involvement.'

The Welsh Group of Labour MPs proved to equally problematic. Few of them proved to be high-profile campaigners. Apart from a small group of outspoken anti-devolutionists (like Llew Smith), there were a number – among them Ted Rowlands and Denzil Davies – who could be described as 'willing to wound, but afraid to strike'. There were others – like Alun Michael and Paul Flynn – who could have played a bigger role, or at least sent out stronger and clearer messages of support. In the interests of unity, the party was not ready formally to discipline 'errant' MPs – which could also be taken as an indication that the devolutionists had only a weak hand to play in relation to the various groupings that form the Labour Party in Wales.

One key part of Andrew Davies's role was to work with the other pro-devolution parties. This task, perhaps not surprisingly, was described by Davies as 'by far the most enjoyable part of my job'. Since a successful campaign depended on building good relations with Plaid (who were nervous about a repeat of 1979), Davies worked hard to build up a relationship of mutual trust. Where it proved impossible to bridge mistrust between Plaid and Labour at the purely *local* level, Davies chose instead to work through the local all-party 'Yes for Wales' campaign groups. Ron Davies was especially supportive of this kind of cross-party co-operation, seeing it as a concrete demonstration of his own commitment to developing a more 'inclusive' style of politics (though, ironically, it often seemed easier to promote an inclusive political culture *across* the parties rather than *within* his own Labour Party).

The publication of the White Paper, *A Voice for Wales*, in July 1997 roughly marked the midway point in Labour's post-election devolution campaign. With the referendum now only ten weeks away, Labour could hardly claim to have in place an effective campaigning machine. The campaign team was scarred by internal tensions; many in the different factions in the party in Wales were giving only grudging and passive support; the party had failed to excite the mass of its own membership over the Assembly idea, and the level of interest in and awareness of the issue among the wider public was low. And yet, if Labour's pro-devolution coalition was tightly stretched, it was, nevertheless, still in place and that, in itself, represented a very considerable achievement for Ron Davies and his allies.

## Notes

1. This is drawn from our book *Redesigning Democracy: The Making of the Welsh Assembly* (Bridgend: Seren, 2000).

2. Philip Gould, a polling expert, was the architect of focus groups within the Labour Party. In June 1997 he organized two focus groups, in Maesteg and Wrexham, to test Labour voters' attitudes to devolution in general and the referendum in particular.

3. The clearest expression of this coalitionist thinking was the leading role which pro-devolution figures, Ron Davies and Peter Hain in particular, played in helping to set up the Yes for Wales Campaign, which was launched in February 1997.

4. The Parliament for Wales Campaign was formerly the Campaign for a Welsh

Assembly Group, founded in 1988 and chaired, initially, by Jon Owen Jones, Labour MP for Cardiff Central.

## References

Anderson, D. (1992). 'Why I changed my mind on devolution', *Western Mail*, 27 January.

Bevan, A. (1944). *Welsh Day Debate*, House of Commons, 17 October.

Bevan, A, (1947). 'The claim of Wales; a statement', *Wales* (Spring).

Davies, R. (1999). Personal interview.

Gould, P. (1997). 'Assembly for Wales: referendum polling' (Labour Party memorandum).

Griffiths, J. (1944). *Welsh Day Debate*, House of Commons, 17 October.

Griffiths, R. (1978). *Turning to London: Labour's Attitude to Wales, 1898–1956*, Abertridwr: Y Faner Goch.

Griffiths, R. (1979). 'The other Aneurin Bevan', *Planet*, 41, 26–8.

Keating, M. and Loughlin, J. (eds.) (1997). *The Political Economy of Regionalism*, London: Frank Cass.

Kinnock, N. (1990). 'Message to the Regional Government conference', Newcastle.

Morgan, K. (1994). 'Beyond the quangos: redressing the democratic deficit', *Welsh Agenda*, 1 (1).

Morgan, K. and Mungham, G. (2000). *Redesigning Democracy: The Making of the Welsh Assembly*, Bridgend: Seren.

Morgan, K. and Roberts, E. (1993). *The Democratic Deficit: A Guide to Quangoland*, Papers in Planning Research, No.151, Department of City and Regional Planning, Cardiff University.

Morgan, K. O. (1989). *The Red Dragon and the Red Flag: The Cases of James Griffiths and Aneurin Bevan*, Aberystwyth: National Library of Wales.

Osmond, J. (1996). *Welsh Europeans*, Bridgend: Seren.

Rose, R. (1982). *Understanding the United Kingdom: The Territorial Dimension in Government*, London: Longmans.

Smith, D. (1997). 'The ashes onto the wind: Bevan and Wales', in G. Goodman (ed.), *The Political Legacy of Aneurin Bevan,* London: Gollancz.

Wales Labour Party (1990). *A Statement on the Future of Local and Regional Government in Wales*, Cardiff.

# 4    Too Important to be Left to the Politicians: The 'Yes' for Wales Story

LEIGHTON ANDREWS

## Introduction

The drama surrounding the referendum result on 18 September 1997 has tended to overshadow the story of the referendum campaign itself. It is now too frequently forgotten that when Ron Davies announced the referendum on 27 June 1996, the main reaction from supporters of devolution was demoralization. Some felt that Labour was backsliding and getting ready for betrayal.

Paradoxically, however, opinion polls in Wales did seem to show a significant majority in favour of devolution in Wales. So why were devolution campaigners themselves so nervous about the prospects for victory, and why were they so disillusioned with the idea of a referendum? The referendum announcement seemed, on the surface, to be a retreat. Many were unhappy with the Welsh proposals, which they saw as timid and inadequate: they argued that the Assembly proposals would not command the support of the people because they did not go far enough. Others feared that Welsh devolution was a campaign that could not be won because they knew that the work had not been done at the grass roots to win over the public to a 'Yes' vote. And they were right. The devolution campaign in Wales – from 1987 the Campaign for a Welsh Assembly, then from 1992 the Parliament for Wales Campaign – had focused principally on winning support amongst the politically active and the chattering classes, rather than on converting public opinion as a whole. In Wales, there was nothing as pluralist or popular as the Scottish Constitutional Convention.

In consequence, there was criticism of Labour's plans for the referendum from both the Welsh Liberal Democrats and from Plaid

Cymru, as well as the Parliament for Wales campaign. Labour's plans were not their plans: they wanted commitment to tax-raising and law-making powers, and to a much more proportional electoral system. They warned that their support for a campaign for a 'Yes' vote was in the balance. Within Labour, too, there was opposition to the referendum over issues such as the electoral system and the powers of the Assembly. The Wales Labour Party had recalled its Policy Commission on devolution to respond to the call from Ron Davies and Tony Blair that there should be an element of proportionality in the electoral system. Some MPs were as hostile to PR as to devolution, and pressed for the party to allow them to express their views in the referendum campaign. Other party activists, such as Gareth.Hughes of Wales Labour Action and Cardiff councillor Kevin Brennan, sought to open up the debate on the Assembly's powers and the electoral system.

### Filling the gap: the creation of 'Yes' for Wales

One person who did not believe that the devolution referendum needed to be lost was Peter Hain, the Labour MP for Neath. A successful campaigner with a thirty-year track record of campaign success (including in the anti-apartheid Stop the Seventy Tour Campaign and the Anti-Nazi League), he had discussed with Ron Davies specifically the need to identify the possible leaders of a non-party umbrella campaign for devolution, and had agreed to get an all-party campaign under way. Hain planned the campaign with the present author from late summer of 1996. We had known each other since the 1970s and used our contacts to test out support for an all-party 'Yes' campaign, and to see whether the Rowntree Trust, headed by Sir Trevor Smith, would be willing to provide initial funds. Several meetings were held in the Commons with potential supporters, and a search for the right person to chair the campaign was indicated.

The views of prominent members of the Welsh Liberal Democrats and Plaid Cymru were canvassed. Hain was able to explain to them that Labour would take the campaign very seriously, recruiting its own organizer and receiving a budget and support from the UK party. This helped to persuade both Plaid and the Liberal Democrats that things would not be the same as 1979. Hain had always been of the view that a new campaign vehicle was needed for mobilizing the 'Yes' vote. Labour saw the Parliament for Wales campaign as something of a Plaid/Liberal front. Its call for a referendum with a multiple-choice set of questions identical to that of Plaid made it look and sound like a Plaid Cymru front. A new campaign, Hain felt, must have one focus: victory in the referendum. This became the basic strategy of the Yes for Wales Steering Committee, outlined in its first paper, the 'Aims of the Campaign'.

The new campaign's objective quite simply was to secure a 'Yes' vote in the referendum on Welsh devolution: 'It is not a forum for debate on the merits of different forms of devolution to or within Wales, or on the nature of the Assembly's tax-raising or law-making powers. Its sole purpose is to secure a yes-vote in the referendum on the terms offered.' Hain explained that people were not being asked to downplay their own views but that they should focus on points of unity. The campaign would be non-party and all-party. The paper recognized that the referendum could be held as early as the autumn of 1997 – about a year away – and identified the urgency of appointing a campaign organizer, establishing local 'Yes' campaigns and specialist groups; e.g. Doctors Say Yes, Teachers Say Yes, etc. Above all, it was agreed that the campaign had to be popular, taking the argument for devolution out to ordinary people, confident about the prospects for Wales after devolution and involving popular celebrities. In Hain's view, 'the campaign will only succeed if it engages with popular contemporary culture.'

## Launching the Yes for Wales campaign

In early December, Peter Hain had identified a potential campaign organizer: Daran Hill, a former vice-president of NUS (National Union of Students) Wales, and a Labour Party member from Neath. He was interviewed and offered the job, conditional upon the money from Rowntree being secured. He agreed to start in January 1997.

The first meeting of the campaign's Steering Committee was held in December 1996. Chaired by Peter Hain, it included the author; Mari James, former organizer of the Parliament for Wales

Campaign; Professor Kevin Morgan (a close adviser to the Shadow Secretary of State on economic development issues); Geraint Stanley Jones, formerly chief executive of S4C and controller of BBC Wales; Derek Gregory of Unison; Alun Jones of the NUT; Eluned Morgan MEP; Peter Polish of Democratic Left; Eleri Carrog of Cefn; Huw Roberts, formerly director of public affairs of Swalec and of ITN, now running his own political consultancy; Angela Pulman of Community Enterprise Wales; Alun Wyn Bevan, soon to join Agenda TV; and Ron Jones of Agenda Television. Other Steering Committee members included Professor Hywel Francis, the historian and adult educationalist; Val Feld, a prominent Labour activist and a former director of Shelter Cymru; David Waterstone, the former chief executive of the WDA; and Russell Deacon of the Welsh Liberal Democrats.

The Shadow Secretary of State, Ron Davies, attended the first meeting, and spoke and answered questions. Hain and the present author outlined the campaign's initial plans, introduced the new national organizer, demonstrated initial ideas for the logo, and took soundings on the campaign strategy. It was agreed to go for a main launch in February 1997, and to set up an organization of business supporters, to undermine possible opposition from business organizations such as the Wales CBI (Confederation of British Industry). Daran Hill began work as planned in January 1997. Mari James obtained the backing of Charter 88 to act as the payroll-handler for the salary of the national organizer, and assumed responsibility for the IT (information technology) needs of the campaign.

On 17 January 1997, *The Western Mail* front page was headed 'Tycoon Forum backs fight for Assembly'. The Business Forum on Devolution took much of Wales by surprise. It had been decided that *The Western Mail* would be given exclusive coverage in recognition that exclusivity would be likely to guarantee prominence. The campaign's thinking was simple. Though *The Western Mail* was not the most widely read newspaper in Wales, it was actively interested in the devolution debate, read by opinion-formers, and helped set the agenda for the broadcasters. The Business Forum statement was endorsed by Geraint Stanley Jones, then working in TV production, Ron Jones, who headed Agenda Television, Mike James, chairman of BJ Construction and of Swansea Rugby Club, Jack Pearce of John Pearce Ltd, the haulage company, and Rhydian

Davies of Consolidated Coal, as well as David Waterstone. The Business Forum's statement described devolution as 'a positive force for the Welsh economy'. The initiative was welcomed by Ron Davies, Shadow Secretary of State for Wales, who said he was confident that the Assembly would be able to enter a partnership with Welsh business and commerce. The Business Forum statement attracted considerable media attention, with a feature and an editorial in *The Western Mail*, as well as broadcast coverage. It was a good start.

Following this, *Wales on Sunday* was given a hint about the Yes for Wales campaign for 19 January, to coincide with Peter Hain's interview planned by HTV for that day, The story ran: 'A rainbow coalition of Welsh devolution supporters ranging from bishops to sportsmen is expected to reveal itself within weeks.' The leak was carefully planned: perhaps too well planned, as very few noticed it. But Hain hinted at the new campaign and made it clear that there would be developments very shortly.

The second meeting of the Yes for Wales Steering Committee was held on 24 January. The following day Clive Betts in *The Western Mail* reported that a group had met the night before to consider launching a 'Yes' campaign. Betts was told: 'Members of the group believe that devolution is too important to be left to the political parties alone.' He wrote that the campaign was looking for supporters from all walks of life and even Conservatives, and indicated that the group had decided to reject the demands by Plaid Cymru and the Parliament for Wales campaign for a multi-choice referendum.

The basic case for Yes for Wales was to be presented in an Agenda-page article in *The Western Mail*, in the name of Professor Kevin Morgan. An informal consensus had emerged on the Steering Committee that he should be chairman of the campaign. *The Western Mail* headlined the article in Morgan's name 'The People's Cause' with the subhead, 'Devolution is too vital to be left to the politicians.' The article said that the campaign would focus on the principle of devolution, rather than wrangling over the details, and that the campaign was supported by people from all over Wales with different views on the details, but who recognized the dangers of division against a united 'No' campaign. 'Unless we win the referendum, there will be no chance even to debate the details of devolution we want. Without a yes vote, the whole project is doomed. This is the last chance Wales has to decide its future for at least a generation.'

*The Western Mail* also reported that the group had occupied an office in Cardiff and appointed a full-time organizer. *Wales on Sunday* was given the name of Tyrone O'Sullivan (one of the leaders of the Tower Colliery miners' buy-out), as one of the prominent Welsh people who would be declaring themselves for devolution, and on the Sunday the broadcasters followed up the story.

The actual launch of the campaign was held in Cardiff City Hall, then thought likely to be the home of the Assembly. On the platform were Kevin Morgan, the broadcaster Mavis Nicholson and the MEP Eluned Morgan. The campaign was anxious to ensure both a gender and linguistic balance in its public personalities. A list of supporters was announced including sports stars, cricketers Tony Cottey and Steve Watkin, hockey player Linda Watkin, rugby player Stuart Evans and boxer Steve Robinson, secretary of the Welsh Rugby Union, Vernon Pugh, actors Siân Phillips and Philip Madoc, playwright Ewart Alexander, and the rock group Catatonia. Yes for Wales (YFW) had worked particularly hard to get one of the upcoming Welsh rock bands on board, and it was Catatonia's album *Way Beyond Blue* that greeted people attending the press conference.

Sensitive to the charge that it might be seen as a Labour front (an issue that was to be raised in subsequent press conferences), the campaign arranged for Alex Carlile, leader of the Welsh Liberal Democrats, to issue a statement of support. Eleri Carrog, a member of Plaid Cymru, also declared her support. Predictably, the launch attracted negative criticisms. The Conservative minister Gwilym Jones attacked the campaign as a collection of 'has-beens and never-weres', prompting the response from the campaign that 'the Minister had demeaned his office by his petty, personal attacks on a wide range of Welsh figures far more distinguished than himself'. Coverage gained by the launch was extensive with Welsh media, and YFW saw this as a success.

In February, the Welsh Labour Party unveiled its own plans in 'Representing Wales', and Tony Blair announced that he would join in the referendum campaign. Backing for Labour's devolution plans was declared by all Labour council group leaders in Wales at the same time. The Welsh Economy Research Unit at the Cardiff

Business School indicated that the cost of the Assembly could be as little as £5 per head, and on St David's Day *The Western Mail* came out in favour of devolution.

## The organization of the Yes for Wales campaign

Campaigns are not linear activities organized around a single narrative. They have to be pursued on many different planes at the same time: there is the internal structure of a campaign with its cycles of meetings and self-imposed targets; there are the external conditions and events which a campaign seeks to influence and which may themselves in turn influence the campaign; there are the different tasks all being undertaken at the same time by different individuals, including fund-raising, message development, rebuttal, event management and group support. In writing an account of a campaign such as this, it is therefore necessary to try to draw out at the beginning of the story some basic threads which run through the organization, before turning to the narrative of the campaign.

## Funding the campaign

The only money available to Yes for Wales was money it could raise itself. Though the campaign had obtained a promise of two years of grant funding from the Rowntree Reform Trust, this would be nowhere near enough to fund a campaign which had to challenge opinion across Wales. Rowntree funds of £25,000 for 1997 paid for office costs and some basic literature. The rest of the money would have to be raised from a range of other sources: voluntary donations from the public and supporters, contributions from unions and political parties, and from business.

On 17 March, Yes for Wales ran its first advertisement asking for funds in *The Western Mail*. That day it launched its website, and mailed its supporters and potential supporters through the mailings of other organizations. Small sums were coming in, but far more would be needed when campaigning for the referendum started. By mid-May, £10,000 had been spent on salaries and publicity materials. If Yes for Wales was to run an effective advertising campaign a sum of £250,000 would be needed, with more for polling. That was never achieved, although the campaign developed a mailing list of 1,500. By the end of May there was a budget of £43,000, and early in June, Rowntree Trust hinted that it might be willing to make further money available. The campaign began expanding its staff during July, and Rowntree's release of extra money, coupled with a steady flow of income from donations, allowed the 'Yes' campaign to embark on at least the elements of an advertising campaign. A van was hired with an advertisement for the 'Yes' campaign and a phone number to ring to support the campaign. This drove throughout Wales and was available to the campaign for local meetings and celebrity photocalls. In August, the Yes for Wales campaign decided it would need to up its level of spending for the duration of the campaign, and made an appeal for an additional £20,000. The announcement was partly made to counter claims that the 'Yes' side luxuriated in government sponsorship. On the night of the referendum, Yes for Wales campaigners knew they needed to find a way to raise an additional £30,000 or so to pay the campaign's bills. In total, the campaign's income was just over £150,000, as it told the Neill Committee in May 1998.

## Operational strategy

Once the campaign was launched, the Steering Committee had to determine its strategy. In its meeting on 21 March it reviewed the campaign so far, conscious that the campaign had not penetrated the tabloid press and recognizing that it would need to speed up with extra staffing and clearer lines of responsibility for the Steering Committee members. The campaign also needed to clarify its relationship with the new government and decided to focus on fund-raising, recruiting celebrities and establishing the infra-structure of the campaign, with local groups in particular. The committee anticipated that the publication of the White Paper would require persuading people to make the change from supporting the principle of devolution to supporting the devolu-tion package on offer. It was decided to focus on the development of the case for devolution for different groups. Women were to be a particular target.

The Steering Committee expanded significantly in the period to July, as some of the political parties joined, and became rather unwieldy. YFW held a national conference in July and announced a restructuring of the Steering Committee to include local group representatives and a reduction in other members without designated tasks. During August, the campaign held two expanded Steering Groups attended by representatives of local groups, at the Eisteddfod in Bala and in Neath three weeks later. These were designed to facilitate co-ordination between local groups and the campaign at the centre and to share information. A campaign pack was dispatched to all groups as they were formed.

In the final months of the referendum campaign, the Steering Committee met less frequently, but the key officers, at least those based in south Wales, were meeting weekly. Vice-chair Mari James worked full-time in the campaign office during the summer and through September, co-ordinating the implementation of campaign activities and liaising with the political parties. Convenor Hywel Francis was on the road as one of the campaign's leading speakers, as was campaign chair Kevin Morgan, who was frequently called on by the media as YFW's main spokesperson. Val Feld, the treasurer, was heavily involved in fund-raising and in organizing Women Say Yes. The present author looked after media relations, supervised the flow of announcements handled by the press officer, Kate Stokes, as well as keeping in touch with the Labour campaign. The other campaign vice-chair, Eleri Carrog, based in north Wales, played a leading role in getting groups off the ground there. Crucial to local liaison were the Yes for Wales organizers based in north-west and north-east Wales (Jill Torkington and Claire Bryant), the Valleys (Darren Evans) and west Wales (Anna McMorrin).

## Communications strategy

In the absence of large-scale funds for advertising, Yes for Wales resorted to local campaigning and national and local media coverage. Local groups were seen as the key to getting the message across to ordinary people. Local groups dealt with local media and encouraged local debate on the benefits of decentralization; mobilized activists to campaign for a 'Yes' vote; acted as fund-raisers; and provided a forum for people from different political parties to come together in a particular geographic area. Yes for

Wales also organized its supporters in sectors (business, arts etc.), and launched several sectoral groups. The Steering Committee also produced a detailed list of Wales-wide events between the election and the expected referendum date.

The campaign's media strategy was based on a series of events, policy statements and celebrity endorsements. The publication of the White Paper provided a vehicle for taking the campaign forward, and a media strategy was devised emphasizing popular and positive elements. At this early stage it was decided that the final week's message would be 'Wales must not get left behind'.

Clearly, the 'No' campaign could not be ignored. It was expected to campaign on divisive themes, setting Welsh-speakers against non-Welsh-speakers, running a highly negative campaign. The Yes for Wales aproach to the 'No' campaign would be to rebut lies and distortions, then to move back on to its own positive themes as soon as possible. These included: 'Wales needs a voice'; 'An Assembly will be good for jobs and for inward investment'; 'Wales needs to decide its own priorities on key issues'; 'An All-Wales Assembly will give Welsh issues more time than the House of Commons'.

The strategy recognized that the Welsh broadcast media were to be the priority, with particular concern for those areas of Wales where people tuned in to English TV programmes. Specific themed articles were prepared for *The Western Mail*. Tabloid papers in Wales (*Daily Post, Wales on Sunday, South Wales Echo, South Wales Evening Post* etc.) were fed a diet of local and celebrity-linked stories. In the last four weeks of the campaign, Yes for Wales set out themes for daily and weekly media coverage. A detailed media briefing pack was sent out to the Welsh and London media. It contained a list of activities, information on the breadth of its sectoral support including business, celebrities, local and sectoral groups, funding, the Just Say No campaign, dissident Labour MPs, polling results and a list of future activities.

**The campaign under way: from the election to the White Paper**

There was a widely held concern in the Yes for Wales campaign that the overwhelming Labour majority might undermine the enthusiasm for devolution. Yes for Wales was aware of research carried out in Scotland that indicated a very low level of understanding of the meaning of devolution, let alone the government's proposals. In the middle of May, we presented a paper to Hain, now a Welsh Office minister, which argued that there was a real danger of presuming the general election result could be automatically translated into a 'Yes' vote in September. The Welsh Office would need to run a basic information campaign on the government's proposals. The 'Yes' campaign would need resources for advertising to invoke the votes of the pro-devolution parties in a kind of popular front against the status quo, represented by the Conservatives. Meanwhile, Plaid leader Dafydd Wigley indicated that Plaid would only oppose Labour's plans if they offered no increase in devolved power. The Liberal Democrats agreed to campaign for a 'Yes' vote if they were consulted by Labour. Even some Conservatives were rethinking their position.

The Referendum bill, unveiled on 15 May 1997, marked the start of the campaign proper. Professor Kevin Morgan was formally appointed chairman of Yes for Wales, and by June the campaign was planning to find ways of using volunteer staff. At the launch Ron Davies told the press conference that it was not appropriate for any Labour MP to take any course of action which would include, for example, associating with others in opposition to the 'Yes' campaign or indeed publicly campaigning on their own behalf against the government's proposals. But the first signs of a 'No' campaign were beginning to be felt. In the Rhondda, two women activists, one a former chair of the Wales Labour Party, declared their opposition. An unnamed senior Conservative spokesperson in Wales said that there would be an all-party 'No' campaign launched during the summer, though by 28 June *The Western Mail* commented that the 'No' campaign had failed to have its first meeting, nor had it yet found an apolitical chair.

Support for the 'Yes' campaign rapidly grew. The Wales TUC joined the Steering Committee and published its document in support of a 'Yes' vote in June. The first local 'Yes' group was launched in Neath on 19 May 1997. A public meeting was held in Caernarfon in late May to get things moving in north Wales. Nine other groups were launched in June: Cardiff, Ceredigion, Newport, Bridgend, Blaenau Gwent, Rhondda, Port Talbot, Ynys Môn and Torfaen. Carmarthen, Monmouth and Swansea were launched in July.

Yes for Wales also promoted more sectoral groups. Christian Ministers Say Yes was launched at the end of May. Students Say Yes was launched in June and concern that women voters seemed less supportive of devolution than men led to Yes for Wales handing in a letter to the Secretary of State from Women Say Yes on 23 June, calling for fair representation for women.

By early June rumours began to circulate about the prospects for a 'No' campaign. There was concern about the way in which the media, particularly the broadcasters, would cover the campaign. Kevin Morgan reported to the Yes for Wales Steering Committee on 6 June about a meeting he had had with the BBC's chief political adviser Anne Sloman. Morgan was very concerned that an inactive 'No' campaign would still get as much coverage as an active 'Yes' campaign on grounds of 'balance'. Within the likely 'Yes' camp, not all was rosy either, as David Jenkins, general secretary of the Wales TUC, attacked Plaid and their 'narrow nationalist agenda'.

July, however, began with better news for the 'Yes' campaign. *The Western Mail's* poll showed that those planning to vote 'No' had dropped from 37 to 27 per cent, while those planning to vote 'Yes' had increased from 34 to 39 per cent. Taking account of a likely differential turnout between 'Yes' and 'No' voters, that gave the 'Yes' camp 43 per cent of the vote. However, 28 per cent were undecided. Most encouraging was the level of support in the Valleys, where most of the anti-devolution MPs were concentrated.

Discontent in Labour's ranks began to emerge at this stage. Llew Smith sought to turn his dispute with Ron Davies into an issue of free speech, and his cause was taken up by the Conservatives, out to embarrass the government. MPs who were seen as devo-sceptic (Alan Williams and Ted Rowlands) expressed their concern that the referendum would precede the actual devolution bill. The 'No' campaign was also starting to shape up. Viscount Tonypandy, touted as a possible leader of the 'No' campaign by the Conservatives, confirmed his opposition to devolution and said he believed that the people of Wales would say 'No' to the Assembly. The Llew Smith case caused the Yes for Wales campaign great concern and rumbled on for several weeks. The 'Yes' campaign feared that, if Labour could not orchestrate its MPs to come out and make the positive case for devolution now, they would not be able to do so in the heat of the referendum campaign. A meeting of the Parliamentary Labour Party confirmed that MPs could express their views without fear of expulsion, but that they should not be involved in a sustained campaign against Labour Party policy. Meanwhile, government ministers were seeking to clarify the extent to which the government itself could campaign in favour of its own proposals. They hoped for a spectacular launch of the White Paper in Cardiff after its presentation in the House of Commons but were told by officials that this would amount to campaigning, and would be ruled out of order. Yes for Wales was asked to make arrangements for the launch. A booking was promptly made for Cardiff Castle on 22 July. The date and planning were so secret that for at least a week only two people within Yes for Wales were aware of the move. Yes for Wales held its national conference in Llandrindod Wells over the weekend of 12–13 July. The campaign had achieved all-party backing for the conference, with Viscount St David, a former Conservative government spokesman on Wales, agreeing to speak. Both Plaid Cymru and the Liberal Democrats agreed to send speakers. Ron Davies spoke for the government. The private lines of communication which Yes for Wales had established with the parties were beginning to pay off. The national conference was attended by 150 people representing many local groups from around Wales.

### Launching the campaign: the White Paper

In the run-up to the White Paper launch, there was more positive news for the 'Yes' campaign. Ryan Giggs came out in favour in the *Daily Mirror*, Tony Blair made his first campaign appearance in Wales, answering questions in front of an invited audience in Llancaiach Fawr with Ron Davies. For both occasions, the *Daily Mirror* produced special Welsh editions, and their circulation in Wales went up. Blair's visit attracted massive TV and radio coverage, exactly the kind of media coverage Yes for Wales was really looking for. The good news continued. As the days to the launch of the White Paper went by, Yes for Wales choreographed the announcement of a number of other groups in support of the Assembly, including teachers, the Presbyterian church, farmers and Welsh writers. John Elfed Jones, former chairman of Welsh Water and HTV Wales, became the most prominent business supporter of the campaign.

The White Paper on Welsh devolution, *A Voice for Wales*, was launched by the Secretary of State, Ron Davies, in the House of Commons on 22 July. It outlined the creation of a sixty-member Assembly, with forty members elected by first-past-the-post and twenty by a form of PR. The Assembly would take over the powers of the Secretary of State and would have powers to reform or abolish the quangos. Following the statement, the three Welsh Office ministers and their advisers caught the train from Paddington to Cardiff in time to join the reception at Cardiff Castle. There were 200 guests from the arts, sports and politics, as well as local 'Yes' groups. The television personality Siân Lloyd hosted the evening. This was not an event for the great and the good, but for people from all backgrounds. Perhaps the speaker who attracted most emotional support was Tyrone O'Sullivan, leader of the miners' buy-out at Tower Colliery. Most of the UK and Welsh broadcasters were represented, and there was widespread coverage in the next day's papers, and extensive coverage on that evening's news. By any measure the event was a media success.

Over the following days, more groups announced their support for a 'Yes' vote. Finally, at their special council meeting on July 26, Plaid Cymru came off the fence and agreed to support the government's proposals.

### From White Paper through the 'silly season'

By the Steering Group meeting at Bala on 2 August, the campaign was ready for the referendum with letterheads, balloons, T-shirts, car stickers, campaign ribbons, stickers, posters, recruitment leaflets and carrier bags.

As expected, the 'No' campaign adopted a negative abrasive tone. At the Eisteddfod, it claimed it had been set upon and spat at, though the Eisteddfod organizers were not able to confirm this. The first signs of disagreement in the 'No' campaign surfaced, with one former Conservative agent attacking it. Elwyn Jones said, 'I now want nothing to do with a campaign which is autocratic and has little understanding of the Welsh way of life.' The 'No' campaign ran two main arguments on the Eisteddfod field, claiming that Assembly members would be paid £78,000 per annum, and that the people of Wales would face an extra tax of £1,200 a year.

Meanwhile, a survey of Labour councillors revealed that 70 per cent of them would vote 'Yes'. Friends of the Earth declared in favour, as did Welsh pensioners. The Federation of Small Businesses came out against. At a local level, the campaigning was becoming more active. Summer fairs and festivals were targeted by local Yes for Wales groups, with the Neath group leading the way with a clear plan for the whole of its area. In a pre-planned process, Newport and Torfaen Councils came out in favour. So did Carmarthenshire County Council, Gwynedd and Ynys Môn Councils. Celebrities continued to come out in favour, with the rock group the Stereophonics declaring their support. Artists Say Yes and Health Workers Say Yes were launched. The government launched its devolution hotline and Yes for Wales groups were launched in Abergavenny, Pontypridd, Pembrokeshire and Llanelli. A campaign shop was opened in Ystradgynlais. Ethnic-minority supporters came out in support of the 'Yes' campaign, as did Cymdeithas Yr Iaith. Meanwhile, the Labour Party campaign started targeting the Valleys, with several minibuses carrying campaigners into town centres for leafleting and canvassing.

To counter the cost argument, the government said that the cost of the Assembly would be met by savings from the quangos.

## The campaign proper

The Yes for Wales Steering Committee met in Neath Civic Centre on Saturday 23 August with representatives from Bridgend and Ogmore, Blaenau Gwent, Llanelli, Neath, Aberavon, Ceredigion, Ystradgynlais/Brecon and Radnor, Swansea and Cardiff, as well as the Wales Labour Party, Plaid Cymru, the Welsh Liberal Democrats, Democratic Left and Unison. The officers outlined the campaign timetable for the final week, explaining how the campaign would be relaunched on the Tuesday following the Bank Holiday. Campaigners were in good heart. The Labour Party had distributed its first leaflet and a second would be unveiled the following week along with bus advertising. Unison had mailed all their members. The Liberal Democrats were active through local 'Yes' campaigns but were producing their own 'Yes' posters. Plaid, while mobilizing their own voters, were working through 'Yes' groups. They were undertaking telephone polling. The Llanelli, Ceredigion and Cardiff groups had been leafleting using their own locally produced leaflets. Cardiff had produced credit-card-shaped pledge cards. Ystradgynlais was working through local rugby clubs. Brecon and Radnor had had a specific focus on farmers. But most groups indicated they were not expecting to canvass as they anticipated local political parties taking responsibility for that.

One aspect of the Yes for Wales campaign was focused on refuting the claims of the 'No' campaign that the business community supported Just Say No. *Wales on Sunday* published an on-the-record quote from the director of the Wales CBI denouncing a 'No' campaign leaflet claiming CBI support as 'a lie'. This story was followed up by the *Financial Times*, enabling the 'Yes' campaign in Wales to undermine the charge that business was opposed to Welsh devolution.

The Yes for Wales Campaign announced a long list of celebrities in support of the 'Yes' campaign at its press conference on 28 August. These included Ruth Madoc, Bryn Terfel, Matthew Rhys, Ioan Gruffydd, Dennis O'Neill, Gwyn Hughes Jones and most of the cast of *Pobol y Cwm*. The tempo of the campaign began to build up. The following week there were leaflet blitzes in Porthcawl, Bridgend, Llanelli, Swansea, Pontypool, Montgomeryshire, Ceredigion, Brynmawr, Neath, Cardiff and Aberavon; public meetings in Wrexham, Ebbw Vale and Cynon Valley, and a concert and meeting in Haverfordwest. Women Say Yes for Wales held a rally at Whitland's Hywel Dda Memorial Park. The Liberal Democrats, Plaid and the Welsh Greens signed a joint declaration in favour of the Assembly, and Yes for Wales issued a joint statement from Labour MEP Eluned Morgan, Liberal Democrat MP Richard Livsey and Plaid MP Cynog Dafis on the benefits to agriculture of the Assembly. That Saturday, the 'Yes' campaigners really felt things were going their way. The atmosphere was good on the streets and *The Western Mail* ran a poll putting the 'Yes' campaign well ahead, by 42 to 22 per cent. But, as the paper pointed out, over a third still said they were undecided.

Then, tragedy struck. The death of Diana, Princess of Wales on Sunday brought a pause to public campaigning. There were phone calls between Cardiff, Glasgow and London as 'Yes' campaigners and the government bowed to the obvious and agreed that there would be no more press conferences until after the funeral the following Saturday. 'Yes' campaigners have no doubt in retrospect about the impact of the moratorium, which undermined their momentum. Several events had to be cancelled including a Business Forum on Devolution conference and several local fund-raising activities.

The campaigns relaunched on 8 September. MPs and ministers returned to the fray and the government announced that several ministers would visit Wales in the last ten days of the campaign, Yes for Wales launched *The Economic Case for an Assembly* and local 'Yes' campaign shops were opened in Llanllyfni and Caernarfon. A campaign bus was launched in the Valleys, and there were public meetings in Cwmbran, Pyle, Pembrokeshire, Brynmawr, Aberdare, Aberystwyth, Maesteg, Llanidloes, Colwyn Bay, Machynlleth, Welshpool, Coity, Bridgend, Monmouth, Barry, Cardiff and Newtown. Leafleting blitzes went on in Clwyd, Alyn and Deeside, Wrexham, Carmarthen, Holyhead, Pwllheli, Arfon, Llangefni, Newtown, Conwy, Bala and Meirionnydd. There was a large Labour rally in Pontypridd with local MP and education minister Kim Howells, the Deputy Prime Minister John Prescott and Siân Lloyd, the weather presenter.

Eyes were now firmly on Scotland, as their poll was now only four days away. The 'Yes' campaign, noting that Mrs Thatcher was campaigning in Scotland, rushed out a release labelling the dissident Labour MPs as 'Thatcher's Friends'. Press conferences were now a daily event. The 'Yes' campaign found Conservative supporters of devolution and held a press conference with them. There was a press conference on education and the Assembly with education minister Kim Howells. A document was released by the campaign on housing and the Assembly. Against all this activity a small doubt entered the perceptions of the activists. A *Guardian* poll suggesting the vote was on a knife-edge was published on 10 September, dubbed 'wobbly Wednesday'. The poll had the vote at 37 per cent 'Yes' and 36 per cent 'No', with 27 per cent undecided.

On the Thursday came Scotland's victory vote. The next day, supporters of Yes for Wales greeted Chancellor Gordon Brown with a congratulations card at Cardiff Station, and a banner stating the final message, 'Wales must not get left behind'. A congratulations card was also handed to victorious 'Yes' campaigners in Scotland by Mari James and a small group of Yes for Wales supporters who had travelled north for the Scottish vote and a BBC *Panorama* devolution debate.

A flying visit by the Prime Minister to Cardiff was supported by 'Yes' banners as Blair urged a 'Yes' vote in Wales as well as in Scotland. Yes for Wales was mindful of the polls and aware that another opinion poll was being carried out for HTV that weekend. At this time, the campaign also became aware that insufficient work had been undertaken to get the message out in Cardiff. On the same day over a quarter of a million 'Yes for Wales' news-papers, bearing the heading 'Don't let Wales get Left Behind' and featuring Neil Jenkins in a Yes for Wales T-shirt, were delivered to campaigners for distribution over the last weekend. But doubts remained whether all would be distributed. On Sunday, Donald Dewar arrived from Scotland to join the Labour Party campaign and 'Yes' campaigners. A photocall held at City Hall, with the slogan 'Scotland voted Yes – Don't let Wales get left behind' was recorded widely on television and became the front page of *The Western Mail* the next day. Eighty people came to the Yes for Wales headquarters that evening to deliver both Yes for Wales and Labour leaflets in those areas of Cardiff which had not yet received them.

The final week saw local campaigning at its peak, with yet more meetings, rallies and leaflet drops. The *Daily Mirror*, which had dropped 'Yes' coverage in the aftermath of Diana's funeral, came back into the campaign in the last few days to urge a 'Yes' vote. A poll for HTV at the beginning of the week found 37 per cent 'Yes', 29 per cent 'No' and 34 per cent still undecided, but a likely turnout of only 50 per cent was forecast. 'Yes' campaigners had to intervene with the Liberal Democrats after their leader said on BBC's *Frost Programme* that it was arrogant to think the people of Wales would necessarily follow the people of Scotland. Ashdown was given private briefings by the 'Yes' campaign and corrected the interpretation of his comments. Further photocalls were held, with minister Tony Banks, Peter Hain and Cardiff rugby captain Jonathan Humphries. In the last few days, Ted Rowlands, one of the MPs with doubts, confirmed he would vote 'Yes'. The Prime Minister returned to Wales to visit Wrexham, where the greeting was quite extraordinary, and the Deputy Prime Minister visited Newport.

In the final day, the 'Yes' campaign joined in the traditional polling-day activities alongside the political parties, leafleting and 'knocking up' in the key areas. An anonymous businessman donated a private plane to fly over the Valleys with the message 'Vote Yes – Support Blair'.

The Park Hotel was the Yes for Wales headquarters on the night of the results. As the early results came in they were in keeping with what Yes for Wales had feared. Defeats in the more anglicized border areas, victories in Bridgend, Merthyr and Blaenau Gwent (this one cheered to the rafters). But by 2.30 a.m. 'Yes' supporters in the Park Hotel could no longer see the way through. It looked likely that the 'Yes' campaign was to be squeezed out by the smallest of margins. Rallying, defiant, if downbeat, speeches were made, first by Peter Hain, then by 'Yes' campaign chair Kevin Morgan, specifically called back to the Park Hotel from the count at the Welsh College of Music and Drama to be with the Yes for Wales 'troops'. Then came the Gwynedd and Powys results: the first better than expected for the 'Yes' campaign, and the second worse than expected for the 'No' campaign. Suddenly, things came alive. Rumours began to circulate that it would, after all, be a very good morning for Wales. Then came the Carmarthen result and there was pandemonium. Shortly after, the leaders of Wales's pro-devolution political parties came over from the main count. The Secretary of State addressed the throng and at 6 a.m. the Yes for Wales campaign was able to host the celebratory press conference that had been planned for three months. Most satisfying of all was the fact that the campaign had helped to produce a victory in every area where there was a dissident anti-devolution Labour MP.

### Lessons

The underlying lesson of the Yes for Wales campaign is a political one. Building a consensus for constitutional reform requires significant cultural change that takes years rather than months. In a sense, Yes for Wales was not only seeking to achieve a 'Yes' vote but also to fill the gap that in Scotland had been occupied by the Scottish Constitutional Convention. Whereas the Convention had had nearly nine years to prepare the way for a Scottish Parliament, it was only in February 1997 that Yes for Wales was launched. It was only in March 1997 that the Wales Labour Party had agreed to adopt an element of PR. It was only in the summer of 1997 that the

Welsh Liberal Democrats and Plaid Cymru finally agreed to come on board, officially, for the 'Yes' campaign. It was all very late.

The second lesson relates to the difficulty of running a referendum in an area lacking homogeneous broadcasting media (see chapter 7). Substantial sums of money were needed to mount a serious campaign, for advertising, leafleting and campaigning, and Yes for Wales never had enough money. No commercial organization seeking to influence Welsh opinion would have spent so little. And yet there were real successes, driven by local activity in particular, reinforced by the media coverage of the central campaign. The campaign achieved most in the areas where campaigning started earliest: Neath and Port Talbot were outstanding examples. In other areas local groups could claim real successes: for example, Blaenau Gwent, Pontypridd and Bridgend. There were some areas with good local groups but disappointing results, such as in Cardiff and Ynys Môn.

At the end of the day, however, the people of Wales signalled a narrow but decisive shift in their views on devolution over eighteen years. The very closeness of the result demonstrated that the work undertaken by the thousands of individuals across Wales involved in the Yes for Wales campaign really mattered. It had, after all, been too important to leave to the politicians.

This article is based on the book by Leighton Andrews, *Wales Says Yes: the Inside Story of the Yes for Wales Referendum Campaign* (Bridgend: Seren, 1999).

# 5 The 'No' Campaign: Division and Diversity

J. BARRY JONES (ed.)

From the outset, the 'No' campaign was obliged to confront serious problems. Soon after the general election it became clear that the Labour government, with an overwhelming majority in the House of Commons, would not be held to ransom by dissident Labour MPs as it had been in 1979. Furthermore, the government was adamant that the devolution referendum would be 'pre-legislative', that is, held prior to the passage of the Government of Wales Bill through Parliament, thus denying the opportunity for the forging of cross-party alliances opposed to devolution. Beyond Parliament, the Welsh Conservatives were demoralized and eliminated as a parliamentary force, and reluctant to take too strong an anti-devolution line lest the referendum became another opportunity for the Welsh electorate to punish them.

The 'No' campaign did not so much launch itself as stutter into existence. While the majority of Conservatives were 'No' supporters, they were anxious to keep the lowest of low profiles and play little or no formal part in the campaign. Indeed, with the exception of Nick Bourne, who was to become leader of the Conservative group in the National Assembly, leading Welsh Tories were conspicuous by their absence for most of the campaign. North Wales Conservatives were outside the organization loop, a situation which generated bitter recriminations and, according to one Tory activist, fatally undermined the campaign in the north. Finance was another problem. Immediately after a general election party coffers were low; moneys would have to be found elsewhere. Eventually, Sir Julian Hodge, a south Wales millionaire, appeared to support the campaign through the involvement of his son, Robert Hodge, who became the campaign chair. However, Sir

Julian's intervention did have its downside; he was a tax exile living in the Channel Islands, which had devolved government. Apparently, Sir Julian was persuaded to provide support for the 'No' campaign by Lord Tonypandy, whose political career had taken several interesting turns. Lord Tonypandy, or George Thomas as he was more widely known, was born and raised in the Rhondda Valley, joined the Labour Party and, in the course of time, became Welsh Secretary of State and then Speaker of the House of Commons. He developed a strong personal admiration for Mrs Thatcher during her premiership and on his elevation to the House of Lords, opted to sit as a cross-bencher rather than take the Labour whip. In the 1997 general election he was a leading supporter of Jimmy Goldsmith's Referendum Party, an enthusiasm he shared with Sir Julian Hodge. Both were significant elements in what might be described as the 'three-Rs connection'; the Rhondda Valley, the Referendum Party and the Welsh Referendum.

Neither of the two central movers in the campaign organization was a Conservative, a deficiency both beneficial and disadvantageous. Matthew Gunther-Bushell, one of the leading organizers of the Referendum Party in the general election, had contributed indirectly to the defeat of several Conservative candidates. Tim Williams was a renegade member of the Labour Party whose political odyssey had taken him from supporter of Plaid Cymru via radical Labour activist to vitriolic critic of Welsh-language policies. The other members of the 'No' campaign team who completed the 'three-Rs connection' were the Rhondda Ladies, Labour party members Carys Pugh and Betty Bowen, who self-consciously presented themselves as the custodians of traditional 'Old Labour' values, were dismissive of the so-called 'New Labour' Party and contemptuous of Tony Blair. They also displayed a streak of chauvinism in their attack on Peter Hain, Minister of State in the Welsh Office, whose origins were South African. The 'No' campaign's central organization consisted of a motley array of political professionals, enthusiastic amateurs and ideologues. Yet, despite its inherent tensions and contradictions, and to the surprise of political observers and many of its organizers, the 'No' campaign almost won.

To understand the motives of this diverse group we need to consider its members' perceptions of the campaign expressed through their own words. David Melding, a Conservative member

of the National Assembly explains the dilemma which faced the
Conservative Party in Wales, stunned by the scale of its defeat in
the general election and uncertain how to deal with devolution,
which seemed all but inevitable. Elwyn Jones, a Conservative Party
agent in north Wales for many years, gives a revealing picture of
the breakdown of 'diplomatic' relations between north and south,
of 'betrayal' and his personal turmoil and dismay. Finally, the two
non-Conservatives who set up what was in effect a 'front
organization', recall their motives in joining the campaign and
their frustrations in trying to run it in a professional manner.
Matthew Gunther-Bushell and Tim Williams, represent a new kind
of politics, issue orientated rather than party driven. They were
political cuckoos in a Conservative nest, an environment which
helped shape the bitter-sweet last moments of the referendum
count, when the shock near-victory was abruptly replaced with the
anguish of marginal defeat.

## The Conservative Party's shy and muted campaign

DAVID MELDING (AM for Wales South East)

Shortly after the 1997 general election, a group of Conservative
parliamentary candidates (add 'unsuccessful' if you want to
complete the syllogism) met to discuss the forthcoming devolution
referendum. The scale of the general election defeat, unequalled in
the modern political era, continued to act as a paralysing
anaesthetic. In Wales the Conservative Party had lost a quarter of
its once routine support and now faced the bleak task of
campaigning without any representatives at national level. The
meeting was held at Penlline Road, the Conservative Party's
headquarters in Wales, but not even the genteel suburban ambience
– with its Churchillian memorabilia – could lift the gloom hanging
over a party seemingly bereft of means or mission. And, indeed,
within minutes, it was clear that this meeting was not a 'council of
war' on how to conduct a 'No' campaign but a despairing
'brainstorm' on ways to fund it. The bemused candidates were
asked to think of ways to raise £50,000 – the Conservative Party,
deep in the red, no longer had the overdraft facility to cope.

The contrast with 1979 could hardly have been starker. Then a tired and moribund Labour government had impaled itself on the spike of a devolution referendum. Now Mr Blair's referendum – personally 'conceded' against the wishes of the Wales Labour Party – was more like a pedestal from which to declaim the importance of devolution to a new youthful Britain. In 1979, the Conservative Party was riding high and confident of sweeping gains at the impending general election. In 1997, however, the principal protagonists were in a state of almost surreal vice versa. The Labour leadership further strengthened its position with a series of dazzling manœuvres: the devolution referendums would be held *in advance* of legislation; the polls to be held quickly just after the dog days of summer; and the referendums staggered, the Scottish formality one week before the less certain poll in Wales. The government's tactics were brilliant and in utter contrast to the maladroit performance of the Wales Labour Party with its arguments about PR or the need for a referendum in the first place.

Under such debilitating circumstances, it was remarkable that the 'No' campaign proved so successful. Although the (by now) Welsh Conservative Party was in swift retreat, it had not quite been routed. Its most carefully chosen redoubt was the decision to separate the 'No' campaign from the Conservative Party. This was a common enough tactic, and one used by the 'Yes' campaign, but it required some deft footwork because the political parties in Wales – maverick members apart – were split three to one. Simply put, if voting 'No' was seen as synonymous with voting Conservative, defeat for the 'No' campaign would have been certain. Given the impossibility of a cross-party 'No' campaign, the Conservative Party entered a period of studied abnegation in an attempt to make the cry 'Just say No!' politically neutral.

Although the 'No' campaign was just about able to appear non-partisan, its base remained narrow. A small band of socialist stalwarts, the likes of Carys Pugh and the heterodox historian Tim Williams, saved the day rather like an eighteenth-century Prussian army by dashing around everywhere to conduct media interviews. In general, the media accepted the non-partisan character of the 'No' campaign, to the relief of those involved. Robert Hodge, a respected businessman, chaired the campaign with an air of independence that bordered on serene detachment. The business community as a whole remained neutral, no doubt wisely in the face of an expected 'Yes' vote. Even the CBI's refrain that an Assembly must not become 'a burden on business' was insipid compared to the more blood-curdling cries of the past. Inevitably, the narrowness of the 'No' campaign necessitated the wider involvement of the Conservative Party despite initial misgivings. The easy days of 1979, with a divided Labour Party, a hostile business community and an irritable electorate, were but a fond memory and a source of nostalgia rather than inspiration.

While the leaders of the 'No' campaign could claim to be heading a non-partisan movement, the activists required to canvass and deliver leaflets were nearly always drawn from local Conservative associations. This proved an inadequate substitute for a broad-based campaign. While many Conservative activists did their utmost, morale was still very low following the severe general election defeat. Inevitably, co-ordination between the 'No' campaign and the Conservative Party was not always slick, and local associations often complained about the lack of campaign materials (actually, given the dismal financial state of the 'No' campaign, the materials often did not exist to be distributed). Afterwards, reflecting on the tiny 'Yes' majority, Conservatives throughout Wales complained that the party should have gone all out for victory. Whether this would have increased the 'No' vote or not can surely be disputed, but the frustration felt by local Conservative activists was acute. It is certainly the case that the intensity of a general election campaign was lacking, and efforts to 'turn out' the vote patchy. There were exceptions, of course, and in some areas there was a close interaction between the 'No' campaign and the local Conservative Party. But even if the Conservative Party had been fully match-fit, the state of Conservative associations in Wales ranged from strong and extensive (Monmouth for example) to weak if not absent (such as Rhondda). It is surely significant that in Labour's heartland – where the electorate switched from a loud 'No' to a quiet 'Yes' – the 'No' campaign reflected the weakness of the Conservative Party.

Rather like celibacy in the Roman Catholic priesthood, opposition to devolution has been an entrenched practice but not a fundamental principle of Conservatism. In abstract, Conservatives have emphasized the simple choice that seems to exist between unitary and federal states. Liberal democracies use both systems of government but rarely (if ever) a hybrid. The Conservative Party has no fundamental opposition to parliamentary federalism and accepts that it works successfully, for example in Canada and Australia. Accordingly, it was the half-baked nature of devolution that attracted most criticism from the Conservative Party. The threat of separatism was largely played down by Conservative commentators who chose instead to question the advantages likely to flow from devolution. Unlike 1979, it was no longer tenable to claim that devolution was anathema to the unity of the British state. Scotland loomed large. Few doubted that Scotland would vote overwhelmingly for devolution (a *de facto* federal Parliament in their case). In Wales, any concerted attempt to claim that devolution would destroy Britain *itself* posed a danger to the Union, given the situation in Scotland. The Conservative Party faced a conundrum: devolution must be opposed but also made safe.

This limitation became increasingly visible. Some Conservatives remained obstinate and claimed that devolution would indeed mean the end of the United Kingdom (with regard to Scotland they remained in a state of complete denial!). Others shifted the focus of criticism to secondary issues: Wales risked losing its seat in Cabinet; the Assembly would be wasteful and bureaucratic; Cardiff could not serve the interests of north Wales, etc. But there was no getting away from the fact that the elephant on the doorstep during this campaign was the realization that, given the situation in Scotland, devolution had to be reconciled with the British state, or that was the end of the United Kingdom. The rhetoric of the Conservative Party became more measured. Prophecies of destruction were replaced by calls for a balanced constitution aided perhaps by a Royal Commission. The need to hear the voice of the English in the devolution debate was also stressed. All this amounted to a rather shy and muted campaign. It was less a case of pulling punches, more an attempt not to knock oneself out. By the time the Scots did what everyone expected them to do, the bizarre argument that the Welsh ought to reject the form of devolution on offer to them because it was so feeble, was offered to an incredulous electorate.

With the balance of probabilities indicating a 'Yes' vote, the Conservative Party had to prepare discreetly for the first set of elections to the National Assembly. The party would face a crucial test soon after an affirmative referendum, although most

Conservatives (and many commentators) assumed that the party would have little difficulty in securing second place. A Conservative boycott of the Assembly was never mentioned as a serious possibility even on the edge of the most reactionary fringe of the party. Indeed, in private many former parliamentary candidates were keen to offer their services and stressed the need to participate constructively in the Assembly should it be endorsed in the referendum. Astute observers could see the Conservative Party preparing for a fundamental reform of Britain's system of government. In the event, the Conservatives were the first party in Wales to have in place a full slate of candidates for the National Assembly elections. In its movements and mannerisms the Conservative Party was rapidly learning the steps for the new devolution dance.

While the situation in Scotland had a deep impact on the devolution campaign in Wales, the influence of Europe was more hypothetical. The tiresome slogan 'a Europe of the regions' was chanted to vitiate more logical argument, but it did also demonstrate a change of mood. The emergence of a European polity in the 1980s started to undermine the adolescent faith some had in an immutable British state. Both those pro- and anti-Europe feasted on a rich stew of hyperbole: lauding the attractions of an ever-closer union or condemning the new Holy Roman Empire. Turning to subsidiarity, not since the sixteenth century, or so it seemed, had the practices of Catholic Spain entered so easily into domestic political discussion. Some commentators suggested that Britain should emulate Spanish regional government with all of its rococo convolutions. More credibly, the modern and innovative attractions of Barcelona were emphasized as a model for Cardiff and Wales. Essentially, devolution was no longer viewed as a nationalist obsession but as a common characteristic of modern European government. Alternatively, opponents of devolution were portrayed as archaic and rather shrill. Throughout, the 'Yes' campaign appeared youthful and confident: a rich pageant of pop stars, transsexual writers, weather forecasters and footballers sought to cajole an oddly indifferent electorate into saying 'Yes!'

The Conservative Party can claim to have had a 'good' devolution campaign. First, the result was far, far closer than generally predicted. Given the shoestring operation, this was no mean achievement. Secondly, either directly or via its participation in the

'No' campaign, the Conservative Party provided an effective opposition to the government's devolution proposals. Without this participation, the electorate would have been deprived of a real choice. It is surely important that all constitutional change is examined and tested through an effective adversarial process. Thirdly, by acknowledging the way the political mood had changed since 1979, the Conservative Party promoted reasoned and measured discussion and successfully prepared the ground for the next stage of constitutional development and the party's participation in that process.

## The campaign in north Wales: negligence and betrayal

ELWYN JONES (former Conservative Party agent for north Wales)

The very next day after the general election of 1997, the national newspapers of Wales carried advertisements for the 'Yes' campaign in the referendum, and supporters knew exactly whom to contact and where. I wish it had been so for the 'No' campaign. Here was I, a fervent and passionate opponent of devolution, not knowing to whom to offer my support, where the headquarters were and who was in charge. The whole of June and July was spent in total frustration watching the superbly well-organized and co-ordinated 'Yes' campaign developing, with something in the newspapers daily and huge cover being given in the Welsh media. The 'No' campaign had not got going, seemed totally to lack any cohesion, and to consist of a scattering of individuals rather than a well-organized and well-thought-out strategy.

As an individual I made several media appearances on both Radio Cymru and S4C, and this culminated in a strong outburst quite deliberately calculated to try to stir some 'No' activity and, in particular, in north Wales, which I had always felt crucial in determining the result. This was on Sunday, 20 July. That very evening I was telephoned by one who later became a prominent member and organizer of the 'No' campaign and told there was definitely going to be a 'No' organization in north Wales, and there would be a meeting held soon. I was asked if I could suggest a list of names of prominent people who could be invited.

The following week I duly submitted a list of prominent mayors, businessmen and councillors (all non-political) in north Wales who should be invited. I had checked with them all and they were all opposed to devolution. One, in particular, headed a very strong and influential organization and would have been an excellent choice to chair the north Wales 'No' campaign committee.

The meeting duly took place on Friday 1 August at the St George's Hotel in Llandudno. I was surprised on arrival to see that the attendance was made up of Conservatives from all over north Wales. They were old friends and acquaintances whom it was on the whole nice to see again. Indeed, as far as I could make out, I was the only genuine non-member of any political party. There was a releasing of balloons on the Promenade followed by media interviews. I did three, for BBC Wales, Radio Cymru and a special programme on the devolution campaign. I was somewhat impassioned, as is my style, went in very hard and was surprised to realize that people around me were uttering 'Hear, hear'. As I was doing the interviews, I could see the looks of jealousy and annoyance on the faces of those in charge. We then trooped into the hotel to arrange the north Wales committee, discuss the strategy and organize the campaign – or so I mistakenly thought.

The first surprise was that none of the people I had suggested should be invited were present. I later checked with some of them and found they had neither been invited nor had any idea that the meeting was taking place. This was typical of the disastrous organization of the 'No' campaign.

The second surprise was that there was nobody from north Wales actually on the platform. In fact, it consisted of Professor Nick Bourne, Lyndon Jones and a Mr Davies who seemed to think we were all hicks and had to be told what to do. The main platform members, Robert Hodge and the two Rhondda ladies, had got stuck somewhere near Welshpool, another indication of the shambolic nature of the campaign. To say that the meeting was acrimonious would be an understatement. The platform seemed unprepared for the very sensible questions, and the audience unprepared for the lack of direction and strategy from the platform. Several strong statements were made from the floor.

I was getting increasingly annoyed at the whole nature of the meeting. Here was Cardiff again telling us what to do. My explosion was inevitable. It came after Davies made what I thought was a patronizing speech, more or less saying that it was our job to deliver leaflets, etc., that I could take no more. I made one of the strongest and most heart-felt speeches of my life. I had after all spent some twenty-six years organizing the delivery of leaflets in north Wales, organizing several general election campaigns, four for European elections and, most of all, the 1979 referendum campaign in Gwynedd. More to the point, we had won it hands down. I felt, therefore, that my expertise entitled me to speak. I asked who was going to liaise with the Welsh-language side of the campaign, S4C, Radio Cymru, Golwg, *Y Cymro*, *Herald Gymraeg*, etc. They hadn't a clue and thought I was some sort of dangerous radical.

I sat down to huge applause. There was then a proposition, which was seconded, that I should head the campaign. I was taken aback and could see the look of sheer horror on the faces of the little coterie of Conservatives who seem to see themselves as running the party in north Wales. I declined. I would have been controversial, yes, that was the nature of the beast, but I would also have raised the profile of the whole campaign and undoubtedly have made very extensive use of the media and got a bit of passion into the whole thing. But most of all my very extensive experience of 1979 could have been adapted and my records and memory of those events extensively used. What followed were two telephone calls the next evening from two different people, telling me that they had been 'appointed' to lead the campaign in north Wales. I felt that there was no role for me to play and that democracy seemingly counted for nothing. I contented myself with doing the odd interview and article and watching the shambles the little group of inexperienced and, in my opinion, thoroughly unprofessional team made of the campaign in north Wales. It is perhaps indicative of their jealousy and power plays that, from that day on, the only communication I received was a begging letter. At about the same time, members of the 'Yes' campaign began to woo me. For the first time ever, I began to think I might switch sides and admit to an agonizing period of indecision (very unlike me). The clincher was that nobody, not even Ron Davies himself, could assure me that devolution would not lead to the break-up of the United Kingdom. I therefore decided that I would take no more active part in the 'No' campaign, but would still vote 'No' which I did. I accuse the 'No' campaign of letting the people of north Wales in particular down. I do so on two major counts:

1. Letting June and July go by with no organization and being too far behind the 'Yes' campaign when they did eventually start.
2. Having an inexperienced, uncoordinated and far too young team trying to organize north Wales. They failed to target in a proper manner, and had no real rapport with the ordinary people, they were in an ivory tower which eventually crashed around them. The good result achieved in north Wales was despite rather than because of the 'No' campaign. The 6,000 additional votes required did not transpire because of the mixture of inexperience, incompetence and negligence of the 'No' campaign.

Meanwhile I and at least half a dozen others with extensive experience of the 1979 'No' campaign were not used, contacted or respected in any way. The new young whizz-kids were in charge, and as a result Wales was destroyed.

In all this saga also there is great sadness over the role of the Conservative Party. They had been in fear and trepidation since 1 May. The then misguided leaders did not allow prominent members to put their heads above the parapet. There was no enthusiasm, leadership or organization. They effectively betrayed the Welsh people.

What should they have done? In my opinion, they should have taken a firm lead, campaigned with vigour, expressed their principles, formed action committees, barnstormed the media, written strong and powerful articles. But we had none of this; instead we had the sad sight of Conservatives hiding behind umbrella committees that consisted of Conservatives. The fear factor led to betrayal. They did not discern the mood of Wales correctly, as Nick Edwards had done in 1979. How sad that we did not get a similar campaign going, targeting for instance Wrexham, Alyn and Deeside as well as specific areas like Holyhead, Towyn and even Caernarfon, as we had to maximize opposition, co-ordinate it and make sure it registered its vote.

On the night of the results I was on BBC Radio Cymru all night, and as the night unfolded I really did have very mixed feelings. On the one hand, I regretted that Wales had made what I think was a very wrong choice for its future. On the other, I felt that now the people had decided, and this must be made to work. More than anything, I felt a personal sense of betrayal that the 'No' campaign had been such a shambles, so negligent and unprepared at the start, and that the political party I had supported and voted for all my life had betrayed Welsh people like myself by their fear of losing and their lack of commitment.

What is done is now done, but I can only hope that some lessons have been learnt and that people are prepared to listen and learn. Sadly, the lessons of the 1979 campaign did not seem to matter or were of no relevance to the 1997 'No' campaign organization. Had they been, the result might have been different.

## Reflections on the 'No' campaign

J. BARRY JONES with contributions from MATTHEW GUNTHER-BUSHELL (strategist and organizer of the 'No' campaign) and TIM WILLIAMS ('No' campaign steering-committee member)

### Motivations
What was it that brought two such political opposites together, one to the right of the Tory Party and 'spin doctor' for Jimmy Goldsmith's Referendum Party and the other an erstwhile Plaid Cymru supporter and Welsh-speaker? Was it an intellectual commitment to an unchanging unitary state or was it a personal belief that the Welsh people could not be trusted with devolution? Or was it simply 'costs'? What emerges from their recollections is more complex. The reader can identify a mix of personal factors: bravado, *noblesse oblige* and, not least, 'the thrill of the chase'. The prospect of fighting the campaign attracted them, although both expected defeat. In short, they saw themselves as making a historic stand against the forces of change.

*Matthew:* Getting involved in the referendum campaign was something that I'd been thinking about for a while following the 1997 general election. I'd been in frequent contact with Nick Bourne back in Wales and we met for dinner one night in Swansea to talk about the referendum. I just said to him, 'As far as you're aware, has anything got going yet?' He said 'No.' And I said, 'Well, I've got an idea. But basically my big fear at this stage is that if it becomes a Conservative campaign Labour is going to play its big card – Vote Yes, Vote Labour – and obviously if they get their objective they will polarize the debate. So the campaign needs to be independent and cross-party.' That conversation with Nick led to the 'No' campaign that was.

*Tim:* I must confess that I was really concerned initially. There did not seem to be any kind of organization and I wondered whether I should have anything to do with this. I had assumed in my head that, in some mysterious way, there was going to be money coming from Jimmy Goldsmith and that I would be supping with the devil with a very short spoon, but that I would be willing to do it, because my enemy's enemy is my friend. And, in this battle, I would fight with anybody against the enemy, and the enemy was my own party. I was suspicious because I didn't want to be used for a Tory campaign, and I wasn't sure that I was willing to burn my boats with the Labour Party. I had no notion of having a conventional career within the Labour Party, that had never been an issue, but I had a sentimental desire not to be despised by my own party. At the end of the day, I decided to put my country before my party. But I had conflicting feelings because of the sense, in the back of my mind, that it was an unwinnable battle so why cause further enmity towards me in Wales on the basis of a campaign that could not be won.

*Matthew:* So what changed your mind?

*Tim:* Well, a couple of things really. A certain amount of gallantry, I hope, in that I did think it was remarkably brave of Betty and Carys to be kind of carrying white flags. Brave, because I knew the kind of hatred they would arouse. Brave, because, although quite experienced themselves, they probably did not know entirely what they were letting themselves in for, and once they did realize, they still carried on. They knew they were in a vocal minority within the Labour Party in Wales and I think, also, just the sheer bravery of going before the cameras. I had done a lot of media work and I didn't think they had and, well, I just decided I couldn't let them do it alone and I thought if they can do it, I must do it.

*Matthew:* I think how the campaign came to be is probably one of the most fundamental questions about the whole 'No' campaign. No one really understands how it came about. Essentially, you have to look at a few forces that existed. You have to look at Carys as an individual force in herself. You have to look at the Conservative Party as a force and you have to look at me as another force. These three all impacted upon each other. Carys, obviously by her own statement, was just personally against the whole idea of an Assembly. So the day after Ron Davies announced that a referendum was going to happen, she just spoke out. I think that she is the kind of Old Labour person who had her own gut instinct that this was going to annihilate the country. She announced instantly that a campaign was going to be formed. From that point on she had been chatting with Lord Tonypandy in a kind of informal way. He had agreed to act as a president or chairman of the campaign but, effectively, it was just Carys and a day later Betty came on board. Carys and Betty, just acting as these two lone soldiers with just one phone line, sending out petitions and doing media interviews – totally funding themselves. I think Tonypandy gave them a cheque for £100, or something like that, and that was it.

### The Referendum Party connection

The connection was evident even before the 'No' campaign came into being. The Referendum Party associates included Matthew Gunther-Bushell, Lord Tonypandy and, it was thought, Sir Julian Hodge. In fact it was Robert Hodge, Sir Julian's adopted son, who provided the cash for the campaign and Lord Tonypandy's association with Carys Pugh and Betty Bowen (the Rhondda Ladies) provided the entrée to dissident Labour Party members in the valleys.

*Matthew:* After that dinner with Nick, I wrote to Tonypandy, with whom I had worked during the Referendum Party campaign. In the letter I asked if I could meet with him and discuss creating a solid campaign. He phoned me and said 'no problem', and so I went up to see him, along with Nick Bourne, in Cardiff the next day. It was at that meeting that Tonypandy first enlightened me as to the existence of Carys and Betty. He also mentioned that Sir Julian Hodge might be doing something but, at that stage, he wasn't sure what.

*Tim:* You had actually been advising Sir James Goldsmith and working on the Referendum Party campaign up to the 1997 election. You presumably had no knowledge of me at that time?

*Matthew:* No. The first time I heard of you was about two weeks after I met with Tonypandy and that was from Carys. I remember her saying 'Dr Tim Williams' – you were this enigmatic figure I had never heard of, and when I spoke to Llew Smith on the phone, he also said I should get in touch with you, but I couldn't track you down. By some miracle you just happened to phone up a couple of days later.

## Anti-devolution Labour MPs

From the start the 'No' campaign was anxious to involve rebel Labour MPs to press home the point that Labour voters could be anti-Assembly without being disloyal. In the 1979 referendum the Labour 'Gang of Six' rebels, led by Leo Abse and Neil Kinnock, had disrupted the official party campaign. The question was whether the 'No' campaign could winkle out enough Labour MPs to join their campaign.

*Tim:* I was old enough to remember the 1979 referendum. I had in fact been involved in it on the Plaid Cymru side. I discovered then that devolution was so unpopular in Labour circles, that it was the nationalists who ended up distributing the leaflets. So I suspected the same would happen again. And in fact it did. I went on the radio, and Alan Rogers, the MP for Rhondda, heard it and was encouraged by it and told Llew Smith MP the same. So I was hoping, because I know Llew as a personal contact, that we would get some MPs backing us actually at the launch. Now I know you had some conversations.

*Matthew:* Yes, I had spoken with quite of few of them myself. I had spoken with Llew. A colleague of mine had spoken with Alan Rogers, and there had been various discussions along the way. Fundamentally, they were keen to get involved, but they would not go on a platform with any Conservative – that is what it had come down to.

*Tim:* They wouldn't actually start anything, would they?

*Matthew:* No. It was strange. Llew was very good in his own right. He'd always phone up the newspapers – *The Western Mail*, or whatever, and he would say what he thought. But that was really the extent of it. I wanted to get a feeling of Labour against Labour through the campaign. I wanted to get as close as we could to it.

*Tim:* Yes, but I think you must have felt in your bones, as I did, that we looked very thin on the ground in terms of the Labour presence.

We needed somebody more substantial, like an MP, to defect at the start.

*Matthew:* When I first contacted Llew Smith we discussed the idea of him and a couple of his colleagues writing a joint article and coming out and making a great play of the fact that they were against the idea of devolution in Wales. They bottled out at the last minute.

*Tim:* Do we know why?

*Matthew:* As I remember the article they were drafting was getting harder and harder by the day. I think it got to the point where it was so vitriolic, not just against devolution in Wales but the Blair regime too that when it was shown to other colleagues, they said, 'You guys are mad if you're going to put that on paper.'

*Tim:* Now that article was going to be in the *Sunday Times* wasn't it?

*Matthew:* Yes, and I'd set the whole thing up to appear on the front page. It was to be the front-page splash a day before the official launch of the 'No' campaign at the St Mellon's Hotel.

*Tim:* I think one of the problems was that although there were probably six or seven MPs in Wales – many of them with considerable backgrounds in the Labour Party – who were against the government's devolution proposals, they didn't agree on much else together and they probably didn't like each other very much.

*Matthew:* But even though they were anti-devolution, they were actually against it for different reasons. Their common bond was that they disagreed with what was in fact being proposed there and then.

*Tim:* So, at the end of the day we didn't get much out of them.

*Matthew:* I don't think we needed to get much out of them. I think what was important was – and I give them credit for this – that they captured the mind's eye and the public eye in Wales with the perception that devolution wasn't just a snowball or steamroller.

*Tim:* Absolutely. Their lack of enthusiasm, their obvious lack of enthusiasm, reminded Labour voters, in particular, to vote against devolution. Now my central mission in all this was by being a Labour Party person, and obviously from south Wales, to say: 'Look, I'm like you in every respect and like you I'm suspicious of devolution. You can be Labour, you can be a Socialist even, but you don't have to go along with this nonsense.'

### The media

The 'No' campaigners, lacking organization on the ground, particularly in north, mid- and west Wales, looked increasingly to the media to get their message across. However, they harboured serious doubts about their treatment by the media, suspecting them of being biased against the anti-devolution cause.

*Tim:* The prejudice on our side about the media was that they were heavily pro-devolution. They would say, 'Whatever our professional preferences (which were heavily pro-devolution) we played the professional objective game throughout.' I don't think that at the start of the campaign I had any criticisms whatsoever. I think that the campaign became largely a media campaign and the media were so concerned to have the semblance of fair play that they actually ended up putting our stories out when probably they didn't deserve it. We know overall that certain areas were pro-'Yes', and we know *The Western Mail* was pro-'Yes', they were openly so.

*Matthew:* I never had a major problem with *The Western Mail*, and I have to say a lot of people on our side really did have a go at the paper. For me they are not the bad guys in all of this. I have to say they were very polite whenever I phoned up and really wanted to hammer a point. They objectively covered what I had to say on behalf of the campaign. Sure, they gave a lot more coverage to the 'Yes' campaign, but they did help as much as they could. I never got the feeling they were genuinely fighting not to print anything I put out.

*Tim:* Our strategy was to try and show Labour Party people that they could be Labour and against devolution. The best thing from our perspective was to show the people of Wales that there were Labour Party people like me who were opposed to devolution. But the media, the broadcast media, either found it impossible to accommodate that or just bent over backwards to accommodate the Labour Party.

*Matthew:* The broadcast media didn't seem know what to do with their weight. They were thinking, 'We've got Plaid, Lib Dems and Labour on one side of the platform. Ron Davies is saying, "I won't debate against anyone who is a Labour Party member". So what do we do? Do we put three Conservatives up? Do we put three 'No' campaign people up? What happens if one of those is from the Lib Dems as well or the Labour Party?' They didn't know what to do. They knew they were being bullied by Ron Davies; he was the big draw, the guy who was pulling the thing forwards. I think it is probably one of the most glaring examples of the broadcast media finding it difficult to interpret the guidelines.

### Money – or the lack of it

Finance was a continuing preoccupation during the 'No' campaign. Its organizer, Matthew Gunther-Bushell, had helped organize the Referendum Party's campaign in the 1997 general election and clearly yearned for access to the levels of financial support provided by Jimmy Goldsmith. Here again the Referendum Party connection came into play.

*Matthew:* No money, you know, that was the biggest point. If someone had turned around and said to me, 'Matthew, here's £500,000', you know what I mean. Then no problem at all because I'd have just bought people in. That was the whole point. I couldn't buy in any additional expertise, so the only people I really got to deal with were you and Nick as spokesmen and Robert doing the occasional interview and article which I had to draft. That was the campaign. It was all about how well I could spread and get interviews for these three people. The rest of it was pure spin, which I had to generate day in day out. There were a couple of chaps from Conservative Central Office who got involved. They tried to get on the ground but, on the whole, these were guys who were just used to running limited campaigns for one constituency and they just couldn't cope. They were lost. I actually phoned Julian Hodge up in Jersey to confront him personally. I was happy for the campaign to be burdened with the label of being financed by a tax exile if he came up with the goodies, but he didn't. I was used to dealing with Jimmy, a guy who put millions where his mouth was. I think Julian Hodge just liked the sound of his own voice and reading about himself.

*Tim:* But we were all under the impression that Sir Julian was going to be like some kind of big Santa Claus, who was going to appear at some point and throw bags of money down at us. Robert Hodge had given the impression that his father would put some money in, which was great. We settled back a little bit in terms of fund-raising.

*Matthew:* You're right. We didn't go looking for money because we assumed it was going to be there from Julian and that everything would be cool. Things then started going slightly awry when Robert said, 'Look, my father's only going to pay for some leaflets and literature.' So, at that point I started to get very nervous. I knew how critical money was; if we were going to have any chance of winning we needed money to swing the balance a bit more in our favour. The next thing was that I received a memo from Robert saying that Sir Julian would not have any financial involvement in the campaign. I thought this was a betrayal of our campaign, nothing short. I started phoning round big players. Jimmy had died right at the start of the campaign, and so I phoned various other characters that I had been involved with to say 'Look, there's seven weeks to go, can I have some money for some advertising? This campaign's got no money.' At that point it was virtually impossible to do. It was too late. The perception was that Julian was bank-rolling the campaign, that it was his campaign, and that we were loaded. As it turned out, it was Robert who heroically stumped up what cash was spent during the campaign. In the end I think the sum was around £100,000. I have to say, I don't know exactly what that £100,000 was spent on. Probably most of it was on leaflets and balloon launches as they were good visuals for the TV news.

### The Conservatives
From the 'No' campaign's point of view the Conservative Party was demoralized and in turmoil following its general election defeat. This was not just the Welsh Conservatives; Major's resignation and the subsequent leadership election had created a policy paralysis in Central Office.

*Matthew:* The Conservatives recognized that some sort of campaign had to come about. But there was a split in Conservative thinking. There had been such a vacuum left after the election with the disappearance of Major, and the coming of William Hague, that Central Office was in absolute turmoil. It really had no idea what it was doing. As far as they had been thinking, it was all focused on Scotland. Scotland had stronger Conservative support than Wales, so they were looking towards Scotland and not really at Wales at all. The Conservatives in Wales knew there needed to be some sort of campaign, but again their thinking was split. One group thought that the 'No' campaign should be spearheaded by the Conservative Party as it was ideologically opposed to devolution. Another group thought they should step slightly back and find an independent figure, some sort of business character who wasn't really officially Conservative to head up what was basically going to be a Conservative campaign. This view was the one that was prevailing.

*Tim:* A non-Tory, Tory campaign.

*Matthew:* Effectively that is what they were after. At the time, I was contacting Conservative friends in London, MPs, very senior ones, saying 'Look, have you thought about this?' And all the time the feedback was, 'Not now, not now.' I don't think, at that stage anyone really cared.

*Tim:* Were they still in trauma, so that they just couldn't focus on Wales?

*Matthew:* Yes, yes. Their thinking was just all over the place. They had suffered a major defeat, everything had gone out of the window, what do you do now? In Wales certain characters in the Conservative Party were trying to influence Robert Hodge through the business community to get involved. Robert ended up giving out a press release saying he was going to get involved in the referendum debate. So I phoned up and said, 'What are you doing?' I explained that all these Labour Party figures, including you Tim, had been lined up and that you were the biggest assets of any structured campaign that was going to get going. The key was to ensure that the 'No' campaign was not a Conservative campaign, as the Government would seize on it instantly, you know, 'Vote Labour, vote Yes. Vote Conservative, vote No.' Robert said that he had been approached by some Conservative businessmen to get involved and had agreed. He said an office had been donated by the Thomases, originally the Peter's Pies people and now TBI. I just immediately thought that this was all wrong, just so wrong. Not just in media terms but in political terms too. My core feeling was that Robert was about to become a puppet of the Conservative Party. This would be sniffed out by the media and any reasonably sharp political operator in about a nano-second and any campaign would be in tatters. If the campaign was going to be convincingly lost, this was the way to go about it. It was, potentially, an enormous error of judgement.

*Matthew:* I found out, eventually, that certain junior secretaries and equipment had been donated to Robert by the Conservative Party. A press release had been drafted on his behalf and sent out to the media saying that the 'No' campaign was to be officially launched that Friday at the donated Windsor Place office. Robert Hodge was going to be there to oversee the launch. This was a disaster about to happen, not only because of the Conservative connection, but because they planned the launch on a Friday. Friday is possibly the worst day to launch anything – you only get a day's press coverage on Saturday and then only in the print press. The broadcast media dies over the weekend. The whole thing was blunderous naïvety from every angle. I demanded that we go and meet the people who were setting up the office. So we went down to the centre of Cardiff and into what became the 'No' campaign headquarters and it was riddled with various Conservative operators, most of whom I knew well. I pulled the most enormous fit and basically told Robert to throw them all out, there and then.

*Tim:* Because they were too high profile?

*Matthew:* Yes, and because they were too Conservative. It was just ridiculous tactics. We decamped across the road to the Hodge Bank offices, and I said that if any journalist had been present with a photographer then the whole thing would have been over here and now. The 'Yes' campaign would have won before the 'No' campaign had even started. I started explaining what I was doing and what should happen. Jonathan Evans, the former Conservative MP and government minister, was one of those present and, to his credit, he listened and agreed; he was one of the few who could see the big picture. From my point of view he saved the campaign by pulling off the Conservative dogs, so to speak. From that point onwards the Conservative Party backed away and didn't reappear until the end of the campaign. They left it to us, totally.

*Tim:* And this strategy worked for us. We didn't launch the campaign until a Monday either, did we?

*Matthew:* Yes and yes. By creating the steering committee we had, including yourself, Betty, Carys, Robert and Nick, it was impossible to label the campaign a Conservative campaign. There were more Labour Party members on the steering committee than anything else. The 'Yes' campaign and the media tried to label us a Conservative front a couple of times and then gave up, as it was so obviously not so. We completely removed their trump card – voting 'No' didn't mean voting Conservative, and so we totally stole their main ammunition. And, as you remember, we officially launched the campaign on that fateful Monday at the St Mellon's Hotel. It was a complete success and we set the news agenda for the week as a result.

In addition to the organizational problems in Cardiff, the difficulties of the strategy to be followed and how low a profile the Conservative Party should adopt, there was also the problem of the north Wales Conservatives.

*Matthew:* North Wales Conservatives, I have to say, created possibly the biggest headache of the entire thing because they were so egocentric. They wanted to be heroes for a day. They all wanted to see their faces on the front page of the latest national – sorry – latest local newspaper.

*Tim:* We couldn't form an effective alliance with these people, partly because we weren't Tories. If we'd been Tories we could probably have formed an effective alliance with some of those dissident Tories, but we couldn't because we weren't really on the same wavelength.

*Matthew:* That's what I'm saying, north Wales Conservatives were a problem. We did have people up there. We had former Referendum Party people up there, we had Labour Party people there and we had a couple of Independents up there. All these people were fine and caused no problems at all. But effectively the north Wales Conservatives wanted to run the campaign themselves and they wanted to be in control. They couldn't work with or co-operate with anyone other than themselves and then only just. They didn't want anyone else involved and if they couldn't do it no one else should be able to it. I spent most of my time trying to clear up their mistakes, like when they were sending out letters during the week following Princess Diana's death and I had to invent a story to explain what had happened.

### Issues

Perhaps the 'No' campaign's biggest success was to establish a central message that appealed to a significant proportion of the Welsh electorate. Their other success was to identify the divisions in the 'Yes' campaign and expose them with considerable skill and regularity.

*Matthew:* One of our strengths was that nobody on the 'Yes' side actually seemed to agree with one another. They all seemed to want more or less but not the actual legislation that was in front of us.

*Tim:* There were two campaigns. The government said it was about devolution, but most of the people in the 'Yes' campaign were nationalists or wanted to go much further. We found nobody willing to say 'the legislation and no more than the legislation'. So they were incoherent on the other side – that was helpful. It allowed us to open up differences between them and say: 'Do you realize that the government says it wants this, but that there are many people who want to use this to go further?' This was one of our campaign issues.

The 'No' campaign issues came increasingly to dominate the later stages of the referendum.

*Tim:* There were the costs; that was an issue. The constitutional crisis was an issue. The possibility of the Barnett formula being revised against Wales after the referendum was an issue. The overall economic prosperity of Wales after the referendum was an issue.

*Matthew:* To me the critical aspect was money. 'This is going to cost you money, it's not going to bring any more money into Wales. All you are doing is giving jobs to sixty fat-cat politicians.'

*Tim:* At the end of the day I think the balance was about right. It enabled us to have a cheap argument about fat cats together with a deeper argument about the serious politics, and I believe people voted on both issues.

*Matthew:* We got that balance exactly right. I remember watching Vox Pops about two days before the referendum and people were being asked what they thought. And they were saying to the cameras: 'No, I'm against the Assembly, I think it would break up the UK' and 'it's going to cost us a lot of money' and 'I hear there's not going to be enough money for schools and hospitals'. And that's what kept coming out, so we got those two messages across very heavily.

*Tim:* So the issues were OK. We were helped, I thought, by the fact that we were saying that devolution would lead, inevitably, to a greater split between Wales and England and half the people on the 'Yes' side wanted that split. They were coming out loud saying 'The Assembly is the first stage of this process.'

*Matthew:* We picked up on that. Our line when it came to the nationalists was: 'Look, the only reason they want it is because they want a Welsh Parliament and independent Wales. This is a stepping stone for them.'

*Tim:* They were helping us by saying it.

*Matthew:* Absolutely.

*Tim:* We thought that one of the strengths of our campaign was the weakness of theirs. Let's sum this up: we were helped by the contradictions between their positions – the fact that there were more extreme positions on one side and less extreme positions on the other side. Our essential argument was that this is the first stepping stone and that was being supported by people on the 'Yes' side. So that was good. I think, also, there was this sense of them being very New Labourish. In so far as they were Labour at all, they were the wrong kind of Labour for Wales. I think we benefited from that.

## Princess Diana's death
The major disruption to the referendum campaign was brought

about by Princess Diana's death in a car accident in Paris. The 'Yes' campaign saw it as a serious interruption to the growing momentum of their campaign. This was not the case with the 'No' campaign.

*Tim:* I think we have an intellectual version of this issue and we have a practical version. Intellectually, did Princess Diana dying make a difference to the thinking of people on the Assembly issue? To which I respond 'I doubt it.' Maybe a few people were inspired by royalty and United Kingdom. Practically, did it make a difference? We were the side without any money so it helped us, since it meant a week's worth of well-planned and financed campaigning that the 'Yes' campaign and the government couldn't do.

*Matthew:* Do you remember the talk of what campaigning you could and couldn't do during the week of mourning? This was hilarious in that we had no plans anyway. We were only looking ahead one day at a time, and we weren't actually doing any campaigning anyway. I just sat in the office for that week, played backgammon with Danny and answered the phone.

### The results
The publication of the results produced a roller-coaster of emotions for Matthew Gunther-Bushell and Tim Williams.

*Matthew:* 'We are quietly confident' was the line that we put out. 'We're not sure that Labour is really going to make the difference in the Valleys.' We were pretty sure of capturing the 'don't knows' if they came out to vote. If they came out and thought 'Am I really going to vote Yes or No?' we thought they'd vote 'No'.

*Tim:* I was over at the Channel 4 studios when the first result came in. To my astonishment we were winning quite handsomely in north-east Wales. In Wrexham, which Blair had visited during the campaign, the vote went 'No'. I was saying things like, 'Well, it shows the people over there that the amateurs have given the professional politicians a bloody nose. This is the people of Wales saying they're not impressed.'

*Matthew:* Well, back in the 'No' HQ I watched it and said to myself, 'This is good.' My gut instinct was, 'We can win this, my God we can win this.' When the first result came in I thought, 'This is possible.' Then the fun started because the media started pouring into the 'No' HQ. They started leaving the 'Yes' HQ and coming to ours.

*Tim:* And then of course the results, the 'Yes' campaign started saying that it had lost. They were going on live television and conceding defeat in front of the nation. The nationalists started blaming the Labour Party, live on air, for not doing enough during the campaign. Then I think Neath was the one which was a bit of a body blow for us, and we knew it would be very tight. Powys came in and it was closer than we had hoped.

*Matthew:* In the end there were 6,000 votes in it. My view at that stage was that it was worth going over to where the official count was being collated to discuss the issue of a recount. You know if you've got a margin of only 0.3 per cent, in any other election anywhere there would be a recount. I approached Professor Eric Sunderland, the returning officer, and said, 'What about a recount? You have to, it's so close.' He said: 'No, it's not possible.' He was very polite. 'No, it's not possible, there's no provision in the legislation for it, therefore that's it.'

*Tim:* By the way, we've forgotten these Tories that we didn't see in the whole of the campaign who suddenly starting flooding into our headquarters.

*Matthew:* Yes, a lot of them turned up on the night but I didn't begrudge them that; they had been our biggest allies for not getting involved. You know, Tim, another £10,000 and we could have done it.

# 6 No Dreads, only Some Doubts: The Press and the Referendum Campaign

KEVIN WILLIAMS

The lack of national media in Wales is seen as a significant factor in the outcome of the 1997 referendum. Much of the information people gained about a Welsh Assembly was from media sources based outside Wales, and the vote against the Assembly was strongest in those areas in which the presence of Welsh newspapers and television was weakest, mainly along the border with England, the north-east of Wales, and in Cardiff and the surrounding area. The contrast in media consumption patterns between Wales and Scotland has been highlighted to account for the difference in the outcome of the vote in the two Celtic countries. In Scotland only 10 per cent of Scots buy daily morning newspapers produced outside their country while nearly 87 per cent of people in Wales buy daily morning newspapers not produced in Wales. A similar position exists regarding broadcast media (radio and television). It is estimated that 35 per cent of Welsh people live in areas which overlap with English transmitters. Only 2.5 per cent of Scots live in areas which receive news and information from England. Overall Welsh television originates around fifty hours of programmes each week, but slightly less than half are in the English language. There are only around twenty-two hours of television every week for English-speakers in Wales, who make up four-fifths of the people living in Wales.[1] These facts and figures confirm for some commentators that there is a correlation between the way in which people learned about the issues surrounding the plans for a Welsh Assembly and the way in which they voted in the referendum.

The press in Wales[2] has been singled out for criticism from a number of quarters for its coverage of the referendum. 'Yes' men and women were unhappy at what they saw as the scepticism and negativity of certain newspapers towards devolution, with the *South Wales Echo* being the butt of such criticism. They also expressed concern that the press compensated for the inadequacy of the 'No' campaign by seeking out and publishing material that supported their arguments. On the other hand, 'No' campaigners saw a conspiracy amongst the leading newspapers of Wales to deny them access. Seasoned commentators on the Welsh newspaper scene berated the failure of the press to inform their readers. Former *Western Mail* editor, John Humphries, accused most of Wales's newspapers of treating the debate as 'having less consequence for their readers than the next episode of Coronation Street', while BBC heavyweight Patrick Hannan bemoaned the 'relentlessly trivial nature' of much of the coverage.[3] Comparison has been made with the press in Scotland, which is seen as having played a significant role in building public support for devolution through its commitment to, and campaigning for, devolution throughout the 1990s. For some, a strong, diverse, indigenous press in Wales would have increased support for the Assembly by developing political consciousness and a better understanding of the issues involved.

This chapter examines these arguments by analysing the press reporting of the campaign for the establishment of a Welsh Assembly in the late summer of 1997. The editorial stance of the press in Wales is contrasted with the position it adopted in 1979, while the news reporting is analysed in the context of the commitment made by most editors to provide necessary and sufficient information for their readers to make up their mind on how to vote. The analysis shows that the Welsh press was, in contrast with the situation in 1979, highly supportive of the case for an Assembly. Many of the leading papers editorially declared themselves in favour of a 'Yes' vote. Those that did not remained neutral. Many of these papers did not see it as their responsibility to tell their readers how to vote or think on devolution. Much of the coverage concentrated on the rituals of political campaigning and electioneering, with the 'substance' of the debate receiving less attention. In some parts of the press – particularly the London papers and the weekly press in Wales – the campaign received limited coverage. Much of the reporting focused on the apathy and indifference of the people in the face of the greatest political event in post-war Welsh history. In the news coverage, more attention was paid to the

'Yes' campaign and its activities than to those putting the case against the Assembly. To understand the nature of this coverage it is important to begin with a background to the development of the Welsh press since the vote against devolution in 1979.

## Changes in the Welsh newspaper landscape since 1979

Major changes have taken place in the newspaper industry in Wales since 1979. The hold of the London press has been strengthened with the decline in the circulation of the Welsh daily press. The total circulation of the daily morning and evening newspapers in Wales fell from around 440,000 sales in 1979 to just over 312,000 in 1997 (see table 6.1).[4] In 1997 the national daily and Sunday press of Wales is London based, and overwhelmingly tabloid. According to Mackay and Powell[5] the best-read newspaper in Wales is the *Sun*, which in 1995 was read by 22.5 per cent of Welsh households. Some challenge the picture of decline. The editor of *The Western Mail* argues that the poor state of the Welsh press is a 'myth'.[6] He believes the press in Wales is 'thriving'. He points out that 55 per cent of people in Wales read a Welsh daily newspaper once a week while 38 per cent read a Welsh daily paper every day. He draws attention to the importance of the evening newspapers in Wales, which have performed more strongly in the last few years than their English counterparts.

As the London press has strengthened its hold over the Welsh newspaper-reading audience, there has been a decline of resources devoted by London newspapers to gathering news about Wales. In 1979 there were Wales-based correspondents for most of the national Fleet Street newspapers. By 1997 they all relied on the representative of the Press Association (PA), Britain's national news agency, in Wales. Trevor Fishlock, writing in 1976 about reporting Wales for *The Times*, bemoaned the failure of the London press to tell their readers what was going on in the countries and regions of Britain. He talked at that time about 'patchy' and 'occasionally silly' reporting as well as the under-reporting of Wales in the British press.[7]

A more significant shift since 1979 is in the ownership of the Welsh press. Today most of the daily, evening, weekly and Sunday newspapers published in Wales are owned by one company. The

Table 6.1: Circulation of English-language morning and evening daily press in Wales

| | |
|---|---|
| *The Western Mail* (Cardiff) | 61,541 |
| *South Wales Echo* (Cardiff) | 74,246 |
| *South Wales Argus* (Newport) | 30,597 |
| *Evening Leader* (Wrexham) | 31,864 |
| *Daily Post* (Liverpool: Welsh edition) | 52,000 (1) |
| *South Wales Evening Post* (Swansea) | 64,405 |
| Total | 314,653 |

*Source:* These figures are drawn from the ABC figures, July to December 1997, published in the UK Press Gazette, 27 March 1998 (except (1), which is based on publisher's own estimates).

Trinity empire includes *The Western Mail*, the *Daily Post*, *Wales on Sunday* and the *South Wales Echo*, as well as the Celtic Press Group, which owns weekly newspapers across south Wales including the *Merthyr Express*, the *Rhondda Leader* and the *Pontypridd Observer*. The decline of competition in the Welsh newspaper industry has consequences for the performance of journalism. A challenging, independent and informative journalism, as Patrick Hannan[8] has recently pointed out, can only thrive in conditions where people can read a diversity of accounts of events and issues. A range of different newspapers helps to provide a platform for different opinions to battle it out, which is necessary for a democratic and pluralistic society. Hannan notes that 'there is little incentive for good journalists to remain in newspapers in Wales since there are few opportunities to advance themselves', and 'if you don't write for Trinity Holdings, you don't write'. He argues that by concentrating all the leading newspapers in the hands of one owner, the performance of journalism is sapped and the democratic process suffers.

### Editorial policy and the devolution referendum

In 1979 the editorial position of most of the English-language press in Wales was hostile to the Labour government's proposals for the devolution of power to Wales. John Osmond[9] states in his review of the press coverage of the 1979 debate that 'the "collective" line of the English language Press was overwhelmingly opposed to the Assembly'. The only exception was *The Western Mail*, which held out in favour, if only 'falteringly'. The situation in 1997 was almost the opposite: the large proportion of local and national newspapers in Wales editorially was in favour of the establishment of a Welsh Assembly; the rest were by and large neutral. Trinity's flagship newspapers, *The Western Mail*, *Wales on Sunday* and the *Daily Post* were, to a greater or lesser extent, on side. The pro-Assembly papers were led by *The Western Mail*, which sought to establish itself as the platform for a national debate. The tenor of the paper's editorial position was set out as early as St David's Day, 1997 when it put 'A case for the right kind of Assembly for Wales'.[10] The paper declared its support by stating that 'an Assembly could be Wales's golden opportunity' to make the country 'fitter, stronger and prepared for the challenges of the twenty-first century'. In July the paper welcomed the publication of the White Paper *A Voice for Wales*, and took up three pages to publish the whole of the document. During the period of the campaign the paper opened up its letters page to provide the opportunity for a wide-ranging debate – a common feature of nearly all the newspapers in Wales. The *Mail*'s letter page acted as a national forum for debate throughout the referendum campaign, and the paper's commitment to the Welsh nation and the proposals for the Assembly was forcefully put in its editorial columns.

## The Welsh national press

*The Western Mail* provided more editorial comment on devolution during the campaign than any other newspaper read in Wales. Each day following the resumption of campaigning after the death of Princess Diana, the newspaper carried editorial comment on the issue (see Appendix). The eve-of-poll comment was carried on the front page. 'Vote Yes for our future', declared the paper, next to pictures of faces representing Welsh men and women of all ages. The newspaper made an appeal to patriotism, to the 'love of country' which 'will be shared by the vast majority of those at the polling booths today, whichever side they are on'. But it reduced the vote for an Assembly to one fundamental issue, 'how Wales is run and its effect on us all'. *The Western Mail* saw an Assembly as the chance to redress the fact that 'Wales has been badly governed for far too long'. It dismissed the opposition to the Assembly, expressing admiration for the Labour Party in standing up for the Assembly in face of 'its more Jurassic supporters' worst instincts' and rejecting the 'silliest criticism' that devolution would lead to the break-up of the United Kingdom. This was a newspaper seeking to live up fully to its logo claim to be 'the national newspaper of Wales'.

*Wales on Sunday*, the populist, more tabloid Sunday stablemate of *The Western Mail*, has throughout its chequered history maintained a commitment to promoting things Welsh. On 14 September it laid out its reasons for voting 'Yes', stressing that 'The Assembly will provide democratic control over the Welsh Office's £7 billion a year budget' and highlighting the 'tremendous opportunity to break down the divisions that have for many years hampered the cause of Welsh unity'. The paper reinforced its view that 'Wales can no longer afford to be without a national body to argue our case' with a front-page cover that made an unashamed appeal to patriotism. A Welsh Uncle Sam loomed out of the page, pointing his finger at the reader, with the caption 'Your country needs you'. Trinity Holdings' main daily and Sunday newspapers in Wales were clear and direct in their commitment for the Assembly.

Trinity's other morning newspaper, the *Daily Post*, was identified by the 'Yes' campaign as 'soft' on devolution. However, the *Post*, on the eve of the poll, after having 'considered very carefully what will be in the best interests of the country which means so much to us and to you', decided to endorse the case for the Assembly. It pronounced that it was 'on balance, the preferable of the two options' (18 September). Prior to this there was little editorializing in the newspaper during the campaign. What there was tended to be light-hearted, inconsequential and flippant. For example, an editorial on 16 September speculated on who should be the chairman of the Assembly: 'With former Eurovision winner Dana among the front-runners for the Irish presidency, what parallels could there possibly be for Wales? Bryn Terfel or Sir Harry Secombe, perhaps? Or what about Mary Hopkin?'

## The evening press

The *South Wales Argus*, another newspaper whose commitment to devolution was seen as uncertain, ran six editorials during the period of the campaign (see Appendix). In 1979 the *Argus* had run only one editorial on devolution, which 'avoided any commitment'.[11] Eighteen years on, the paper was again determined not to take sides, pleading on the eve of the vote, 'We will not tell you how to vote. We did not do so at the General Election, we will not do so today. We do not believe that is the role of a local newspaper' (17 September). However, the *Argus* appeared to have been wrestling with its position up to this declaration. It had told its readers that the Assembly was 'too important to the future of this country to be bogged down by internal Labour Party squabbles' which 'only serve to play into the hands of opponents of the Assembly' (29 August), and reminded them that 'we said immediately after the General Election that we wanted to see more control by the people of Wales over their own destiny, especially after 18 years of colonial rule by Tory secretaries of state' (9 September). It also complimented Secretary of State Ron Davies, on making 'a pretty good fist of marshalling the government's arguments' (10 September).

The other south Wales evening newspapers raised questions but remained firmly on the fence throughout the referendum. In 1979 the *South Wales Echo* was the newspaper most opposed to devolution. As Osmond[12] says, 'no paper matched the *South Wales Echo* in its sustained campaign of vindictive fury against the Assembly proposals.' In 1997 the newspaper was considerably less 'vindictive'. Under the byline of its editor, Robin Fletcher, the *Echo* disowned its editorial stance of 1979. On the day after the overwhelming vote for devolution in Scotland, he commented that 'our stance on devolution for Wales in 1997 has nothing to do with this paper's previous posturing – and particularly its anti-devolutionary campaigning editorials of 1979' (12 September). In its most lengthy editorial comment of the campaign, the newspaper drew attention to the Welsh electorate's being 'split right down the middle' and 'a public thirst for more information on the Government's proposals'. The newspaper's telephone polls in the Cardiff area were revealing much doubt, confusion and a contest too close to call. The paper stated that in the midst of such indecision and confusion it would be 'deeply unhelpful to declare in favour of one camp or another' and that the *Echo*'s job should be to 'give every voter enough information to decide their own views'. Hence the heading of the editorial 'Helping you make the right decision'. In making its claim to be an 'impartial standard bearer on the biggest issue to face Wales this century', the *Echo* compared itself favourably with its sister papers, *The Western Mail* and *Wales on Sunday*, which it nailed as having been 'Yes supporters for some time' and whose coverage 'inevitably reflects this fact'. On the day of the vote the *Echo* repeated its opinion of 1979 that if 'you are not convinced you should vote NO', but the overwhelming thrust of its eve-of-poll editorial was to be non-committal. This represented a significant shift from the position it took in 1979, and was adopted in the face of evidence that many in its circulation area were not in favour of the Assembly.

Doubt was reflected in the position of the *South Wales Evening Post*, the Swansea evening newspaper, which produced six editorials between 26 August and ballot day (see Appendix). The paper acknowledged that the 'issues and implications involved are . . . immensely important' and commented at length on public apathy and inertia, which it described as 'the enemies of democracy and a successful future'. The *Evening Post* found the number of people who did not know which side to vote for 'alarming'. While it accepted that more accountability in the decision-making process was a 'very persuasive argument for voting yes', the editorial column the day before the vote focused on the case of the doubters. The *Post* believed that the response to their doubts had been unhelpful: too many of them had 'simply been insulted and called anti-Welsh'. The paper felt that the 'Yes' side had a lot of work to do to convince the doubters, and 'in the absence of convincing responses to these concerns, we must wait and see what the don't knows have to say.' However, the *Evening Post* did not see the role of the paper as one of helping to convince people how to make up their minds. It stressed the importance of an informed debate with rational and common-sense consideration of the issues which the paper had done much to lay out in its editorial comment. On the day of the vote, the paper's editorial concluded: 'We respectfully suggest, however, that those who still don't know, and who are heading for the polling station tonight, remember to vote with their head and not their heart. As with all important decisions, emotion should not get in the way of common sense.' The *Post*, on the publication of the White Paper, had drawn attention to the 'confusion and lack of enthusiasm for the devolution debate' (24 July), and throughout the campaign mentioned the importance of the need to 'galvanize debate'. But the *Post* itself left its readers without guidance when it refused to take a position on the Assembly during the campaign.

The Wrexham *Evening Leader* did not express many doubts about the benefit of a Welsh Assembly. Its editorial the day before the vote was clear: 'Yes: give Wales a chance', it stated. The opening sentence of the editorial said: 'Wales must change to progress', and proceeded to argue that the Assembly was the way forward, as it had a better chance of 'unifying the country' than the quangos and the Welsh Office, and of allowing local people to influence the services they receive. The paper conceded that there would be problems: 'There may be an aspect of jobs-for-the-boys in it; North–South antipathies won't suddenly cease; Cardiff will continue to see itself as the centre of the Welsh world.' However, the paper saw the new body as a vital step to rebuilding democracy in Wales following the years of Conservative rule. The day after the Scottish vote, the paper emphasized that 'democracy is the real goal' of the proposals for an Assembly.

One theme that emerged in the editorial comments of all the daily newspapers in Wales was the exhortation that everyone should cast their vote. Both the *Daily Post* and the *Argus* vigorously presented the case for the need to vote. For the *Argus*, those who did not go out to vote 'will be doing a great disservice to their fellow citizens' (17 September), while the *Daily Post* stated that the failure of many Welsh people to turn out to vote would send a negative message to the rest of the world (18 September). *Wales on Sunday* told its readers that 'you owe it to Wales to cast your vote' (14 September), while the *Echo* simply said: 'Everyone should VOTE' (18 September). *The Western Mail* appeared so convinced of the importance of the issue that it saw no need to urge its readers to get out and cast their vote. The attack on apathy was seen as helpful by the 'Yes' campaign, but with the eventual turn-out of around 50 per cent, the editorial exhortation of the Welsh daily press appeared to have been less than successful.

## The weekly press

Encouraging people to vote was the theme of the editorial comment in the local weekly press around Wales. The *Cambrian News* urged local people to 'Get out there and vote in Wales's vital referendum' (18 September). If voting was of 'paramount importance', the paper was less than forceful in making its position known during the campaign. It welcomed the 'commitment to consensus politics' which characterized the campaign for the Assembly, and concluded that 'at the end of the day it seems likely the dominant opinion among the people of Wales must be that an Assembly is undeniably a modest and healthy step towards democratic accountability' (18 September). The *Pontypridd Observer* and the *Rhondda Leader* encouraged readers to use their 'precious votes'. While telling readers that 'being a "Don't Know" is one thing; being a "Don't Care" is another', neither paper 'cared' enough to state where they stood on devolution. These newspapers had shared editorials with others in Mid Glamorgan, including the *Glamorgan Gazette* in Bridgend and the *Merthyr Express*. On the eve of poll the readers of all these papers were told in a common editorial, 'To devolve or not to devolve', that 'there are no easy answers and it is not part of the duty of this newspaper to arrive at them for you' (18 September). This editorial was not written by the editors of these newspapers but by the group's editor-in-chief in Cardiff. The consequence was that the leading weekly newspapers in four major conurbations in south Wales did not tell their readers where they stood on the eve of what one newspaper had called a 'critical day in Welsh history'.

However, these areas were better served by their weekly paper than those in other parts of Wales. In areas of west Wales readers of the weekly press would not have known that the campaign existed. The *Western Telegraph* did not pay attention to the issue, let alone comment on the merits or disadvantages of a Welsh Assembly. In Powys no specific editorial comment was made by either of the two leading weeklies in the region, the *Brecon and Radnor Express* and the *County Times and Express*, which serves Newtown and Welshpool. More surprising was the lack of comment by the *Carmarthen Journal*. In the north, the *North Wales Weekly News* did provide its readers with a statement from the editor, Mark Brittain, who 'sings the praise of Britain'. The column, however, did not deal with any of the specific issues of the devolution debate but simply presented its readers with a rosy-tinted outline of emotional attachment to the sceptred isle. Brittain argued that 'people of these Isles, regardless of race, religion or creed, will when the chips are down or the eyes of the world are upon us, with very few exceptions, join ranks and present a united front with dignity, good humour, flair and imagination'. For him the 'character of the British people totally transcends our own internal borders' and no referendum would change the essential character of the British people. With some exceptions, the main feature of weekly-press comment during the campaign was the reluctance to come down on one side or the other. Many weekly newspapers did not attempt to give a lead to local opinion, but were happy to reflect public apathy or ignorance, while criticizing people for their indifference.

## The London press

If the Welsh press was either friendly or indifferent to the establishment of the Assembly, the editorial stance of the London press that bothered to comment reflected the political disposition of each newspaper to the Blair government. The *Independent* expressed the view that 'Wales's past can make a difference to Britain's future', and in a tour of Welsh history the paper identified the difference between Scotland and Wales, laying stress on the 'spiritual and cultural' resistance of the Welsh to English domination to explain the 'lesser appetite for Welsh independence' and the 'weaker form of devolution offered'. The paper supported the Assembly as it would be able to promote the distinctiveness of Wales in the global market place: it 'would prove its utility by stressing, strengthening and marketing those differences to investors and customers outside' (17 September).

The *Guardian* on the other hand stressed the 'kinder and more gentle' nature of Welsh nationalism. Jonathan Freedland sympathized with the difficulty the Welsh campaign had in making itself heard over the 'larger struggle for home rule' in Scotland. 'You almost feel sorry for them. For the months they have been a blip on the political radar screen, first forgotten by the distractions of summer . . . shoved further into obscurity, silenced by the death of the principality's first lady' (8 September). His point was reinforced by his own paper, which found the Welsh referendum not worthy of separate editorial comment. But Freedland saw Wales as a 'much likelier model' for the way in which Britain could be governed.

The *Daily Telegraph*'s Unionist tradition led it to oppose devolution for Wales and Scotland. Following the large vote in favour of a Scottish Parliament, an editorial (13 September) stated that 'Wales is not Scotland' and berated the 'vacuity' of the argument that Wales should vote 'Yes' not to be left behind. The paper was critical of 'telling the people of Wales to fall in obediently behind the Scots', particularly when the proposals for Wales were 'second-rate' – the *Telegraph* made the comparison between a 'Caribbean cruise' for the Scots and 'a weekend in Blackpool' for the Welsh. The editorial accused 'Yes' campaigners of employing the 'wisdom of the Gadarene swine' rather than addressing real concerns such as whether devolution would improve services, a view dismissed by the paper as 'implicitly dishonest'. The day before the vote, the newspaper's leading political columnist, Boris Johnson, issued 'A warning for Wales'. In a piece of political invective almost unmatched in the press coverage, Johnson called forth a number of hoary political clichés to mobilize people against the 'bully-boy tactics from the New Labour nomenklatura' which had been employed against anti-devolution Welsh Labour MPs, whom he described as 'lilting veterans with mountainous majorities, men with nothing to gain from speaking out'. Conspiracies abounded as Johnson spoke of 'jobs increasingly reserved for Welsh-speakers, the cultural élite who know a taxi is really a tacsi' and of the influence 'within the European Commission' of a 'cell of politically motivated Welshmen, who yearn for the day when Wales will be independent within Europe'. Johnson's most telling point, about the Barnett formula and the consequences of an Assembly for the subsidy to Wales from the UK Exchequer, was drowned in a welter of flabby rhetoric and silly caricatures of Welshness.

*The Times* was also dismissive of the 'don't be left behind' argument for voting 'Yes' (17 September). The Assembly was described as a 'toothless dragon' compared to the Scottish Parliament, and the paper seemed to argue that not following Scotland's example would leave Wales 'better subsidised and more influential than the majority of the United Kingdom'. However, the paper found it 'persuasive' that 'Wales should accept this imperfect solution' as there were several good reasons for it. These included the potential of an Assembly to encourage the 'spirit of pluralism' in Wales which 'had suffered for too long from clientism and cronyism'. For *The Times*, 'Wales deserves better government and better arguments.' The newspaper's political columnists also went down this road. Simon Jenkins's 'poor Wales' was being 'offered in marriage to the village idiot', compared with the glamorous wedding for Scotland. Jenkins was highly critical of the legislation for the Assembly, seeing the government's proposals as not providing the new body with any substantial power to determine and manage its own spending priorities. Described as having 'less freedom than a local council' and representing only a 'paltry slice of devolution', the Welsh Assembly, for Jenkins, was only a 'half-hearted stumble down Britain's crowded road to constitutional reform'. However, he saw the stumble as being 'in the right direction'. His views were echoed in a column by William Rees-Mogg (15 September), who worried that devolution, together with the European movement, 'may lead to the destruction of England as a nation'. However, while Rees-Mogg saw the Assembly as 'half-baked', he stated that if he lived in Wales he would vote 'Yes' 'in the hope that something better would come out of this feeble Cynulliad'. Despite these reservations, Britain's 'paper of record' was sympathetic, if not strongly so, to Wales's voting 'Yes'.

At the popular end of the newspaper market, the *Mirror*, as expected of a Labour-supporting tabloid newspaper, was strongly for devolution. The front page in a special edition for Wales on the day of the ballot carried a picture of the Welsh flag with the caption 'Vote Yes – and give Wales a voice', and for the first time in British newspaper history the Welsh language appeared at the top of the front page: 'Dwedwch IE dros Gymru.' The voice of the *Mirror* was unequivocal – 'Yes for a new Wales'. At the beginning of the final week of the campaign the newspaper stated its position in an editorial entitled 'Too much at stake to ignore' (15 September) in which it argued that a 'Yes' vote was needed to turn back eighteen years of 'Tory misrule' during which, to cap all the indignities that were heaped on Wales, 'John Redwood was inflicted on the principality', a man described as having 'as much understanding for the people of Wales as Dracula had for necks'.

To vote 'No', that is 'to vote the Tory way', was not an option, but the *Mirror* regarded not voting as being 'more shameful', as it was 'to chicken out of playing a part in this momentous time in Welsh history'. The *Sun* was not convinced of the need for an Assembly, which would only produce 'more windbags' (17 September). 'What on earth will its sixty members find to talk about?' asked the paper, as 'away from the north and south coasts there's not enough going on to excite a sheep'. The paper concluded its comment by asking readers to 'imagine sixty Neil Kinnocks in one room'. The mid-market tabloids, the *Express* and the *Mail*, did not find Wales interesting enough to devote any specific editorial comment to the referendum vote.

## News coverage

To assess the nature of the reporting of the campaign by the press, the output of the newspapers was examined for the period of the official campaign, from 26 August to the vote on 18 September, punctuated as it was by the death of the Princess of Wales which brought a halt to all campaigning for the first week of September. Three kinds of newspapers were examined: London-based quality and popular newspapers (the 'national' press of Wales); the Welsh-produced national daily and evening newspapers, and a selection of the local press around Wales.

The study of the news coverage of the campaign in the London press, Welsh national newspapers and Welsh local papers began with the documentation of all the stories and items devoted to the campaign and the issue of devolution during the sample period.[13] While the main focus was on news stories, other items, including columns, vox pops (the comments of the man and woman in the street) interviews and question-and-answer pieces, were examined. The main themes that emerged in the news stories were itemized and categorized. Several themes in the campaign debate emerged from the analysis:

(a) **modernization**, relating to constitutional reform, better government, more efficient decision-making in Wales and getting government closer to the people's priorities;

(b) **'giving Wales more voice'**, referring to the Assembly's providing Wales with its own mechanism to speak for and represent specific Welsh concerns and positions in Britain, Europe and the rest of the world;

(c) **impact of the Assembly on the economy** and public services in Wales, which related to the ability or otherwise of Assembly to create jobs, bring increased prosperity to the people of Wales, improve education and health services, assist internal investment and enhance economic decision-making and performance;

(d) fuelling **internal divisions**, exploring the consequences of the Assembly on division inside Wales, between north and south, east and west, Cardiff and the rest of Wales, rural and urban communities and local communities throughout Wales as well as English- and Welsh-speakers;

(e) **break-up of Britain**, covering concerns about the impact of devolution on the integrity of the British Isles and the fears of separatism and Welsh nationalism;

(f) **cost**, regarding the amount of money needed to establish and maintain an Assembly and possible consequences for spending on other services in Wales;

(g) **apathy** of the public response to referendum debate, the level of interest in the debate and whether people would turn out to vote;

(h) **party divisions**, concerning internal political party differences over devolution and the establishment of an Assembly;

(i) the Assembly as a **talking shop**, with little effective power or clout to do anything serious or substantial about the problems that face Wales;

(j) **jobs for the boys**, involving who would participate in the Assembly and whether they would be the same people who had served in local government throughout Wales and gained a reputation for inefficiency and incompetence;

(k) **more bureaucracy**, expressing the view that the Assembly would create another tier of government;

(l) **greater accountability** of an Assembly, making government more accountable to the Welsh public in the spending of public money and the development of economic, social and cultural policies;

(m) **campaign events and personalities**, covering the comings and going, of the referendum campaign, the stunts and activities organized by the Yes for Wales and Just Say No campaigns, as well as the political parties and government, and stories about the personalities at the forefront of the campaigns;

(n) **'getting left behind'**, referring to the consequences of Wales's voting 'No' with reference to the future of Wales inside the UK and Europe, as well as by comparison with Scotland.

The most substantial coverage of the referendum was in *The Western Mail*, which produced 120 news stories and news features on devolution between 26 August and 18 September. In addition, the paper carried seventeen columns, which primarily consisted of leading political figures putting forward their opinions. Thus, the day before the vote, Prime Minister Tony Blair told the paper's readers, 'Vote Yes to a better future', while the leader of the opposition, William Hague, told them to 'Vote No to avoid the blank cheque'. Spokespersons for the Yes for Wales and Just Say No campaigns in the same edition fielded responses to the 'Twenty questions we're all asking'. The paper's regular columnists also had a stab at commenting on different aspects of the campaign. But the most interesting columns were the penned pieces that appeared on the news pages. A number of interested parties were allowed to state their case in a relatively unmediated way. These included Graham Benfield of the Welsh Council for Voluntary Action (15 September), Alan Kreppel, managing director of a Welsh bus company (13 September), Anna Terron, Spanish MEP (13 September), and Freddie Watson, former civil servant at the Welsh Office (10 September). These commentators were by and large sympathetic to the establishment of the Welsh Assembly. Nowhere in the paper during the sample period was there a piece penned by a 'No' figure not directly linked to the political campaign.

There were also disparities in the news stories. *The Western Mail*, like most of the other daily and evening newspapers in Wales in our sample, carried a large number of single-sourced stories. These were primarily reports of speeches or press events, and photo opportunities organized by the campaigns or political parties. They were reported as uncritical accounts, a form of 'stenographer journalism'. The 'Yes' campaign was able to organize more of these events than the coalition that supported a 'No' vote. Hence more access was accorded to views in favour of an Assembly, which created problems for the press in producing balance in their coverage of the debate. This was also highlighted in the 'hierarchy of access' to the news stories of the newspaper. These findings provide some support for the claim made by the *South Wales Echo* that *The Western Mail*'s stance on the Assembly had shaped its reporting of the campaign. However, this does not mean that the newspaper was biased. Most of the politicians and all the political parties except the Conservatives, as well as the government machine, were pro-devolution. This was, by and large, the perspective of official Wales, and *The Western Mail* simply reflected the situation that many in official circles wanted some devolution of power to Wales. The paper's coverage of the views of the 'Yes' and 'No' groups during the period of the campaign was fair, but *The Western Mail*, like most newspapers, relied on official bodies, institutions and groups for routine political stories. The outcome was that *The Western Mail*, along with the rest of the Welsh press, underestimated popular opinion, which was much more opposed to the Assembly.

*The Western Mail*, however, went further than any other newspaper in providing a context within which readers could make judgements about the claims of the different camps. The newspaper's coverage was broader and more comprehensive than the rest of the press, and stories appeared during the campaign on a range of issue areas including housing, education, business, investment and Europe. This complemented regular features on background issues that appeared in the newspaper prior to the campaign. For example, in July the paper devoted a week to how the establishment of an Assembly could 'improve' or 'change' health, transport, environment, education, housing, business and industry and politics in Wales. This series of articles was launched under the heading 'Case for an Assembly is as strong as it was before the change of government' (7 July). The paper was careful to talk about how the 'right type of Assembly' should play a part in all of these aspects of Welsh life, but the clear underpinning of the pieces was that devolution was right for Wales.

The coverage of the *Daily Post* contrasted sharply with that of *The Western Mail*. It carried thirty-four news stories on devolution during the period of the official campaign, and nearly half of these focused on the events and personalities of the campaign, with little attempt to place their reporting in a broader context. Visits to the north Wales region by British national politicians were a common feature of these reports. Just under a quarter of these stories were about the north–south division, including the warning by Denzil Davies, MP for Llanelli, that the less populated areas of Wales would get less grant aid under an Assembly (28 August), the findings of a poll that indicated the majority of businesses in north Wales believed that devolution would harm investment into the region (30 August) and an account of the 'old rivalry' between north and south that 'Blair must conquer' (16 September). Overall, the *Post*'s coverage of devolution was not that of a newspaper attempting to serve a nation – despite its detailed coverage of the White Paper in July. The paper presented the perspective of a regional newspaper for north Wales with its horizons confined to its own backyard.

The evening press in Wales provided roughly the same amount of news coverage of the referendum. The *South Wales Evening Post* had fifty-nine news stories during the period, while the *South Wales Echo* carried sixty-four, the *South Wales Argus* forty and the *Evening Leader* in Wrexham twenty-six. A large proportion of these stories consisted of short, three or four paragraphs at most, single-sourced reports of events relating to the campaign. The activities of local Members of Parliament were regularly reported, highlighting the strong relationship between local MPs and local newspapers. Thus the *Argus* carried news stories about Newport West MP Alan Howarth on the campaign trail in Caldicot ('MP brings "Yes" message', 29 August) and Monmouth MP Huw Edwards commenting on the business manifesto launched by Labour ('Assembly "a better deal" for Wales', 1 September), while the *Evening Post* reported the views of Gower MP Martin Caton ('MP says Assembly is vital for the future', 27 August), the *Echo* covered a speech by Cardiff Central MP Jon Owen Jones to local business leaders ('It's good for Wales', 13 September) and the *Evening Leader* reported that the view of local MP John Marek that 'A yes vote will give voice to everyone' (17 September).

The passive reproduction of the views and positions of the campaigns was a notable feature of the coverage of the 'substance' of the referendum debate throughout the Welsh press. Prominence was given to what could be described as 'political advertorials', that is, pieces penned by leading political figures that outlined their reasons for voting one way or the other in the referendum. This format was adopted by nearly every Welsh newspaper. Thus, side by side, we had the *South Wales Echo* publishing authored pieces by Prime Minister Tony Blair and Opposition leader William Hague, on the eve of the poll, with, the previous day, Welsh Office minister Peter Hain and Just Say No chair Professor Nicholas Bourne answering questions put to them by the paper. The *South Wales Argus* pitted Welsh Secretary Ron Davies against William Hague in their eve-of-poll 'guide to the arguments for and against', with Peter Hain joined by Robert Hodge of the 'No' campaign in their 'Assembly question time'. This was the second occasion on which Ron Davies had been provided with an opportunity to present his views directly to *Argus* readers, the first being on 11 September when he told them why 'We must not miss out on our day of history'. The 'Yes' case was also put forcefully by Tony Blair writing exclusively for the paper on 'Why I want you to vote Yes' (16 September). The 'No' campaign did not have similar access to the pages of the *South Wales Argus* for one of their supporters to present their case. The nearest approach was by the paper's parliamentary correspondent who was 'On campaign trail with Llew the rebel' (16 September). The *South Wales Evening Post* preferred to give space to representatives of the local 'Yes' and 'No' campaigns, historian Rob Humphreys and Independent Swansea councillor John Bushell, to state their position, while the *County Times and Express* pitted the local MEP Eluned Morgan against the former Tory MP for Brecon, Jonathan Evans, in their 'Time to choose' page of 12 September, which also included smaller contributions from a 'Yes'-voting Australian and an anti-Assembly Liberal Democrat. These are just a few examples of the unmediated access politicians and campaign spokespersons gained in the press. The decline of political advertising in the press can be seen as a consequence of the growth of these more direct means of reaching the readers.

The subtle shift in the *Echo*'s coverage of devolution from 1979 was perhaps the most significant development in the press coverage. The paper which made the greatest effort amongst the local press during the campaign to lay out the issues was the *South Wales Echo*. On 11 September it provided a free, twelve-page 'reader's guide to devolution', *Wales Decides*. This guide included two pages on the impact of devolution in the areas of health, councils, education, jobs, elections, quangos, Welsh Secretary and

taxpayers, accompanied by an overview by the paper's parliament-
ary correspondent under the title 'May 1999: a new dawn for
Wales?' The impact pieces focused on how the chosen areas of
Welsh life would benefit from the arrival of an Assembly. The
positions of the Conservatives, Liberal Democrats and Plaid
Cymru, as well as the 'Yes' and 'No' campaigns, were also carried.
A centre double-page spread focused on business and the Assembly.
The main article, 'Welsh business hedging its bets over devolution',
drew attention to there being 'no uniform business' voice on the
issue, while two shorter articles, 'Small firms against Assembly'
and 'Wales set to receive economic boost from devolution',
balanced each other out on the economic impact of the new body.
One page was a 'Guide to how every MP in Wales stands on the
devolution vote', replete with pictures with a bold 'Yes' or 'No'
against them – thirty-five 'Yes', four 'No' and one who would not
say (Denzil Davies). History was also featured with stories on what
happened in 1979, with a wrap-up of what leading 'Yes' and 'No'
campaigners of today were doing then, including details of Carys
Pugh's early political career in Plaid Cymru, and a profile of 'one
of the most famous Welsh freedom fighters, Owain Glyndwr'. The
guide ended with the views of the 'ordinary people' of Cardiff –
eighteen faces, the majority of whom were going to vote 'Yes'. The
thrust of this guide, while factual, certainly made a better job of
presenting the 'Yes' case. If the *Echo* never came out in favour of
the Assembly, it certainly was not anti-devolution.

The metropolitan bias of the London papers led them to focus on
the UK political aspects. Dissent inside the Labour Party over the
Welsh Assembly proved an important focal point. The *Telegraph*
devoted coverage to the dissent inside Welsh Labour with stories
such as 'Ex-minister joins dissenters over devolution plan' (16
September) and 'Labour MPs join protest against Welsh Assembly'
(10 September). The paper's focus on internal Labour wrangles over
devolution provided the framework for the reporting of Blair's visit
to Wrexham. 'Blair shrugs off devolution critics', the headline
trumpeted (17 September). *The Times* gave copy to the 'one-by-one'
coming-out strategy of those MPs against the Assembly – for
example, 'Two more Labour MPs defy the party on Wales' (10
September). For the London papers these kinds of stories perhaps
represented a greater interest in the impact of the vote on the Blair
'project' than the consequences for democracy in Wales.

The general pattern points to the overwhelming focus of the news reporting during the campaign being centred on the 'horse-race' aspects of the electoral process,[14] stories describing campaign activities as distinct from those which deal with the 'substance' of the referendum debate, that is those that discuss the range of issues involved. Despite commitment to informing readers of the issues, most of the press reporting concentrated on the race to win the vote. It was only in papers such as *The Western Mail* in Wales and the broadsheet press in London, with more commitment to more 'serious' journalism, that stories of substance held their own with accounts of the campaign.

Within this pattern it is possible to see a few themes dominating the press agenda in the reporting of the referendum campaign. The apathy of the Welsh people was a key theme. Reasons for the apathy included voting fatigue following the May general election, ignorance of the issue of devolution, flaws in the Welsh character and the campaigning confusion caused by disunity inside Wales's leading political party, the Labour Party. The political fortunes of the government, Labour Party and the Prime Minister were another theme, with Blair's plans for constitutional reform and moderniza-tion, the consequences of an Assembly for Wales's relationship with Britain, the future of the quangos and the political career of Welsh Secretary Ron Davies being to the fore. While stories of internal division inside the Labour Party were prominent, the lack of stories about Plaid Cymru highlighted the low profile of the party during the campaign. Economic considerations were less prevalent as stories, and usually tended to concentrate on the cost of the Assembly and the impact of the Assembly on the fortunes of the Welsh economy. What was largely absent was any passion about democracy and the development of Welsh society.

## Pressures on the press

The reporting of the referendum has to be seen in the context of the pressures that were exerted on the press. Decisions that shaped the coverage were made at a number of levels in the production process, from reporters' interaction with their sources through to editors' decisions on policy. Throughout the campaign – as well as the weeks leading up to it – the press in Wales was subjected to unprecedented political pressure. The Millbank propaganda machine attempted to cultivate and influence newspaper editors – a few months before the vote editors of major newspapers in Wales were invited to Downing Street for cocktails and a friendly chat with the Prime Minister. Such overtures were not seen by most editors as having any impact on their paper's position. But it is not every day that members of the Welsh press take drinks with the Prime Minister.[15] The political pressures on the press were identified by many journalists as coming mainly from the pro-Assembly parties and organizations. One reporter described the 'Yes' campaign as 'overwhelmingly' populated by professional public-relations people, while the 'No' campaign was thinly spread throughout Wales and run by 'two ladies and a dog'. The early start of the 'Yes' campaign was also contrasted with the late and sluggish arrival of the anti-Assembly coalition. The better organization and earlier start, according to some journalists, accounted for the greater prominence of 'Yes' stories. But others said the 'Yes' campaign began too early, which led to the 'boredom factor' creeping in by the end of the campaign.

The decision not to take an editorial stance on what they all described as a defining moment in the life of Wales was seen by some as an abnegation of responsibility. One editor asked, 'What is the point of having an editorial comment column if you don't state your opinion on the major issues of the day?' He bemoaned what he saw as the tendency 'not to expect passion from non-London newspapers', although he saw it as easier for national Welsh newspapers to have an opinion on national issues than the weeklies. Another editor took the view that a newspaper should 'not pretend we've got a view if we haven't'. For some, the decision not to take a strong line was a 'pragmatic thing' because 'in pleasing one reader we could put off another'. Increased competition in the newspaper market has resulted in greater sensitivity to matters which might impact negatively on circulation. To take a strong stand requires editors to have either a sound knowledge of their readers or immense bravery.

Commercial concerns weighed heavily on the press coverage of the referendum. One reason given for the limited press coverage was the response of readers. Market research for the *Daily Post* is said to have found that every time a referendum story appeared on the front page casual sales declined. As one employee of the paper put it, 'When we went big on devolution on page one, sales went down. The feeling was that the public were underwhelmed, turned off by the campaign.' One editor acknowledged that his newspaper 'rarely put a devolution story on the front page because it didn't see it as a seller. It was a turn-off subject.' A weekly newspaper editor in south Wales said the 'Yes' and 'No' campaigns in his area 'did not get a great deal of attention in the street, most people wanted to get on with their shopping'. However, editors in other parts of Wales pointed to devolution being 'very important to a lot of people' in their area. Throughout Wales newspaper letter columns were full of views on devolution. The referendum 'generated a huge amount of correspondence' and, as one editor said, even their own 'social market research' found it 'being talked about in the pubs'. In certain parts of Wales the referendum was more news-worthy; popular interest in Swansea appeared greater than that in Cardiff and parts of north Wales. The extent to which newspapers reported the referendum is explained by the differences in their audiences. The greater the local interest the more likely the paper is to provide copy.

There is also the question of who reads a newspaper. *Wales on Sunday*, which locates itself at the popular end of the market with its emphasis on 'a lot of humour and not taking things too seriously', was more resistant to heavy political stories, preferring to seek out the human interest or personality angle. *The Western Mail*, on the other hand, devoted a lot of space to devolution stories because their audience is seen as more upmarket and therefore more interested in the issues. The newspaper, according to one competitor, 'has done well out of it from the sales point of view because they were speaking to a lot of people who were interested . . . people who run businesses and are more politically minded'. The decision of papers that stress their 'Welshness' to support the Assembly made strong commercial sense. But com-mercial criteria were dismissed as being significant in determining editorial policy. One editor agreed that 'the Assembly will be good for the sales of Welsh newspapers and that does affect decisions but when it comes to deciding the policy of the paper that was just a factor, it is not an overriding factor'. The crucial thing as far as he was concerned was that 'I'm a Welshman editing a Welsh newspaper. I want Wales to be a nation and I want Wales to have its own newspapers so the commercial thing flows from that.'

## Conclusion

There is no simple correlation between the reporting of the press around Wales and the outcome of the 1997 referendum. Most of the Welsh newspapers (and even most of the much-complained-about London press) were either supportive of devolution or committed to not taking sides. In certain parts of Wales – such as Wrexham – strong editorial support for a 'Yes' vote was not reflected in the local result. For the daily and evening newspapers the story merited some coverage, whereas the weekly press largely neglected the story. Much of the coverage focused on the rituals of political electioneering rather than on sober and serious accounts of the issues. Some newspapers did try to use their editorial columns to explain some of the issues, and in one or two cases special supplements laid out these issues in some detail. But overall news stories focused on personalities and events, not issues. This decision was a reflection of market choices and commercial considerations. The perception of many editors that their readers were not interested or did not want to read about the referendum determined their coverage. Editors who did go strong on devolution stories did so in the knowledge that their readers were interested and keen on reading about the topic, and that commercial benefits could accrue. Sometimes commercial benefits correspond with political commitments. The growth of market-driven journalism has led to increased sensitivity in the press to the role of a newspaper as an opinion leader in the community. Unpopular campaigns that might lose readers have to be treated with care. But perhaps the most significant characteristic of the Welsh press is the problematic way in which it related to something called 'Wales'. While over the years there have been signs that some newspapers are becoming more 'all-Wales' in their perspective, the referendum shows the importance still attached to locality by the Welsh press and the difficulty of finding local angles to Welsh events.

## Appendix

Editorials on devolution during the referendum campaign, 26 August to 18 September 1997

*The Western Mail*

| | |
|---|---|
| 18 September | Vote Yes for our future |
| 17 September | Hope must look beyond Blair factor |
| 16 September | Time is short and battle is yet to be won |
| 15 September | Keep it clean and let the voters decide |
| 13 September | Breathtaking attacks on the Assembly |
| | Puzzled by Sir Wyn |
| 12 September | Scots have set loose a genie of change |
| 11 September | Local party fury |
| 10 September | The personal touch crucial in the run-in |
| 9 September | Labour needs to tackle its dissenters |

*South Wales Argus*

| | |
|---|---|
| 17 September | Future of Wales is in your hands |
| 15 September | It's your £7bn – so vote on it |
| 12 September | The battle is not yet over |
| 10 September | Expect the big guns on our turf |
| 9 September | Assembly on agenda again |
| 29 August | Devolution row splits Labour |

*South Wales Echo*

| | |
|---|---|
| 18 September | 18 years on, our advice is same – go and VOTE |
| 12 September | Helping you make the right decision |
| 11 September | Considering our future |

*South Wales Evening Post*

| | |
|---|---|
| 18 September | The big day arrives |
| 17 September | Third of electorate undecided |
| 15 September | Hardly a calming influence |
| 13 September | Scots' Yes should move public debate |
| 10 September | Let's get back to the real debate |
| 30 August | Party politics not relevant to devolution |

*Wrexham Evening Leader*

| | |
|---|---|
| 18 September | Yes: give Wales a chance |
| 12 September | A lead for Wales? |

*Daily Post*
18 September      Stand up and be counted
16 September      *Daily Post*: our view
9 September       *Daily Post*: our view

*Wales on Sunday*
14 September      The future rests in your hands


## Notes

The author would like to thank the following people for their assistance in gathering material for this chapter: Tim Lewis, Francesca Rhydderch, Helle Michelsen and Miranda Morton.


1. For overviews of the Welsh media system see Hughie Mackay and Tony Powell, 'Wales and its media: production, consumption and regulation', *Contemporary Wales* 10 (1998); David Skilton, 'More words and pictures in the air', in David Cole (ed.), *The New Wales* (Cardiff: University of Wales Press, 1990); Kevin Williams, *Shadows and Substance: The Development of a Media Policy for Wales* (Llandysul: Gomer Press, 1997).
2. The Welsh-language press was not examined. This is a gap in our understanding of the press coverage of the referendum. However, the Welsh-language weekly press has declined even more rapidly than its English-language counterparts. This has been counteracted to some extent by the growth of *y papurau bro* which are estimated to have a circulation of around 50,000. It is also worth noting that in 1997 *Yr Herald Gymraeg* increased its circulation by 24.8 per cent in the second half of the year (*UK Press Gazette*, 27 March 1998).
3. See John Humphries, 'Attitude: media coverage of the referendum', *Planet* 127 (February/March 1998), 93; Patrick Hannan, 'Who's asking the questions?', *Planet* 126 (December/January 1998), 10.
4. For 1979 figures see John Osmond, 'The referendum and the English-language press', in D. Foulkes, B. Jones, and R. Wilford (eds.), *The Welsh Veto: The Welsh Act, 1978 and the Referendum* (Cardiff: University of Wales Press, 1983), p. 155. The arrival of *Wales on Sunday* in 1982 did establish for the first time a successful Sunday newspaper produced in Wales for Welsh readers. The average sales figure for July to December 1997 was 61,541, as reported in the *UK Press Gazette*, 27 March 1998.
5. Mackay and Powell, 'Wales and its media'.
6. N. Fowler, 'Banishing the myth: newspapers are thriving in Wales', *Y Barcud Coch* (September 1997).
7. T. Fishlock, 'A foreign correspondent in Wales', *Journalism Studies Review* 1 (1976).

8. Patrick Hannan, 'The real democratic deficit is journalism in Wales', *British Journalism Review* 9, and 'Who's asking the questions?', 7–12.

9. Osmond, 'The referendum and the English-language press', 161.

10. Some see *The Western Mail*'s commitment to providing a platform for the move to the devolution of more power to Wales as beginning in June 1996 with its series of penned articles entitled 'The nationhood debate'.

11. Osmond, 'The referendum and the English-language press', p. 160.

12. Ibid., p. 162.

13. There were problems in collecting a sample of newspapers for this period. Material had to be gathered from several sources. This difficulty highlights the need for a complete national newspaper archive in Wales and draws attention to the use of sources such as the the CD-ROM which presents only a partial picture of newspaper accounts. The result is that there may be some material omitted in the sample.

Other material was deliberately omitted including articles in the special supplements and sections that some newspapers print. Thus *The Western Mail*'s Country and Farming supplement had articles on Assembly-related matters as did the Business section of the paper. The decision was to focus on news articles aimed at the general reader. The main reason for these omissions was time and resources.

The sample focuses on the period of the official campaign which is not sufficient to make any long-term assessment of the impact and influence of the newspapers on the outcome of the referendum. This work still remains to be done.

14. See Keith Sinclair, ' "Horserace" versus "Substance" in coverage of election by British prestige press', *Journalism Quarterly* 5, 4 (1982).

15. For a more detailed discussion of the 'spin' during the campaign see David Williams, 'Campaign of the spin doctors', *Agenda: The Journal of the Institute of Welsh Affairs* (Winter 1997/8).

# 7 Television and the Referendum*

IOAN BELLIN

After the Labour victory in May 1997, it was obvious that the broadcasters would have to prepare for a referendum campaign carefully. The government published its White Paper, *A Voice for Wales*, on 22 July 1997, which announced that the government planned a sixty-member assembly to be responsible for schools, hospitals and other key public services in Wales, after the referendum vote on 18 September. There had been debate about the devolution plans beforehand. However, it was from this moment that the campaigns for and against an assembly began to increase their activity. Against this background, television and radio were required to maintain 'due impartiality', unlike newspapers, which could be as partisan as their potential audience would let them.

In July 1997 the BBC had drawn up a policy for 'Coverage of the referendums on a devolved Parliament for Scotland and a devolved Assembly for Wales' based on their obligation to provide 'comprehensive, authoritative and impartial coverage of news and current affairs and to support fair and informed debate at local, regional and national levels'. The lack of public awareness of devolution meant that the broadcasters needed to explain what devolution meant to the audience. For the BBC this was seen as at the heart of its public-service remit. Between the publication of the White Paper and the middle of August, the main thrust of its coverage was explanatory rather than adversarial. Words such as 'devolution' or 'constitutional reform' are not popular with the audience. Journalists had to relate the decision to the effects of the decision on people's lives. It was seen

*The author would like to thank Aled Eirug, head of news and current affairs, BBC Wales, Nick Powell, head of HTV's political unit, and Hywel William, ITC.

that programmes needed to be 'authoritative and impartial. Balance (would) be achieved by asking tough questions, not by an arithmetical formula' ('Policy for coverage of the referendums', 1997).

The BBC also attempted to address the issues of devolution. One issue was the question of whether the economy would benefit from devolution, and it was accepted that this type of issue would be covered by interviewing experts rather than politicians. The primary objective always was to achieve fairness on the issues, but it was also important to ensure a proper balance in the political parties' contributions. As a guideline, the following ratio across programming as whole was used:

| | |
|---|---|
| Labour | 2 |
| Conservative | 1 |
| Scottish National Party/Plaid Cymru | 1 |
| Liberal Democrats | 1 |

This was kept under review, but was the starting-point for coverage. The reason for this ratio was that the devolution debate was multifaceted. It was the Labour government's proposition that was being scrutinized. Therefore, they had the main responsibility for arguing for/answering to it. Labour spokespeople were to be balanced by the 'opposition', represented, as appropriate, by one or more of the three other parties. This policy was monitored by the BBC from 21 July to 18 September using a 'double tally'.

1. For/against (experts, umbrella groups, sectors)
2. Party activists: Lab./Cons./SNP/PC/LibDems.

Appearances were listed, but not their duration. During the monitored period equal balance was achieved overall in the entirety of the BBC's output in Wales, including coverage on Radio Wales, Radio Cymru, BBC Wales and BBC-produced programmes for S4C. Therefore, on a single programme one of the sides could have more say than the other, but balance could be maintained with the counter-argument on another programme (BBC, 'Policy for coverage of the referendums').

The independent sector also had to exist within a regulatory framework, in both languages. The Broadcasting Act of 1990 requires the ITC (Independent Television Commission) to do all that it can to secure 'that due impartiality is preserved on the part of the person providing the service as respects matters of political or industrial controversy or relating to current public policy'.

The term 'due' is significant; it should be interpreted as meaning adequate or appropriate to the nature of the subject and the type of programme. While the requirement of due impartiality applies to all area of controversy covered by the Act, it does not mean that 'balance' is required in any simple mathematical sense or that equal time must be given to each opposing point of view, nor does it require absolute neutrality on every issue. (ITC, Code: 14, 1998)

In the case of 'debate' programmes: 'participants in a political discussion programme will normally be chosen more with a view to reflecting the principal opposing viewpoints.' The provision that due impartiality must be preserved 'on the part of the person providing the service' is also significant. It puts the burden of compliance on licensees rather then individual programme-makers (ITC Code: 14–15, 1998).

The guidelines for S4C's programmes are similar to the ITC code. According to the Broadcasting Act 1990, 'the S4C service must maintain due impartiality in matters of political or industrial controversy or matters relating to current public policy.' It goes on to say: 'In dealing with a major matter of controversy, S4C must ensure that justice is done to all significant views and perspectives, and must do so during the period when the matter is still controversial' (S4C Compliance Guidelines 1996: 1/13). This means that S4C and its suppliers must give coverage to both sides of the devolution argument. This raises the question of who represents both sides of the argument. In the case of the Welsh referendum there were only two choices for the electorate on the ballot paper: 'I agree that there should be a Welsh Assembly' or 'I do not agree that there should be a Welsh Assembly', admitting of only a 'Yes' or 'No' answer.

As indicated above, the 1990 Broadcasting Act ensures that S4C, rather than individual programme suppliers, has to face the burden of impartiality. The compliance guidelines make it clear that 'Impartiality does not mean that broadcasters have to be absolutely neutral on every controversial issue, but it should lead them to deal even-handedly with opposing points of view. Opinion should be clearly distinguished from fact [but] judgement will always be called for' (S4C Compliance Guidelines 1996: 1/12). The devolution referendum was an issue of 'current and active controversy', and therefore broadcasters needed to ensure that the principal opposing viewpoints were reflected in a single programme, i.e. the proponents of a 'Yes' or 'No' vote. It is clear in the ITC code that there are some occasions when the principal opposing viewpoints must be reflected in a single programme or programme item, either because it is not likely that the licensee will soon return to the subject, or because the issues involved are of current and active controversy. Balance can also be achieved over a series of programmes as a whole rather than in just one single programme. The ITC defines a series as more than one programme broadcast in the same service, each one of which is clearly linked to the other(s), and which deal with the same or related issues. It is not sufficient to claim that programmes on other channels or other media will ensure the opposing views will be heard (ITC Code: 14–15, 1998). Therefore, S4C's *Refferendwm '97* series by the BBC, or *Wales Decides* on HTV, would have to be judged by whether they had a tendency towards the 'Yes' or 'No' camp. Furthermore, as all the programmes on the referendum were factual, the suppliers had to follow the guidelines in:

> dealing with controversial issues already the subject of public debate [and ensuring] that all the main opinions on the issue are fairly represented. Programmes which extend the current public debate, or which offer a view on the authority of evidence presented, may single out one aspect of an issue for detailed examination. Programmes which extend the political agenda in this way must be fair to their subject matter. (S4C Compliance Guidelines 1996: 1/13)

News is important in any campaign. It can set the agenda, and has a larger audience than current-affairs programmes. Owing to this importance,

> the Act requires that any news, given in whatever form, must be presented with due accuracy and impartiality. Reporting should be dispassionate and news judgements based on the need to give viewers an even-handed account of events. In reporting on matters of industrial or political controversy, the main differing views on the matter should be given their due weight in the period during which the controversy is

active. Editorial discretion will determine whether a range of conflicting views is included within a single news item or whether it is acceptable to spread them over a series of bulletins. (ITC Code: 16, 1998)

News, in whatever form, must be presented with due accuracy and impartiality. Reporting should be dispassionate. News judgements should be based on the need to give viewers an even-handed account of events. In reporting on matters of industrial or political controversy, the main differing views on the matter should be given their due weight. Provided that due impartiality is maintained, a range of conflicting views may be included within a single news item or spread over a series of bulletins. (S4C Compliance Guidelines 1996 1/14)

Clearly, a regional newsroom will have a different set of priorities from that of a network programme serving the nation as a whole. In dealing with major matters of controversy, licensees must ensure that justice is done to a full range of significant views and perspectives during the period in which the controversy is active. (ITC Code: 16 1998)

This would mean the period from publication of the Government of Wales bill until the Welsh referendum on 18 September.

Also relevant is the section on 'The conduct of interviews' which states that sufficient information has to be given to interviewees about the programme and impartiality must be maintained when editing as well as when conducting interviews. The editing should not distort or misinterpret the opinion of the interviewee. 'The appearances of politicians in news and current affairs programmes are governed by the requirements of due impartiality. The obligation to ensure due impartiality relates to issues, not to parties, and some important issues do not divide opinion along existing party lines' (S4C Compliance Guidelines: 1/16, 1996). This was true of the devolution issue, and therefore a person's party position was not important, but whether they were likely to vote 'Yes' or 'No'.

The agreement associated with the BBC's charter requires the BBC to do all it can to secure that all programmes

treat controversial subjects with due accuracy and impartiality, both in the Corporation's news services and in the more general field of programmes dealing with matters of public policy or of political or industrial controversy, and do not contain any material expressing the opinion of the Corporation on current affairs or matters of public policy other than broadcasting.

Paragraph 5.2 also states: 'In applying paragraph 5.1(c) a series of programmes may be considered as a whole' (BBC producers' guidelines: 290).

The 1979 result constituted a refutation of the theory that support for a political party in a general election also constitutes support for the particular policies outlined in its manifesto. The Wales Act was officially supported by three of the four political parties in Wales – Labour, the Liberal Party, and Plaid Cymru – which had recommended devolution in their October 1974 manifestos and had gained 75.8 per cent of the Welsh vote in the general election of October 1974 and 65.6 per cent in 1979. The only party opposing devolution was the Conservatives, who had received only 23.9 per cent of the vote in October 1974 and 32.3 per cent in 1979. Yet the referendum revealed that the parties supporting the Wales Act did not, on this issue, represent the views of their supporters. The referendum ensured that a major constitutional change would not occur if it was not supported by a popular consensus. According to opinion polls, there had been a change in attitude to devolution; for example in June 1997 it was found that 39 per cent were in favour compared to 27 per cent against, with 34 per cent 'don't knows' (Beaufort Research/*Western Mail*, 2 July 1997). After discussions between London and Cardiff it was decided that if the BBC was to remain impartial the organization would have to give equal coverage to the two groups, 'Yes' and 'No'. Moreover, with regard to the referendum, traditional party lines seemed blurred, with some Labour members campaigning against the Assembly and somewhat fewer Conservatives supporting devolution. This meant that it was too simplistic to give air time to the two sides according to party positions. However, it was difficult for the broadcasters to achieve balance in their coverage because there were three parties publicly campaigning for a 'Yes' vote, and there needed to be an appropriate division of time between them.

If one looks at the number of appearances on HTV, ITV and BBC news programmes between 22 August and 18 September, 'Yes' appearances were more frequent than 'No', apart from coverage of the Welsh devolution debate on ITN's *News at Ten* (Appendix). One of the main reasons for the difference in the figures is that the 'Yes' campaign was better organized and funded. The 'Yes' campaign organized events such as ministerial visits and public 'Yes' launches which gave the chance for the cameras to film something. In comparison, fewer events were organized by the 'No' campaign, and many of those opposed were difficult to get on camera; an example would be dissident Labour MPs. This made balancing the argument even more difficult.

The balance also had to take account of those figures not associated officially with either campaign, but publicly in favour of or against devolution. For example, the Labour MP Llew Smith for Blaenau Gwent was taken as being in the 'No' camp, whereas Plaid Cymru president Dafydd Wigley MP was seen as a 'Yes' advocate, although he may have wanted to go further. One problem was where to place Elwyn Jones, who was critical of the 'No' campaign, yet still voiced powerful arguments against devolution. Guidelines suggested counting any spokesperson or any interview that was obviously in favour of one side over the other. Yet there was a lot of ambiguity: some public figures, such as Ted Rowlands MP, criticized the government scheme while saying he was going to vote 'Yes', and Sir Wyn Roberts said he was going to vote 'No', but at the same time maintained that once in the House of Lords he would attempt to strengthen the existing proposals. The other major problem was where to place Denzil Davies MP. By the second month of campaigning he was being used by the broadcasters as a counter to 'Yes' arguments, which meant he could be counted in the 'No' camp.

If one times the appearances of spokespersons for the 'Yes' and 'No' campaigns, one can see that there was a tendency for 'Yes' to have more time on HTV's *Wales Tonight*, the BBC 9 p.m. news and ITV's *News at Ten*. For example on HTV's *Wales Tonight*, 63 per cent of spoken appearances were 'Yes' supporters, compared with 37 per cent who represented the 'No' campaign. During the BBC 9 p.m. news reports on the Welsh campaign, the 'Yes' campaign had 69 per cent and the 'No' camp had 31 per cent. Rather differently, ITV's news coverage had a 63/37 per cent split in favour of the Welsh 'Yes' campaign. It could be said that these figures reflect the support received by the three parties that fought the 1997 election who were in favour of devolution, and the vote of the party opposed to devolution, that is the Conservatives. But, as was in the case in 1979, many people who vote for a party do not necessarily agree with everything for which it stands.

In the final analysis, the journalists themselves can ensure balance by including a reference to the 'No' campaign's message in reply to a spokesperson by the 'Yes' campaign. An example of this was BBC1's late-evening news on 30 August, when John Major's claim that devolution would lead to the break-up of the UK was quoted by the Scottish correspondent. This was then followed by the counter-arguments given by Donald Dewar and Winnie Ewing.

Viewing HTV's *Wales Tonight*, the 'Yes' campaign can be seen as dominated by the Labour Party. Of the forty-six spokespeople, nineteen can be easily identified as Labour, seven are Liberal Democrats, four Plaid Cymru, two Conservatives, with one each from the Greens and the SNP. The 'No' campaign was Conservative dominated, with sixteen of the thirty-six spokespeople identified as party members, although Labour rebels such as Ray Powell and Carys Pugh are represented, with eleven speakers.

The trend of a 'Yes' campaign identified with the Labour Party and a 'No' campaign seen as Conservative continued in reports by the network agencies, with the exception that the SNP were prominent in the Scottish campaign.


## Conclusions

The headlines from 22 August to 18 September indicate that devolution was not very prominent compared with other British and international news. There were few headlines about the respective referendum campaigns. Devolution made the main headline only twice on the BBC and three times on ITV's news bulletins. This may have been due to a lack of interest by the news teams, or a symptom of a lacklustre campaign.

Finally, if one looks at the amount of time devoted to devolution on network news, more attention was given to Scotland than to Wales. The total for BBC reports of the Welsh devolution campaign was less than a third of the time devoted to the Scottish devolution campaign. ITV's news coverage was more balanced, but the Scottish devolution campaign still attracted almost eleven minutes more air time than the Welsh campaign.

Table 7.1 Network news coverage of the referendum campaign

| News network | Scotland | Wales |
|---|---|---|
| BBC | 39 mins. 51 secs. | 12 mins. 48 secs. |
| ITV | 36 mins. 18 secs. | 25 mins. 40 secs. |

The problem this caused for those campaigning in Wales was increased by the fact that many viewers are able to tune their television aerials to sources outside Wales. Approximately 35 per cent of the Welsh population live in overlap areas, enabling them to choose to watch programmes from English transmitters. This compares with only 2.5 per cent in Scotland. Most people (approximately 70 per cent) watch television as a source for their world news rather than reading papers or listening to the radio (ITC 1995). As there was less coverage of Wales on the network and if Welsh viewers watched other regional news providers such as HTV West, Granada or BBC West, they could quite easily have forgotten that there was a referendum campaign going on.

## Appendix

Spoken appearances by 'Yes' and 'No' campaigns on HTV *Wales Tonight* and their party, 22 August to 18 September

| Party | Yes | No |
|---|---|---|
| Labour | 19 | 11 |
| Conservatives | 2 | 16 |
| Plaid Cymru | 4 | 0 |
| Liberal Democrats | 7 | 1 |
| SNP | 1 | 0 |
| Green | 1 | 0 |
| Independent/Non-identifiable | 12 | 8 |
| Total | 46 | 36 |

Spoken appearances by 'Yes' and 'No' campaigns on BBC 9 p.m. *News* and their party, 22 August to 18 September

| Party | Yes | | No | |
|---|---|---|---|---|
| | Scotland | Wales | Scotland | Wales |
| Labour | 7 | 6 | | 3 |
| Conservative | 0 | | 5 | 3 |
| Liberal Democrat | 6 | 2 | | |
| SNP | 7 | | | |
| Independent/Non-identifiable | 2 | 2 | 4 | |
| Total | 22 | 10 | 9 | 6 |

Spoken appearances by 'Yes' and 'No' campaigns on ITV's *News at Ten* and their party, 22 August to 18 September

| Party | Yes | | No | |
|---|---|---|---|---|
| | Scotland | Wales | Scotland | Wales |
| Labour | 7 | 4 | 1 | 2 |
| Conservative | | | 7 | 3 |
| Liberal Democrat | 2 | | | |
| SNP | 4 | | | |
| Plaid Cymru | | 1 | | |
| Independent/Non-identifiable | 2 | 1 | 4 | 1 |
| Total | 15 | 6 | 12 | 6 |

## References

BBC *Producers' Guidelines 1996* (BBC London).

V. Bogdanor, 1981. *The People and the Party System: The Referendum and Electoral Reform in British Politics* (Cambridge: Cambridge University Press).

ITC *Programme Code Autumn 1998* (Independent Television Commission, London).

I. Lightman, J. B. Jones, R. Jarman, D. Balsom and J. Osmond, 1996. *The Road to the Referendum: Requirements for an Informed and Fair Debate* (Cardiff: Institute of Welsh Affairs).

A. Sloman, 1997. 'A Policy for Coverage of the Referendums on a Devolved Parliament for Scotland and a Devolved Assembly for Wales Based on our Obligation to Provide "Comprehensive, authoritative and impartial coverage of news and current affairs and to support fair and informed debate at local, regional, and national levels" ' (BBC Internal Document, London).

*S4C Compliance Guidelines and Suppliers' Handbook* May 1996 (Cardiff: S4C).

# 8 The Referendum: A Flawed Instrument

J. BARRY JONES (ed.)

The decision by Tony Blair that the Scottish and Welsh devolution legislation would only be introduced after the government's proposals had been endorsed by referendum has, almost certainly, established the principle that all future 'constitutional reforms' will require the prior approval of a referendum. This view is reinforced by the Labour government's commitment to hold referendums for a London elected mayor, Westminster electoral reform and British entry into the European Monetary Union.

The referendum agenda represents a significant departure from the British tradition of a representative democracy, closely linked to the convention of a sovereign Parliament, and a concept of representation which extends considerable freedom of action to individual MPs.[1] This tradition fits ill with referendums predicated upon the presumption that ultimate authority rests with the people. Despite the inherent contradiction, Britain has had increasing recourse to the use of referendums. Since 1973 there have been seven referendums in the United Kingdom as well as a series of septennial plebiscites in Welsh local authorities. In the last case, a clear legal framework was laid down by Parliament, but for the seven referendums no comprehensive rules have been established. Instead, each referendum was treated as a one-off non-repeatable event. In each case, rather more questions were raised than answered.

In the Northern Irish Border Poll in 1973 the high abstention rate (over 40 per cent) recommended by the nationalist parties vividly illustrated the limitations of a referendum in a highly polarized society. The 1975 European Community referendum blew a hole in the convention of Cabinet government and opened up deep fissures within political parties which have persisted and continue to distort the debate on British European Union membership. The devolution referendums in 1979 raised the question why, if devolution was about good government and the maintenance of the United Kingdom, the UK electorate did not participate as a whole. Furthermore, why was an electoral threshold necessary for the devolution referendums but unnecessary for the EC referendum?[2] In 1997 there was no threshold and, in Wales barely 25 per cent of the electorate approved the government's devolution proposals. Finally, if Scotland was given the power to decide the range of devolved powers, why was this dispensation not extended to Wales? The evidence of the referendum experiences in the UK suggests that no coherent, consistent principles were applied. Rather, successive governments responded to the pressures of political circumstances by doing what was expedient. If there was a constitutional principle involved, it was that the supremacy of Parliament should not be infringed. And yet we now appear to have arrived at a situation in which all constitutional reforms require ratification through referendums.

Not all referendums are the same. The circumstances in which they can be employed and the conditions under which they will be administered vary considerably.[3] In some countries the written constitution lays down the requirements for a referendum, which relate usually to constitutional amendments. Lacking a codified constitution, this provision would not apply to Britain. In other countries referendums can be called by popular petitions in circumstances prescribed by the government. This system applies to Welsh local authorities and the Sunday opening of public houses. Finally, there are government-controlled referendums in which the whole operation of the referendum is decided by the government: the subject matter, the wording of the proposition, the definition of what constitutes a majority and the determination of whether the outcome will be mandatory or advisory. This was the type of referendum used to test the issue of Welsh devolution in 1979 and 1997.

The Welsh experience of referendums, including the local authority septennial plebiscites, is the most extensive in the United Kingdom and offers evidence of the strengths and weaknesses of the referendum in deciding fundamental or controversial questions.

It is clear from this experience that circumstances surrounding the use of the referendum – the political culture, the popular standing of the government, the organization of the media and the demographic pattern – have a profound impact on the utility and legitimacy of the referendum. Furthermore, any study of the role of the referendums in Wales must take full account of the Welsh context, the fact that Wales is a nation of minorities, linguistic, geographic and economic. It has a very high proportion of in-migrants, and is more culturally and economically linked to England than either Scotland or Northern Ireland.[4] These factors invest Wales with a complex identity (what has been described as a community of communities) and make the operation of a referendum more problematic.

## Comparing the 1979 and 1997 referendums

The two devolution referendums in 1979 and 1997 addressed virtually the same questions, but in vastly different circumstances. In 1979 the Labour government was physically exhausted, politically weak and peculiarly susceptible to 'events'. Its slim and eventually disappearing parliamentary majority rendered it vulnerable to a Conservative Party sensing victory, backbench revolts and pressures from the Liberal Party which resulted in the 'Lib-Lab' pact. Outside Parliament, the government was subjected to similar strains. A mounting financial crisis required intervention by the International Monetary Fund, and the consequent implementation of harsh economic policies led directly in the disintegration of the government's 'social contract' with the trade unions. There followed a succession of industrial disputes in late 1978 and early 1979, the so-called 'winter of discontent'. Such was the backdrop to the 1979 referendum. By contrast, the referendum in 1997 was introduced by a fresh, newly elected government with an overwhelming majority in the House of Commons and a demoralized Conservative Opposition. A young, energetic Prime Minister, and an expanding economy resulted in increasing levels of public support for the new government in the run-up to the Scottish and Welsh referendums in September 1997.

The contrast between the 1979 and 1997 experiences can also be identified in the organization of the referendums. The 1979 referendum took place after the legislation had been passed by Parliament. It was an exhaustive process which extended over twenty months and three devolution bills and culminated in two parliamentary Acts. Serious consequences flowed from the parliamentary process. The government suffered a series of demoralizing defeats, and its decision to hold a referendum was forced on it by anti-devolutionists who were able to claim, during the referendum campaign, that the Labour government had been unwilling to trust the people. The government was also obliged to accept a referendum threshold of 40 per cent of the registered voters. In effect, this requirement equated abstentions with 'no' votes and set what was generally regarded as an impossibly high hurdle, particularly in Wales. Another referendum impediment was unique to Wales. Welsh devolution was completely overshadowed by Scottish devolution, both during the passage of the parliamentary legislation and in the popular media's coverage of the referendum campaign.'

In 1997 there was a similar tendency for Scottish issues to dominate the media. The strength of the Scottish National Party seemed to threaten the United Kingdom to an extent that Welsh nationalism did not; Welsh devolution was not really newsworthy outside Wales. Partly because the Labour government recognized this, and partly because of lobbying by the Institute of Welsh Affairs, a concession was made to Welsh concerns. The Welsh referendum was held one week after the Scottish referendum. Cynical observers interpreted this as a means of bringing in Welsh devolution as part of a Scottish 'bandwagon'.[6] The issue surfaced during the election campaign but the evidence indicates that the Scottish referendum victory had only a marginal impact on Wales. There were other differences in 1997. The government decided that a simple majority in the referendum would suffice, and that the referendum would be pre-legislative, on the basis that it would be pointless to waste Parliament's time if the Welsh people were not to support devolution. In consequence, the referendum campaign debate was short, sharp and focused on the relatively simple general principles of devolution rather than the complex, constitutional details which had tended to confuse the 1979 debate. All these changes helped the presentation of the devolution case and further ensured that the referendum would be held while the government still enjoyed its 'honeymoon' with the electorate. The consequent 30 per cent swing to devolution in Wales – greater than the swing in Scotland – owed much to eighteen years of Conservative governments, but the changed organizational framework in 1997 also contributed to the Welsh referendum result.

## The 'national' media?

The success of a referendum depends upon an informed electorate, which in turn requires the free flow of information which is both accurate and comprehensive. There are grave doubts whether this was so in the 1979 Welsh referendum. There is an obvious explanation for this deficiency. In the case of a national referendum the national media will focus on the relevant issues, which will be explored at length in the press and on radio and television. In the national referendums in Denmark and France on ratification of the Maastricht Treaty, and in New Zealand on the approval of a new electoral system, the issues were fully explored and the electorate was well informed. In the case of Wales there is no such match between a 'national' referendum and the 'national' media. Wales's media are overwhelmingly located in London. In 1979 the daily circulation of the Welsh morning papers (*The Western Mail* and the *Daily Post*) was slightly less than 150,000 copies, whereas the London morning papers had a circulation in excess of 700,000 in Wales.[7] The London press was largely uninterested in the devolution issue, but when it did consider the subject, concentrated far more on the United Kingdom Scottish dimensions (see chapter 6). Although not so extreme, a similar pattern emerged in the coverage of the two referendum campaigns on the BBC and ITN main evening news programmes (see chapter 7). Stories reflecting the Scottish devolution debate were allocated 51 minutes 17 seconds, while those covering Welsh devolution amounted to 31 minutes 10 seconds.[8]

The situation today with regard to the London media penetration of Wales is cause for even greater concern. The two Welsh dailies have suffered a significant decline in circulation. *The Western Mail* and *Daily Post* now have a combined circulation of barely 110,000. The contrast with the position in Scotland is striking. There, 90 per cent of the daily papers in circulation are produced in Scotland. The figure for Wales is 13 per cent. Nor can the situation be easily rectified by the radio and television. Approximately 35 per cent of the Welsh population live in what are described as 'overlap areas', enabling them to choose (as many do) to watch the programmes from English transmitters. This compares with only 2.5 per cent for Scotland. In addition, although the Welsh broadcasting companies transmit 88.8 hours of programmes a week, 63.6 hours are transmitted in Welsh and only 25.2 hours in English.[9] Nevertheless, there is evidence that Welsh broadcasters recognized their responsibility to make up for the deficiency of the London-based printed media in covering the referendum debate (see chapter 7). Their apparent willingness to give expression to the various parties in support of the 'Yes' campaign led some leading members of the 'No' campaign to complain of media bias against them (see chapter 5).

## A 'national' campaign?

There is another problem. There is no guarantee that each referendum group will be equally well organized. Much evidence has been cited above to indicate that the 'No' campaign was less well organized and funded than the 'Yes' campaign. However, it could well be asked whether the steady flow of press releases from the 'Yes' campaign really met the needs of a doubtful and sceptical electorate. Would a more volatile intervention by the Conservative Party have galvanized electorate support for the 'No' campaign or polarized opinion along a Conservative/Labour axis with consequent benefit to the 'Yes' campaign? (This point is raised below in some of the local campaign reports.)

These questions are pertinent but they suffer from a common flaw. They presume singular, nationwide campaigns, one for 'Yes' and one for 'No'. The evidence from the 1997 referendum is that there was no such singular campaign; the absence of Welsh national media frustrated that objective. Instead there was a variety of traditional campaigns across Wales, fitting their respective canvassing tactics to the locality. Different issues were raised on the doorstep, and different answers given. For some 'Yes' campaigners, the devolution proposals went too far, and only party loyalty kept them 'on message'; for others, the devolution scheme presented to the Welsh people did not go far enough. Yet both had to persuade the voter of the virtues of accepting the Labour government proposals.

The Welsh referendum campaign in August/September consisted of locally based campaigns each with its distinctive tone and message. What follows is a brief selection of some of the key local campaigns as reviewed by local activists.

## The Rhondda campaign

KEN HOPKINS
Chair of the Assembly Preparations Group

On the last night, before going down to Cardiff for the public declaration of the results, and anxious to know how our campaign had gone in Rhondda, I visited the count taking place at the Ystrad Sports Centre. I was greatly cheered and relieved as the first ballot boxes were emptied – from Treherbert, Treorchy and Tonypandy – to see that there were three times as many 'Yes' votes as 'No'. Just as I had promised Tony Blair and Ron Davies, we had, despite our little local difficulties, delivered the Rhondda vote.

I then drove down to Cardiff to see how the rest of Wales was doing and, as the first results came in, became a little anxious. Wrexham down. Cardiff down. Newport down. Ominously, we had lost the urban vote. It seemed that with the Lucky Goldstar investment, Cardiff and Newport felt no need for an Assembly. Already the division was clear. The haves were saying 'No', and the have-nots 'Yes'. It is a division the newly elected Assembly must try to erase. As far as Valley Labour voters are concerned, it had better not once again be a case of hope triumphing over experience.

I was still optimistic, however, and I sent a note to Wayne David MEP, who had worked hard with us in Rhondda and who was then taking part in an HTV discussion panel, to tell him he could be positive and say the Valleys would deliver. I also told an ebullient Mari James of the 'Yes' campaign about our Rhondda boxes and she agreed it was significant that some of the Labour strongholds in the Valleys were still to declare. Earlier I had encouraged a melancholy Professor Hywel Francis with the same message. Then at last the results: Rhondda Cynon Taff and Neath Port Talbot, between them representing six constituencies, all with five-figure Labour majorities. Neath Port Talbot had the highest percentage of 'Yes' votes, and Rhondda Cynon Taff with over 50,000 the highest number of 'Yes' votes.

After the final result I went over to the Park Hotel. It seemed to be full of drunken nationalists dreaming of a law-making and tax-raising Assembly and independence in Europe. How misguided they were to forget that in 1979 in Mid Glamorgan the vote for 'Yes' had been 20.2 per cent, but that in the Assembly referendum in its successor authorities it had almost trebled to reach 58.5 per cent in Rhondda Cynon Taff, 57.9 per cent in Merthyr, 54.7 per cent in Caerphilly and 54.1 per cent in Bridgend. The Valleys had delivered the Labour vote, but that was all. It had never been a vote for a separate Wales.

## A capital campaign

KEVIN BRENNAN and GEOFF MUNGHAM
Members of the Executive of the Cardiff Yes for Wales Campaign

Getting the biggest possible 'Yes' vote in Cardiff was important. As the capital city and the future home of the Assembly for Wales, the Cardiff result was always going to be of more than local interest, something well understood by the Cardiff Says Yes Campaign Group. The portents, though, were not good. In 1979 Cardiff had come out strongly against devolution, and no one was sure how much public opinion had shifted. In the 1997 general election Labour in Cardiff had shown itself to be a formidable campaigning machine. But would this machine be mobilized to help turn out a 'Yes' vote?

The Cardiff Says Yes Group was launched, at Cardiff Castle on 10 June 1997. Around sixty people were there, from all parties and none. One of us, Kevin Brennan (a Cardiff County Labour councillor) was elected as group chair; Jenny Randerson (LibDem group leader on the county council) as treasurer; and Geoff Mungham (former Cardiff City Labour councillor) as secretary. A few days later we held the first of what was to become our weekly campaign committee meetings in Cardiff City Hall. No limit was set on committee size; any 'Yes' supporter could join, though numbers settled around a dozen regular attenders, who became the core of the campaign team. The 'Dirty Dozen' included a clutch of party activists from Labour, Plaid, the Communist Party and the LibDems, a lone Tory and two people – Sally Davies and the Revd Aled Edwards – who had no party affiliation then, but were to play major roles in our campaign.

Our first steps were to raise money, devise campaign material and decide on tactics. Cash was raised by tapping local business supporters (the owners of Splott Market proved especially generous), approaching the 250 people in Cardiff already signed up as supporters of the national Wales Says Yes campaign and from a hefty donation from Rhodri Morgan MP. We built up a war chest of close to £4,000 – enough for our purposes and to donate £1,000 to help pay off national campaign bills when it was all over.

We came up with three main ideas for campaign material. First, to have a campaign ribbon, which Sally designed and produced in hundreds (before we gave the work to a local company), a form of sweated labour which put her on par with a nineteenth-century back-street seamstress. Next, we adapted the successful 'pledge card' ideas used by Labour in the general election. Finally, we persuaded the Splott Market owners to make (and pay for) a gigantic banner in support of the Assembly. They did us proud, producing an emblem 150 feet long and 15 feet deep, bearing the logo 'Splott Market Says Vote Yes for the Assembly'. Most of the time the banner fluttered over the market; when it was needed for campaign events, we simply folded over the 'Splott Market Says' part of the panel and displayed the rest.

Campaign tactics were shaped to match our numbers and resources. We decided against door-to-door leafleting and canvassing, assuming that the political parties would do this – an assumption that proved unfounded, since in much of the city local parties failed to show.

Much of our early work was geared to staging 'stunts' aimed at trying to raise public awareness. We targeted early–morning commuters at Cardiff's Central and Queen Street stations, turned up with leaflets and cards at every public event in Cardiff that summer and tried every trick to entice local media coverage. Our first attempts at getting TV time were frustrated by the dead hand of the Representation of the People Act. Because we were up and running before the 'No' lobby had organized, the broadcasters –

especially the BBC – were reluctant to report for fear of not giving 'balanced' coverage. While this struck us as absurd, there wasn't much we could do about it, though this insistence on 'balance' hurt us in two ways. It meant that the first two weeks of our campaign went largely unrecorded by local radio and TV. And second, the 'Yes' campaign was far more active than the opposition, so that 'balanced treatment' gave the antis far more attention than they deserved.

We did better elsewhere on the media front. During the campaign, the *South Wales Echo* ran a phone-in poll on voting intentions. Although this type of poll has about as much scientific validity as medieval alchemy, we did our best to 'influence' the result by arranging for supporters to call in and register a 'Yes' vote (guessing the other side was doing the same thing). In the end, for what it was worth, our attempts at a 'fix' were marginally more successful than theirs, which pretty much reflected the eventual national vote. Other attempts to try and give a 'spin' to our campaign were through organized letter-writing to the local press and lining up our people to lob in prepared questions/points to live radio and TV phone-in programmes.

The big open-air Splott Market became a key campaign site. Over 20,000 people visit its Sunday market, from all over south Wales. We set up a stall, giving out publicity material (including balloons and carrier bags carrying the 'Yes' logo) and selling ribbons and T-shirts. The market also provided the setting for visiting Labour 'stars' to press the flesh. Successive Sundays in the run-up to voting day brought in Ron Davies (twice), Chris Smith and Donald Dewar. Dewar's visit – coming just after the Scots had voted 'Yes' and only four days before Wales voted – attracted huge media interest. The accompanying hack-pack included a dozen British media outlets and TV crews from seven EU countries. These Sunday outings provided a pick-up for our campaign, which lost some momentum when we had to suspend activities in the week after Princess Diana's death.

About a week before the vote it became clear we needed to rethink campaign tactics. Reports coming in indicated that in much of south and central Cardiff the political parties had done little or no work on the ground. In response, we decided to switch campaign tack and go for a house-to-house leaflet drop. The Sunday evening before voting day we called a meeting of our supporters at the national Wales Says Yes campaign offices in Cardiff; 150 people turned up. We outlined plans to 'blitz' south and central Cardiff in the last three days of the campaign with Labour leaflets – since the target areas were mainly Labour territory. One Plaid member present objected, but was shouted down by the other Plaid supporters. What followed was an extraordinary logistical exercise, made possible only by cross-party co-operation. In just seventy-two hours, close to 30,000 households were leafleted by teams made up of Labour, LibDem, Plaid, Green and Communist Party activists, plus a couple of 'renegade' Tories.

None of us really expected to win in Cardiff – nor did we. But we did get 44.2 per of the vote, a huge advance on the 1979 result. Any lingering disappointment we might have felt about not doing even better was wiped out by the final outcome. It may have been a damned close-run thing, but no one was brooding over margins of victory at a wild night of celebration in Cardiff's Park Hotel. Victory was not the only legacy of a campaign which built new friendships and gave us some great memories. Maybe – just maybe – the co-operation between people from different parties we saw during the campaign will carry over into the Assembly when it starts its work.

## The Powys campaign

GLYN DAVIES
Conservative AM for Mid and West Wales

On 18 September 1997 the County of Powys rejected a proposal to establish a Welsh Assembly by 30,966 votes to 23,038. This was the result that I had expected, even if the margin by which the 'No' side won was surprisingly decisive. Any complete record should also note that Powys was one of the areas where some 'No' votes were incorrectly declared to be invalid as a result of confused instructions given to the local accounting officer, even though the numbers were too small to make a material difference. While all the above is factually accurate it gives us very little idea of how the people of Powys actually voted or why.

Powys is an artificial creation in which there is no natural affinity between its parts, and only those who were present at the

Llandrindod Wells Leisure Centre as the ballot boxes were tipped out can appreciate how inconsistently these different parts of the county voted. The experience for those who observed the count in the early hours of 19 September was akin to being on a roller coaster, with the biggest thrill coming at the end.

The early boxes came in from Radnorshire and within minutes the 'Yes' camp's smiles had gone. My guess is that 80 per cent of the Radnorshire people who voted said 'No'. An hour later and the Welsh Assembly looked dead and buried. I can still see the panic and disappointment in the eyes of Gwilym Fychan, a committed 'Yes' man who looks rather like the image I have of Owain Glyndŵr.

And then the vans brought in the boxes from Breconshire and Montgomeryshire. The picture changed as votes were more evenly divided. The 'No' side was still winning but some boxes from villages that I had expected to say 'No' actually said 'Yes'. My guess was that 60 per cent of east/north Breconshire and east/central Montgomeryshire people who had voted said 'No'. Two hours gone, and Gwilym Fychan looked perky; although I thought he still expected to lose, at least it would be a defeat with honour.

And then the vans arrived from Ystradgynlais and Machynlleth and Llanerfyl, where my own roots lie. The 'Yes' camp blinked disbelievingly. We had all expected western Montgomeryshire to vote 'Yes'; because of population sparsity this would not make a significant difference, but we had not expected ballot box after ballot box from Ystradgynlais to pour forth 'Yes' votes like runner beans in a wet summer. With hindsight we should have taken more note of the massive 'Yes' vote in Neath which borders the southwest corner of Powys. My guess is that at least 80 per cent of the Ystradgynlais and western Montgomeryshire people who voted said 'Yes'. Gwilym Fychan's home patch had put a sparkle born of real hope of victory back in his eye.

Between midnight and the final dramatic result from Carmarthen the evening resembled a tug-of-war contest between two evenly matched teams. For anyone who shares my interest in politics and human behaviour, it was a memorable night, so absorbing that, when the incredible final result came through and the 'Yes' supporters celebrated with genuine tears of relief and joy in some cases, I had to be reminded that I was supposed to be in the 'No' camp.

In the weeks leading up to the referendum, almost everyone with whom I had discussed the subject had expected an overall 'Yes' vote, the anticipated size of which had decreased as the days passed. By the eve of the poll most guesses were that Wales would vote 'Yes' with a margin of victory between 5 per cent and 20 per cent. Most people I knew thought Powys, having been encouraged to 'Just Say No', would indeed say 'No' – just.

At several stages in the counting process many of us thought the government was going to be defeated, and the final closeness of the result inevitably led to several 'if onlys'. If only the 'No' campaign had worked harder! If only the Conservative Party had openly campaigned for a 'No' vote! I am a Conservative, and my party had decided not to take a leading role in the 'No' campaign. We felt that the sheer comprehensiveness of the defeat we had suffered at the recent general election would have made our direct involvement as a party in the campaign unhelpful. We felt the best strategy was to let Labour and Liberal Democrat devo-sceptics make the running. It almost worked. There were the usual hindsight experts who suggest a stronger line from the Conservative Party would have made the crucial difference. I suspect that history will record that the Conservative Party missed an opportunity to derail the devolution process. I also believe that history will be mistaken.

Perhaps the most disappointing aspect of the referendum was the failure to generate interest amongst the people in Montgomeryshire. I arranged several public meetings, inviting people of all views to ask questions and discuss what I advertised as an important issue affecting the future of government in Wales. Because of the Conservative Party's overall strategy, we decided at a local party level that I should adopt a neutral position, something some local members found difficult to accept. The largest turnout was twenty-five people.

I have reflected on how different parts of Powys voted in the referendum, citing personal observation as evidence. I can only guess, with the help of nothing but anecdotal evidence, why people voted as they did. I believe that the reasons differed from one area of Powys to another. In the Labour heartland of Ystradgynlais the voters backed the new Labour government, perhaps accepting the assertion by ministers that a 'Yes' vote was an anti-Conservative vote. In the Welsh-speaking areas around Machynlleth voters felt an emotional commitment to an Assembly as a symbol of national pride, something that I, with ancestral roots in the Llanerfyl area, can fully understand. I would like to think that the reasons Powys voted 'No' were that a Welsh Assembly would threaten the integrity of the United Kingdom and lead to a resurgence of nationalism and the marginalization of mid-Wales. Unfortunately, the real reasons were much more likely to have been less sustainable issues such as the costs of running an Assembly and a belief that everyone would be forced to speak Welsh.

On 6 May 1999 the National Assembly for Wales will be elected into office and for most people the Powys referendum vote will be no more than one insignificant statistic. I shall remember it as the compilation of a myriad of conflicting judgements. Only time will tell which of them were right for Wales.

## The Neath campaign

STEVE KELSHAW
Secretary of Neath Constituency Labour Party

As the first local branch of Say Yes for Wales, the experience in Neath provided lessons for the national body which proved useful in engaging the voting public in a more meaningful manner than the reliance on party loyalty. The Neath campaign encompassed the town and the surrounding communities in the Aman, Swansea, Dulais and Neath Valleys. These are strong communities, rooted in a mining past with strong Labour movement traditions, but also retaining a Welshness and strong bilingual base. The ability of the 'Yes' campaign to accommodate all these interests was central to its success.

As is often the case, a core body based around the party officers and activists provided the main focus for organizing activity. A significant addition was a group of young Welsh-speaking students and school-leavers who brought on extra dimension of ideas, energy and willingness to the campaign. There was no inter-party conflict, no barrier of language and no parochialism.

An immediate priority was the provision of information and the establishment of a database of local contacts in business, political, church, community and other organizations that could be used as channels of distribution for publicity material. To satisfy the need for information, a pamphlet was written in a question-and-answer style to provide basic facts on the purpose, structure and cost of the Assembly. Such was the demand for this basic information early in the campaign that the first print-run of 200 eventually extended to thousands. Extra information was also provided in the form of a newsletter to update readers on campaign events, meetings and contacts.

Many of the communities in Neath and the Valleys hold festivals and carnivals during the summer, and these were prime targets for the delivery of publicity material and a chance to engage people in discussion and raise awareness of the campaign. A 'Yes' petition was started which collected hundreds of signatures and gave another chance to approach people and encourage them to support devolution. Again the mix of young and older people, bilingualism and the non-party base of the campaign proved beneficial. The non-party basis of the campaign gave a significant advantage when accessing groups such as pensioners, churches, and Women's Institute groups. Letters were sent offering speakers and information; this proved especially popular with the extensive network of pensioner groups. First-time voters were delivered personal letters and the usual mix of street stalls, stickers, T-shirts and balloons was adopted for town use. However, as the referendum date approached, little popular coverage was provided by the national media, and local newspapers were reluctant to give space to the 'Yes' campaign in the absence of any 'No' campaign.

The responsibility of a door-to-door canvass was left to the Labour Party and the local MP, who played a key campaigning role in ensuring that the Labour vote turned out. To mobilize the support of party members, senior officers toured branches appealing to loyalty and commitment to party policy, but many local party members were not apparently motivated by this approach. Canvassing, compared with the general election, was limited, and local branches often only barely managed to distribute material provided by the national party. This passive approach may be partly explained by the lack of confidence of members in their ability to persuade voters, as well as a degree of apathy and agnosticism towards the policy of devolution. This reluctance was obviously recognized by national strategists, who based their material on appeals to party loyalty, the popularity of Tony Blair and the equation a 'No' vote with a Tory vote. The local MP, Peter Hain, characteristically played an active and high-profile role. His wider national and ministerial remit meant that he had to spend considerable time outside the constituency, but loyal core activists ensured that his influence was felt. When he did meet members of the public on the streets, his popularity allowed him to make swift converts. As with the general election his high-profile tactics brought results.

## Conclusion

J. BARRY JONES

The referendum result fell so far short of an overwhelming endorsement of devolution that one must question why the issue was given such a priority by the new Labour government. Partly, no doubt, it arose from the general agreement hammered out by Labour and Liberal Parties, while in opposition, to reform the British constitution, of which devolution was a part.[10] It could also be argued that devolution to both Celtic countries established a constitutional-reform programme whereas devolution to Scotland alone, with the 'West Lothian question' unanswered, could have been dismissed as a mere political expedient.

Alternatively, Welsh devolution may have been so marginal that the Millbank electoral strategists failed to understand fully the complexity of the political situation in Wales (this is raised in chapter 3). Andrew Davies, special project officer for the referendum campaign, took up his post on 1 April 1997, a late date and symbolic of the lack of preparation given to the whole devolution project. In his view, devolution was largely an activists' agenda in Wales, unlike Scotland where the debate had been longer, more intensive and more inclusive of party members. Davies is still haunted by his experience of the first focus group organized in Maesteg by Philip Gould, Labour's chief pollster. It soon became apparent that the group lacked awareness, knowledge and support for the devolution referendum. In Andrew Davies's words, 'Philip Gould paced around the room afterwards saying: "they don't want it, they just don't want it." '[11]

In fact Maesteg and the Welsh Valleys did deliver the 'Yes' vote, but even here the 'Yes' vote failed to match Labour's general election vote. A devolution policy devised so as not to alienate anti-devolutionist MPs and party activists could apparently only be secured at the expense of a limited and confusing model of devolution that would fail to arouse Welsh public opinion. In retrospect, this would seem to be the way the constitutional circle was squared.

But there are other factors, relating to the nature of Welsh society, which could provide an explanation for Wales's hesitant endorsement of devolution in the referendum. The results of the referendum revealed significant socio-economic divisions in Wales. The more affluent parts of Wales, the north-east and south-east coastal areas and Welsh border lands, returned a 'No' majority. The less affluent western half of the country voted for devolution. There were other correlations: the incidence of Welsh-speakers and the distribution of the 'Yes' vote, and the pattern of English in-migration and the size of the 'No' vote. Important though these indicators may have been, there is a more fundamental explanation: the Welsh are a cautious people, the product of centuries of living alongside a powerful and dynamic anglophone culture. For centuries survival was the prime directive, even if, as some historians have claimed, it required Wales to reinvent itself periodically.[12]

As we have seen, devolution, anticipated by its proponents as the 'rebirth of a nation', was almost stillborn. However, once the deed was done, no matter by how slim a majority, a new reality was brought into being. On the night of 6 May 1999, just eighteen months after the referendum, votes were being cast for the new Assembly for Wales. The BBC/ICM election-night poll earlier that week had randomly sampled 4,000 voters across Wales. On election day, 1,000 were recontacted after they had voted and interviewed. The findings revealed that Welsh opinion was hardening around the new constitutional status quo. The National Assembly was regarded as a good thing by 58 per cent with only 31 per cent disagreeing; 46 per cent were of the opinion that the Assembly would lead to better government for Wales, with only 11 per cent of the opinion that Wales would be worse off.[13] Welsh voters were learning to live with the new constitutional settlement.

## Notes

1. D. Balsom, 'The United Kingdom: constitutional pragmatism and the adoption of the referendum', in P. Uleri and M. Gallagher (eds.), *The Referendum Experience in Europe* (1996).

2. For a discussion of the procedures for the EC referendum, see A. King, *Britain Says Yes* (1977).

3. For a categorization of referendums see D. Butler and A. Ranney, *Referendums: A Comparative Study of Theory and Practice* (1979).

4. This is a historical factor and is explored in M. Hechter, *Internal Colonialism* (1975).

5. See D. Foulkes, B. Jones and R. Wilford (eds.), *The Welsh Veto: The Welsh Act 1978 and the Referendum* (Cardiff: University of Wales Press, 1983).

6. Polls published prior to the Welsh referendum suggested that the Scottish 'Yes' vote might be worth up to 10 per cent additional 'Yes' votes. But this is difficult to prove, especially as the 'No' campaign used the Scottish vote to show that Wales was different and need not follow suit.

7. J. Osmond, 'The referendum and the English-language press', in *The Welsh Veto* (1983).

8. G. Talfan Davies, 'The role of broadcasting in the referendum', in *The Welsh Veto* (1983).

9. G. Talfan Davies, *Broadcasting in Wales in the Digital Age* (BBC Wales), 1996).

10. M Summer, 'Only connect: towards a new democratic settlement', in M. Perryman (ed.), *The Blair Agenda* (1996).

11. Andrew Davies, letter to author, 16 May 1998.

12. Gwyn A. Williams, *When Was Wales?* (1988).

13. J. Barry Jones, 'The first Welsh National Assembly election', *Government and Opposition* 34, 3 (1999).

# 9   The Referendum Result

DENIS BALSOM

The 1997 devolution referendum was novel in several respects, most importantly, however, in the fact that it was a pre-legislative consultation of public opinion. The public was not being asked to endorse a piece of government legislation, as had been the case in 1979. The referendum was designed to secure a popular mandate, after which parliamentary passage of the legislation was assumed likely to be less problematic. Managers of the Labour Party were fully aware that devolution remained a contentious issue for many of the party's MPs and ordinary members. A pre-legislative referendum kept the argument to one of general principle rather than detailed proposals. It was also hoped that this strategy would enable the principle to be endorsed by those from other parties who favoured devolution, but would be likely to vote against Labour legislation merely because it originated from Labour. At the general election, three of the mainstream parties were in favour of the concept of devolution to Wales. Secretary of State Ron Davies worked hard to sustain this all-party consensus and to identify opponents of the proposals as allies of the Conservative Party. Although not all Welsh Labour MPs played a full part in the referendum campaign, there was not a repeat of the highly damaging counter-campaign led by a Gang of Six or other configuration of rebel MPs, as had been the case in 1979.

As in the previous referendum, local authority areas were used as the key enumerating districts. Whilst this had the administrative convenience of working within an existing electoral framework, it also embodied the distinct political advantage that very few of these areas aligned precisely with parliamentary boundaries and the constituencies of individual MPs. In 1979, however, Wales had only eight county councils. Following local government reorganization, there were now twenty-two counties and boroughs, which did not necessarily coincide with parliamentary constituencies. Notwithstanding this, by comparison with 1979, very few MPs entirely broke ranks and campaigned against the government. Opponents of devolution tended to object on grounds other than that of the core principle. Hence a number of MPs, who played little part in the campaign, held back ostensibly because of their objection to the inclusion of an element of proportional representation in the new electoral system proposed for the Assembly.

Following the closure of individual polling stations, ballot papers were verified and counted in each individual local authority. Results were then relayed to the overall national returning officer, Professor Eric Sunderland, based at the Welsh College of Music and Drama in Cardiff. Here the results were announced and added to the cumulative national totals. Results came in relatively slowly, creating an evening of increasing drama and intensity. Victory was finally claimed by the Secretary of State in the early hours of Friday morning 19 September.

At first sight, the results from the various counties and county boroughs appear highly differentiated. Levels of support, however, clustered between 66:33 in both directions. Broadly, in no part of Wales were less than one-third in support of devolution and nowhere were there less than one-third opposed.

The aggregate results of the devolution referendum held on 18 September 1997 show some peculiar parities. Not only was the outcome a virtual dead heat, with fewer than 7,000 votes dividing opinion from over one million ballots cast, but the local authority areas of Wales, used as the enumeration units, divided eleven for devolution, eleven against. The overall turnout just exceeded 50 per cent, but this average covers a variance from 41.1 per cent in Flintshire in the north-east of Wales to 60 per cent in Gwynedd in the north-west. The outcome of the referendum, however, was based on the total number of votes cast across Wales, and therefore, whilst the variations between areas are of psephological interest, they are of no statutory consequence. The significance of the result, however, was to legitimize a far-reaching constitutional reform for Wales, and therefore the distribution of votes was examined very closely. In particular, the opponents of the reforms were quick to calculate that only a quarter of those eligible to vote

Table 9.1: Results of the 1997 devolution referendum

| | Turn-out % | 'Yes' votes | % | 'No' votes | % |
|---|---|---|---|---|---|
| Blaenau Gwent | 49.6 | 15,237 | 55.8 | 11,928 | 43.7 |
| Bridgend | 50.8 | 27,632 | 54.1 | 23,172 | 45.4 |
| Caerphilly | 49.5 | 34,830 | 54.7 | 28,843 | 45.3 |
| Cardiff | 47.0 | 47,527 | 44.2 | 59,589 | 55.4 |
| Carmarthenshire | 56.6 | 49,115 | 65.3 | 26,119 | 34.7 |
| Ceredigion | 57.1 | 18,304 | 58.8 | 12,614 | 40.6 |
| Conwy | 51.6 | 18,369 | 40.9 | 26,521 | 59.1 |
| Denbighshire | 49.9 | 14,271 | 40.8 | 20,732 | 59.2 |
| Flintshire | 41.1 | 17,746 | 38.1 | 28,707 | 61.6 |
| Gwynedd | 60.0 | 35,425 | 63.9 | 19,859 | 35.8 |
| Isle of Anglesey | 57.0 | 15,649 | 50.7 | 15,095 | 48.9 |
| Merthyr Tydfil | 49.8 | 12,707 | 57.9 | 9,121 | 41.6 |
| Monmouthshire | 50.7 | 10,592 | 31.6 | 22,403 | 66.9 |
| Neath Port Talbot | 52.1 | 36,730 | 66.3 | 18,463 | 33.3 |
| Newport | 46.1 | 16,172 | 37.2 | 27,017 | 62.3 |
| Pembrokeshire | 52.8 | 19,979 | 42.8 | 26,712 | 57.2 |
| Powys | 56.5 | 23,038 | 42.7 | 30,966 | 57.3 |
| Rhondda Cynon Taff | 49.9 | 51,201 | 58.5 | 36,362 | 41.5 |
| Swansea | 47.3 | 42,789 | 52.0 | 39,561 | 48.0 |
| Torfaen | 45.6 | 15,756 | 49.7 | 15,854 | 50.0 |
| Vale of Glamorgan | 54.5 | 17,776 | 36.6 | 30,613 | 63.1 |
| Wrexham | 42.5 | 18,574 | 45.2 | 22,449 | 54.6 |
| **WALES** | **50.3** | **559,419** | **50.3** | **552,698** | **49.7** |

had endorsed the government's intention. This low level was contrasted with the legal requirement, at the previous referendum in 1979, that 40 per cent of the eligible electorate had been needed to endorse the proposal for the Wales Act 1978 to be enacted.

The drama of the night of 18 September was also heightened by the required majority of votes cast not being achieved until the last declaration of the evening, that for Carmarthenshire. In a strange twist of fate, the constituency which had elected the first Plaid Cymru MP in 1966, and in doing so had, arguably, initiated the trail of events that eventually led to Labour's 1997 election commitment to devolution, now delivered the vital votes required to further these plans.

It must be remembered, however, that only the single all-Wales result was valid at the referendum. Each vote cast was of equal weight and value. As Paul O'Leary has demonstrated, overall it is irrelevant that Carmarthen delivered the majority; it was purely a coincidence of the timing of the declaration. It could equally be claimed that 6,721 of the 'Yes' voters in deeply sceptical Newport made the critical difference, and it was their determination to vote against the prevailing mood of their community that successfully brought the Assembly to Wales.[1] For analysis purposes, however, correlates of referendum voting patterns can provide a key insight into the structure and attitudes of the contemporary Welsh electorate. Analysts would also argue that voting decisions are not taken in abstract but are closely related to other social and political phenomena.

The remarkable feature of the pattern of the referendum results is that they appeared to cross-cut the traditional divisions of Welsh politics. The commitment to devolution appeared to be an issue for which a majority exists in both the Welsh-speaking heartland of north and west Wales and the former industrial heartland of south Wales. Notwithstanding O'Leary's analysis, we are used to thinking of the majority view within an area as representing the collective will and personifying the place concerned. Clearly Torfaen, which voted 'No' with a majority of only ninety-eight cannot be considered to be made up of implacable opponents of devolution, but as a community Torfaen did reject the proposal, however marginally. With the usual caveats, it seems appropriate to identify clusters of communities within Wales that voted in the same direction and see what other factors might similarly join them together, either socially, economically or politically. The post-referendum search for explanation of the result has focused upon two principal models. Firstly, that support for devolution represented a victory of the 'have-nots' over the 'haves'. In other words, the referendum outcome is essentially explained by issues of social class. The second thesis looks to aspects of Welsh national identity as the key explanatory variable.

## Social class

The great difficulty of using social class as an explanatory variable is its highly subjective nature. Whilst individuals may retain a sense of their own class identification, this may differ wildly from any objective assessment that a sociologist may have of the same individuals' socio-economic status. Any behaviour deemed to follow from a sense of class-consciousness is inevitably governed by deeply subjective motives. If I believe that I am working class, I may choose to act in a manner I believe to be in the best interests of the working class and, therefore, in my own self-interest. That my self-assessment may be, to an outside observer, inaccurate is of no consequence. This ambiguity also creates a major difficulty in sourcing effective data with which to measure class. When concerned with behavioural outcomes, subjective self-assessment is the only reliable measure of class-consciousness. Unfortunately, standard opinion-poll data measure socio-economic status purely on the basis of occupation and are therefore, at best, a part-measure. Similarly other aggregate measures for communities based on data such as unemployment rates, educational standards

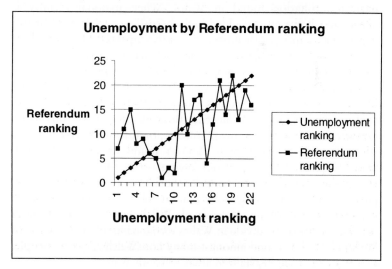

Chart 9.1

or housing quality are only partial surrogates for effective measures of social class.[2]

An analysis plotting unemployment rates against support for devolution in chart 9.1 shows a very imperfect fit. The relationship is plotted on a rank-order basis, ranking the twenty-two local authorities, in order of their rate of unemployment, against the ranking of the authorities by their support for devolution. The closer the symmetry, that is the closer the two lines mirror each other, the higher the rank-order correlation. The assessment that the 'have-nots' supported devolution is an anecdotal response for explaining why some areas with a high Labour vote proved much stronger supporters of devolution than others.

## National identities

An alternative approach has sought to identify a sense of Welsh national identity as being the key explanatory variable of Welsh voting behaviour.[3] Previous models of voting behaviour for Britain have been unable to account satisfactorily for the distinct patterns of partisan affiliation found in Wales. When national identity is considered, however, and added to the prevailing correlates of British voting, any explanatory model is greatly improved. As with class, however, national identity is a subjective concept. A simple measure can be used in sample surveys where respondents choose to describe themselves as British, Welsh, English or something else, but the extent to which their subsequently observed political behaviour is, in part, motivated by this identification is, of course, unknown. Empirical evidence has shown, however, that, for example, the high level of middle-class Labour support found in Wales is almost wholly explained by those voters having a strong sense of their own Welsh identity. Those who consider themselves to be British display patterns of political behaviour that match more closely those of voters from elsewhere. A sense of Welsh national identity also bridges the linguistic divide in Wales, recognizing the strong sense of Welshness that is found amongst many non-Welsh-speaking people, especially in the industrialized areas of south Wales.

Unfortunately, a subjective measure of identity is not available for the population base of the local authorities of Wales. A surrogate measure, however, the proportion of people born within

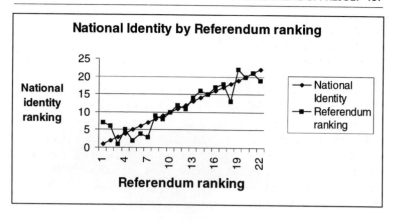

Chart 9.2

Wales in each authority, is available from the census. Using a rank-order procedure as before, one would hypothesize that areas with the highest number of those born in Wales would correlate with support for devolution. As 9.2 demonstrates, whilst the fit is not perfect, it is considerably stronger than that for unemployment.

## The three Wales model

An earlier study set out to bring together the impact of both the level of Welsh-speaking amongst the electorate of Wales and the level of self-assigned Welsh identification.[4] When plotted on the map of Wales, Welsh-speakers were naturally concentrated in north and west Wales, but significant concentrations of self-assigned Welsh-identifiers were found in both the north and west and in traditional south Wales. In the areas peripheral to this, the border counties, Severnside and the Vale of Glamorgan, north-east Wales and Pembrokeshire, British-identifiers were found to pre-dominate. Although first identified in data pertaining to the 1979 election, similar patterns have been observed in subsequent surveys. Although a rather simple analysis, this 'three Wales model', identifying Welsh Wales as the industrial heartland of the old coalfield, *Y Fro Gymraeg* as the linguistic heart of Wales, and British Wales as the surrounding parts, found strong support. The

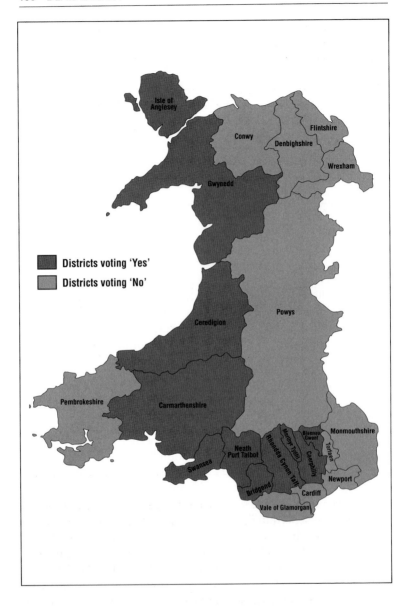

Map 9.1: Voting in the 1997 devolution referendum

interpretation was always broad, but intuitively matched people's experience of the diversity that is represented in modern Wales. The close resemblance between the map demonstrating the three Wales model and the results of the referendum was quickly noted following the declaration and used as an interpretative tool.[5] As noted above, Paul O'Leary and others have cautioned against too literal an interpretation of maps, but the overlap remains striking.

## Conclusion

The outcome of the 1997 referendum on devolution was decided by the magnitude of the change in attitude and behaviour that had occurred since the previous referendum in 1979.

Table 9.2: Change in support for devolution 1979–1997

|              | 1979 % | 1997 % | Change % |
| ------------ | ------ | ------ | -------- |
| Clwyd        | 21.6   | 41.2   | +19.6    |
| Dyfed        | 28.1   | 57.1   | +29.0    |
| Gwent        | 12.1   | 42.5   | +30.4    |
| Gwynedd      | 34.4   | 52.9   | +18.5    |
| Mid Glam     | 20.2   | 56.4   | +36.2    |
| Powys        | 18.4   | 42.7   | +24.3    |
| South Glam   | 13.1   | 41.8   | +28.7    |
| West Glam    | 18.7   | 57.7   | +39.0    |
| **WALES**    | **20.3** | **50.3** | **+30.0** |

The swing between the two referendums of 15 per cent is larger than that experienced in Scotland and should be borne in mind by those endeavouring to diminish the significance of the Welsh result. To broadly similar propositions of reform, a considerably greater degree of support was expressed, whilst the level of participation, when controlled for the age of the electoral register being used, was comparable. Neither should the outcome of the devolution referendum be portrayed as especially divisive. As table 9.2 demonstrates, the areas with the lowest levels of support for devolution in 1979 were also those which recorded the highest swings in favour in 1997. That these are also the most populous areas of Wales makes the referendum result a basis of unity rather than division.

## Notes

1. See *Planet* 127 (1998).

2. For a discussion of the relative merits of aggregate level data analysis and individual level data see Denis Balsom, 'Voting patterns in Wales: an aggregate data analysis', University of Wales Ph.D. thesis, 1982.

3. D. Balsom, P. J. Madgwick and D. Van Mechelen, 'The red and the green', *British Journal of Political Science* 13 (1983).

4. Denis Balsom, 'The three Wales model', in J. Osmond, *The National Question Again* (1985).

5. *Economist*, 26 September 1997.

# 10   Voting Patterns in the Referendum

RICHARD WYN JONES, DAFYDD TRYSTAN and BRIDGET TAYLOR

After a generally lacklustre campaign, the declaration of the results of the 1997 referendum on the Labour government's devolution proposals for Wales provided one of the most compelling and memorable nights of political theatre in living memory. As previous chapters in this book have underlined, for the small if vociferous minority with strong views on devolution, it was a night of unbearable tension. But abundant anecdotal evidence also suggests that even those with no strong opinions on the subject – in Wales and beyond – were drawn into the drama that unfolded in the early hours of 19 September 1997.

Given that the 6,721 votes which separated both sides represented only 0.3 per cent of the electorate of 2,218,850, it is understandable that attention since has focused on the narrowness of the margin of victory for the 'Yes' camp. In particular, commentators have discussed the implications of this most grudging of endorsements for the future legitimacy of the National Assembly, especially given the fact that barely half of the electorate (50.1 per cent) bothered to vote at all.[1] Observers have also questioned the implications of the low turnout, not only for the devolution process itself, but for the credibility of the political class in Wales as a whole. After all, both sides of the argument – including all of the political parties – presented the referendum as deciding upon a question with profound and lasting implications for everyone living in Wales. Yet a substantial proportion of the electorate appears to have remained resolutely unmoved.

The overall result of the referendum portrays a Welsh electorate evenly divided on the devolution issue: approaching half having apparently so little interest in the subject that they declined to

Table 10.1: 1997 Welsh referendum result

|  | Votes | % |
|---|---|---|
| I agree that there should be a Welsh Assembly | 559,419 | 50.3 |
| I do not agree that there should be a Welsh Assembly | 552,698 | 49.7 |

*Official turnout: 50.1%.*

express an opinion in a democratic ballot; and of those who did, half supporting the government's devolution proposals and the other half rejecting them. Once the result is disaggregated, however, it is apparent that the divide it revealed is not even, in the sense that different areas showed markedly different levels not only of enthusiasm for devolution, but also of interest in the subject. Map 9.1 shows the result as it was declared on a unitary authority basis, while Map 10.1 shows the differences in turnout. But it is also salutary in this context to consider the result of the referendum in terms of how far different areas deviated from the all-Wales result. Map 10.2 therefore differentiates between those unitary authority areas where the vote ranged within plus or minus 7.5 per cent of the all-Wales result and the rest. It demonstrates that in only ten areas did the vote fall within this 15 per cent band.

To seek to explain the apparent east–west division exposed by the result in simple geographical terms is surely to misunderstand the dynamics of the devolution referendum, and indeed the very nature of contemporary Welsh society.[2] After all, the evidence suggests that not only were there strong differences *between* unitary authority areas, but also deep divisions *within* them. In the immediate aftermath of the referendum, Dafydd Trystan contacted activists present at the counts in eleven out of the twenty-two areas in order to try to ascertain how the referendum vote broke down on a more localized, ward-by-ward basis.[3] Although incomplete and inevitably somewhat impressionistic, Trystan's survey indicates that within both 'Yes' and 'No' areas there were very significant differences between wards – even those which are geographically adjacent – in terms of both turnout and voting preferences, reflecting differences in their socio-economic and cultural composition.

This chapter begins the task of teasing out the complex relationships between attitudes towards devolution and patterns of

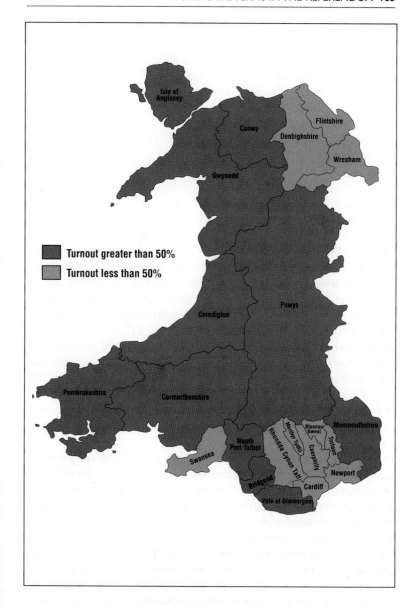

Map 10.1: Turnout in the 1997 devolution referendum

social cleavage and differentiation within Welsh society.[4] It will do so by drawing on data from the 1997 Welsh Referendum Survey conducted by CREST in collaboration with a team at the Department of International Politics, University of Wales, Aberystwyth.[5] The significance of the survey is that it provides data at the level of the individual elector, thus allowing us to relate attitudes towards devolution directly to individuals' socio-economic circumstances and cultural backgrounds without having to rely on aggregate data which both are severely limited in range and entail problems of direction of causality in interpretation.

## The 1997 Welsh Referendum Survey

The 1997 Welsh Referendum Survey was based on a representative and geographically dispersed sample of the electorate in Wales.[6] Fieldwork was carried out within three weeks of the referendum at over seventy sampling points throughout Wales. Trained survey interviewers administered face to face a structured questionnaire with respondents who were also asked to fill in a short self-completion questionnaire. A good response rate of 70 per cent was achieved, so that the survey reflects the views of a representative sample of almost 700 people aged eighteen or over in Wales. The 1997 Welsh Referendum Survey, based on high-standard sampling and surveying techniques, represents the most detailed and comprehensive survey of political attitudes undertaken in Wales at least since 1979.

At the aggregate level, it is worth noting the close correspondence between the actual outcome of the referendum and the vote share recorded by the survey. Of the sample, those who had voted in the referendum were split 50:50 on the government's proposals for a Welsh Assembly which thus matches very closely the actual referendum result (see table 10.1). A higher proportion of the survey sample (61.9 per cent) claimed to have voted in the referendum than was the case in the poll itself (50.1 per cent).[7] However, this is consistent with findings from other surveys in Britain, which regularly report higher percentages claiming to have voted than actually did so. This discrepancy arises from three sources. First, survey response bias: those who turn out and vote are more likely to participate in a political survey, and vice versa.

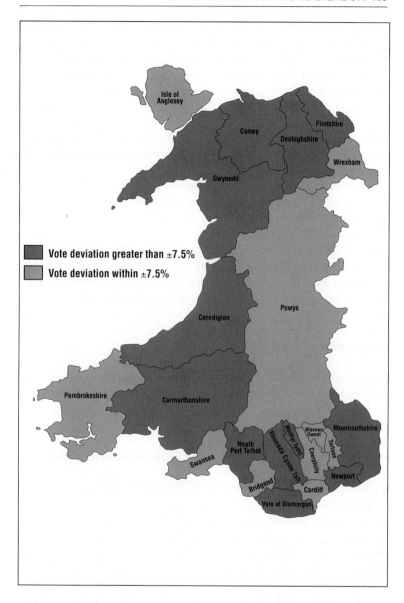

Map 10.2: Deviation in vote in the 1997 devolution referendum

Second, bias in survey report of turnout: respondents have a tendency to overreport turnout, as a result of misremembering, acquiescence bias or pressures for social conformity – particularly in the context of an interview about politics.[8] Third, redundancy in the electoral register – not everyone on the register is actually eligible to vote. In particular in this case, the electoral register used for the referendum was almost twelve months old, serving to deflate the official measure of turnout and inflate the discrepancy with the survey measure.[9] This discrepancy does not invalidate any of the relationships identified below.

In order to explore how attitudes towards devolution in Wales were transformed between the 1979 referendum and the 1997 vote,[10] we draw on data from the 1979 Welsh Election Survey (WES), conducted by Denis Balsom and Peter Madgwick.[11] Although not very closely comparable, not least in that the WES was conducted after the general election in May of that year rather than following the referendum itself, which was held in March, it none the less enables some useful broad-brush comparisons to be made.

## Voting patterns in the 1997 referendum

The remainder of the chapter explores some of the factors that seem to be associated with voting patterns in the referendum.

### Age
The 1997 survey suggests a clear association between age and vote in the referendum. People aged under forty-five were more likely to

Table 10.2: Age and referendum vote 1997

| Age | Yes % | No % | N |
| --- | --- | --- | --- |
| 18–24 | 57 | 43 | 21 |
| 25–34 | 60 | 40 | 62 |
| 35–44 | 59 | 41 | 75 |
| 45–54 | 42 | 58 | 96 |
| 55–64 | 49 | 51 | 61 |
| 65+ | 45 | 55 | 105 |
| All | 50 | 50 | 420 |

*Base:* Referendum voters.
*Note:* Percentages have been rounded to nearest whole number.

vote 'Yes' by a relatively small margin of 3:2, while older people tended to vote 'No', though again by a small margin (with the 55–64 age group being slightly anomalous in this regard).

Second, there is a clear association between age and turnout. Younger people were far more likely to abstain than older people. Again around forty-five seems to be an important threshold. The apparent apathy among the youngest age group (18- to 24-year-olds) is particularly striking. In our sample, 67 per cent of this group did not vote, compared with 38 per cent overall. However, it should be noted that this pattern is not specific to the Welsh referendum, nor is it a new phenomenon. The findings of successive British Election Surveys show that young people are consistently less likely to vote in elections than their elders.[12]

Table 10.3: Age and referendum turnout 1997

| Age | Voted % | Did not vote % | N |
| --- | --- | --- | --- |
| 18–24 | 33 | 67 | 61 |
| 25–34 | 52 | 48 | 119 |
| 35–44 | 55 | 45 | 134 |
| 45–54 | 74 | 26 | 132 |
| 55–64 | 73 | 27 | 84 |
| 65+ | 71 | 29 | 147 |
| All | 62 | 38 | 677 |

Base: Whole sample.

The 1979 survey showed little significant difference in the level of hostility towards devolution across the age groups, though people in the 45–54 age group were somewhat more hostile than others. What this suggests is that while there was a general swing towards the 'Yes' camp across all age groups between 1979 and 1997, this was most pronounced among those under the age of forty-five.

Turning to turnout, in contrast to the 1997 survey, the 1979 data showed no clear pattern across the age groups, except that, as in 1997, people in the youngest age group were the least likely to vote. Thus the association between age and turnout in 1997 differed significantly from 1979. While there was no clear association between age and turnout in 1979, in 1997 those over the age of forty-five were considerably more likely to vote than were younger people.

Table 10.4: Age and referendum vote 1979

| Age | Yes 79 % | No 79 % | N (79) | Change 79–97 % |
|-----|----------|---------|--------|----------------|
| 18–24 | 28 | 72 | 47 | +29 |
| 25–34 | 28 | 72 | 113 | +32 |
| 35–44 | 25 | 75 | 100 | +34 |
| 45–54 | 16 | 84 | 90 | +26 |
| 55–64 | 27 | 73 | 92 | +22 |
| 65+ | 31 | 69 | 116 | +14 |
| All | 26 | 74 | 558 | +25 |

*Base:* Referendum voters.

Table 10.5: Age and referendum turnout 1979

| Age | Voted % | Did not vote | N (79) |
|-----|---------|--------------|--------|
| 18–24 | 52 | 48 | 90 |
| 25–34 | 65 | 35 | 175 |
| 35–44 | 73 | 27 | 137 |
| 45–54 | 64 | 36 | 140 |
| 55–64 | 73 | 27 | 126 |
| 65+ | 62 | 38 | 187 |
| All | 65 | 35 | 855 |

*Base:* Whole sample.

### Party identification

One puzzle concerning the referendum is how successful each of the four political parties was in persuading 'its' supporters to support the party line on the Assembly. According to the Welsh Referendum Survey, the parties met varying degrees of success.

Survey respondents who identified themselves as Labour supporters and who reported voting in the referendum came out approximately 3:2 in favour of the government's proposals. However, over 40 per cent of Labour identifiers did not vote, a higher abstention rate than among supporters of any of the other parties. Meanwhile, voters who were Plaid Cymru supporters voted in favour of an Assembly by an emphatic 12:1 margin. Plaid Cymru supporters were also more likely to vote than supporters of the other parties; only 24 per cent of them reported that they did not vote in the referendum.

Respondents who identified with the Conservative Party and who voted in the referendum came out at around 9:1 against the government's proposals. More surprisingly, given the Liberal Democrats' long-standing commitment to Welsh devolution and the party leadership's endorsement of a 'Yes' vote, Liberal Democrat identifiers who turned out in the referendum voted *against* the proposals by a margin of 7:3.

As Table 10.6 demonstrates, the biggest shift compared with 1979 was among Labour supporters. In the final months of the Callaghan administration they had rejected the then Labour government's devolution proposals by a margin of 7:3. Thus the 1997 vote represented a 31 percentage point shift towards devolution among Labour identifiers. There was also a pro-devolution shift, albeit a smaller one, among Liberal Democrat supporters, although on balance they remained opposed to the establishment of an Assembly.

**Table 10.6: Party identification and referendum vote 1979 and 1997**

| Party identification | 79 YES % | 79 NO % | N (79) | 97 YES % | 97 NO % | N (97) | Shift 79–97 % |
|---|---|---|---|---|---|---|---|
| CON | 10 | 90 | 162 | 10 | 90 | 96 | 0 |
| LAB | 28 | 73 | 272 | 59 | 41 | 213 | +31 |
| LIB (DEM)* | 17 | 83 | 48 | 29 | 71 | 31 | +12 |
| PC | 93 | 7 | 40 | 93 | 7 | 55 | 0 |

*Base:* Referendum voters who identified with a party.
*Liberal supporters in 1979, Liberal Democrat in 1997.

**Table 10.7: Party identification and referendum turnout 1979 and 1997**

| Party identification | 79 Voted % | 79 Did not vote % | N (79) | 97 Voted % | 97 Did not vote % | N (97) | Change 79–97 % |
|---|---|---|---|---|---|---|---|
| CON | 74 | 26 | 219 | 70 | 30 | 138 | −4 |
| LAB | 61 | 39 | 448 | 58 | 42 | 366 | −3 |
| LIB (DEM) | 74 | 26 | 65 | 63 | 37 | 49 | −11 |
| PC | 82 | 18 | 49 | 76 | 24 | 72 | −6 |

*Base:* Whole sample.

As might be expected, given that turnout in the 1979 referendum was higher than in 1997 (58.3 and 50.1 per cent respectively), comparison of the 1979 and 1997 surveys shows a fall in turnout across supporters of all parties. It was most pronounced among Liberal Democrat identifiers.

### National identity

Another crucial issue in considering the referendum is the role played by competing senses of national identity in influencing voting patterns. Wales is not only a bilingual country, but a country where a significant proportion of the population was born elsewhere – in England in the main. Consequently, issues of overlapping and competing identities are posed in a far more pronounced way in Wales than is the case, for example, in Scotland.[13] In earlier work, Denis Balsom argued that identity has played a significant role in determining voting behaviour in Wales.[14] We might reasonably expect that this would be so in the 1997 vote on devolution also.

Measuring national identity is a particularly difficult task, given the complexity of the phenomenon. Among the many factors which may impact upon an individual's sense(s) of identity are place of birth and language.

When the association between place of birth and referendum vote is examined, the survey data reveal that those born in Wales (67 per cent of the sample) favoured devolution by a small margin (55:45) while those born in England (21 per cent of the sample) were opposed by a margin of almost 2:1. People born in Wales were also somewhat more likely to turn out to vote. In contrast, in 1979 there was no clear association between place of birth and either referendum vote or turnout.

### Table 10.8: Country of birth and referendum vote 1997

| Country of birth | Yes % | No % | Did Not Vote % | N |
|---|---|---|---|---|
| Wales | 35 | 29 | 36 | 454 |
| England | 18 | 36 | 46 | 141 |
| All | 31 | 30 | 39 | 595 |

*Base:* All respondents born in Wales or England.

A clear association between language and referendum vote is revealed by the 1997 survey. The survey distinguished three categories of linguistic competence: fluent Welsh-speakers, non-fluent Welsh-speakers, and English-speakers. Of the sample, 16 per cent said they spoke Welsh fluently, 12 per cent spoke Welsh but not fluently, and 73 per cent spoke only English. Fluent Welsh-speakers supported the establishment of an Assembly by a ratio of over 7:2; non-fluent Welsh-speakers were fairly evenly split on the issue, while English-speakers voted 'No' by a ratio of almost 3:2.

Table 10.9: Ability to speak Welsh and referendum vote 1997

| Welsh language | Yes % | No % | N |
| --- | --- | --- | --- |
| Welsh, fluent | 77 | 23 | 88 |
| Welsh, not fluent | 48 | 52 | 54 |
| No | 42 | 58 | 278 |

*Base:* Referendum voters.

There also appears to be an association between language and turnout. Fluent Welsh-speakers were much more likely to vote than people who spoke English only.

Table 10.10: Ability to speak Welsh and referendum turnout 1997

| Welsh language | Voted % | Did Not Vote % | N |
| --- | --- | --- | --- |
| Welsh, fluent | 79 | 21 | 111 |
| Welsh, not fluent | 65 | 35 | 83 |
| No | 57 | 43 | 485 |

*Base:* Whole sample.

When comparing the findings for Welsh-speakers from the 1979 Welsh Election Survey with the 1997 survey results, several patterns emerge. First, in 1979 as in 1997, Welsh-speakers were more likely to support the government's devolution proposals. Thus the relevance of language to preferences regarding devolution appears to be of long standing. Second, the magnitude of the shift in support between 1979 and 1997 is similar among Welsh-speakers and non-Welsh-speakers alike: an aggregate shift of 26 percentage points among Welsh-speakers, and 24 points among non-Welsh-speakers.

When we break down voting patterns in the 1997 referendum by self-ascribed national identity, we find further evidence that identity played an important role.[15] Two clear associations may be noted at this stage. First, those identifying themselves as Welsh supported devolution by the margin of 56 to 44 per cent, while those identifying themselves as English were hostile to devolution by a margin of over 3:2. Furthermore, both those with Welsh identity and those describing themselves as British were far more likely to turn out to vote than those defining themselves as English.[16]

Table 10.11: Self-ascribed national identity 1997

| National identity | Yes % | No % | Did not vote % | N |
|---|---|---|---|---|
| Welsh | 37 | 29 | 35 | 427 |
| British | 27 | 37 | 37 | 175 |
| English | 18 | 29 | 53 | 41 |

Base: Respondents identifying themselves as Welsh, British or English.


The information deficit – the challenge for the Assembly

In this chapter we have suggested that demographic factors, competing party loyalties and different senses of national identity all played a role in voting patterns in the 1997 referendum. But this is only the beginning of the story. All these factors are themselves related in complex ways – ways that need to be explored before we can come to a clearer understanding of their relative importance, and indeed the salience of other factors, in explaining the outcome of the vote. This task of analysis is ongoing. In the meantime, politicians will be selected and elected to serve in the National Assembly for Wales. Even in their preliminary form, these findings underline the extent of the challenge that politicians will face in the coming months and years in trying to develop a political structure in which all those living in Wales can participate. These challenges relate not only to the divisions within Welsh society, but also to a basic deficiency in the country's political infrastructure – namely the lack of mass-media coverage, accessible by all, of developments in Wales.

Table 10.12: Television viewing and referendum vote 1997

| TV Channel | Yes % | No % | Did not vote % | N |
|------------|-------|------|----------------|-----|
| BBC1 Wales | 35 | 29 | 36 | 482 |
| BBC1 other | 23 | 34 | 43 | 185 |
| HTV Wales | 35 | 26 | 38 | 470 |
| ITV other | 20 | 36 | 45 | 152 |

*Base:* Whole sample.

The Welsh Referendum Survey findings indicate that up to a third of the Welsh population depends on English-based trans-mitters for television and therefore does not receive any of the dedicated Welsh news and current affairs programming broadcast on the Wales-based terrestrial TV channels. Moreover, as table 10.12 indicates, this appears to have had an impact on the referendum vote itself. Given that television is acknowledged to be the main source of political information, and that the audience of Wales-based mass print-media is even more limited, this has major implications for the future legitimacy of the National Assembly.[17] As Welsh politics become increasingly distinct from politics east of Offa's Dyke, overcoming the information deficit facing this substantial minority may well be the Assembly's biggest challenge.

## Notes

1. The advanced age of the electoral register, compiled almost a year before the referendum, means that turnout was not as low as the official measure suggests, but it was still low by any standards.
2. A point strongly underlined in Paul O'Leary, 'Of devolution, maps and divided mentalities', *Planet* 127 (February/March 1998), 7–12.
3. See Dafydd Trystan, 'Dosbarth, cymuned, cenedl . . . a threfn', *Barn* 417 (October 1997), 18–22.
4. A more comprehensive account of the referendum vote can be found in the chapters in Bridget Taylor and Katarina Thomson (eds.), *Scotland and Wales: Nations Again?* (Cardiff: University of Wales Press, 1999), and in particular in the

chapter by Richard Wyn Jones and Dafydd Trystan on 'The 1997 Welsh referendum vote'.

5. The Centre for Research into Elections and Social Trends (CREST) is a research centre funded by the Economic and Social Research Council (ESRC) and based at Nuffield College, Oxford, and Social and Community Planning Research (SCPR) in London. The Welsh Referendum Study, and the parallel Scottish Referendum Study, were funded by an additional grant to CREST from the ESRC. See Taylor and Thomson, *Scotland and Wales*.

6. Details of the survey can be found in the technical appendix to Taylor and Thomson, *Scotland and Wales*.

7. The survey sample was drawn from the Postcode Address File of postal delivery points, and was not subject to the same sort of decay due to ageing.

8. K. Swaddle and A. Heath, 'Official and reported turnout in the British general election of 1987', *British Journal of Political Science* 19 (1989), 537–70.

9. For further general discussion of electoral registration see B. Taylor and A. Heath, 'Electoral turnout 1964–97: new sources of abstention?', in P. Norris and G. Evans, *A Critical Election? The 1997 British General Election in a Long-Term Perspective* (London: Sage, 1999); and S. Smith, *Electoral Registration in 1991* (London: HMSO, 1993).

10. For a comprehensive account of the shift in voting behaviour between 1979 and 1997 see Geoff Evans and Dafydd Trystan, 'Why was 1997 different?', in Taylor and Thomson, *Scotland and Wales*.

11. The Welsh Election Study was funded by the SSRC and directed by Denis Balsom and Peter Madgwick at the Department of Political Science, University of Wales, Aberystwyth. The survey was undertaken by Gallup Poll.

12. See R. Jowell and A. Park, *Young People, Politics and Citizenship – a Disengaged Generation?* Report for a colloquium on the values, attitudes and behaviour of young people in the 1990s (London: Citizenship Foundation, 1997).

13. For a comparative discussion of identity in Wales and Scotland see Richard Wyn Jones and Lindsay Paterson, 'Civil society in Wales and Scotland', in Taylor and Thomson, *Scotland and Wales*.

14. This work, based on data from the 1979 Welsh Election Survey, includes: D. Balsom, P. J. Madgwick and D. Van Mechelen, 'The red and the green: patterns of partisan choice in Wales', *British Journal of Political Science* 13 (1983), 299–325; D. Balsom, P. J. Madgwick and D. Van Mechelen, 'The political consequences of Welsh identity', *Ethnic and Racial Studies* 7 (1984), 160–81; D. Balsom, 'The three Wales model', in J. Osmond (ed.), *The National Question Again* (Llandysul: Gomer, 1985).

15. The question relating to self-ascribed identity asked respondents, 'Please say which, if any, of the words on this card describes the way you think of yourself. Please choose as many or as few as apply.' They were offered the choice of British, English, European, Irish, Northern Irish, Scottish, Welsh and Other. Respondents were then asked to choose which description was most appropriate if they had given more than one response to the first question.

16. There are particular complications with the comparability of questions

relating to self-ascribed identity between the 1979 and 1997 surveys. This issue is therefore not addressed here but is examined in detail in Geoff Evans and Dafydd Trystan, 'Why was 1997 different?'.

17. See also Richard Wyn Jones and Bethan Lewis, 'The 1997 Welsh devolution referendum', *Politics* 19 (February 1999), 37–46.

# 11   Post-Referendum Politics

J. BARRY JONES

On Saturday 20 September 1997, *The Western Mail*'s front page was dominated by the train crash in Southall. The intercity service from Swansea to Paddington, packed with journalists covering the declaration of the Welsh referendum result, had crashed into another train killing six and injuring 160. Detailed coverage of the referendum results was pushed off the front page, apparently no longer newsworthy. It appeared that the Welsh referendum – in which marginally more than 50 per cent had voted and, of these barely 50 per cent had voted 'Yes' – had already become a non-event.

Such an assessment, although understandable, was wrong. Despite the marginality of the result, the 1997 referendum marked a decisive shift in Welsh politics. The parameters of political debate were changed, new policy issues emerged, and the parties in Wales devised new roles for themselves in an emerging and specifically 'Welsh' political process. The most profound questions were asked of the Welsh Conservatives, but the victorious parties, Labour, Liberal Democrat and Plaid Cymru, also had to redefine themselves for the new devolution context. Labour was to discover that the task of winning general elections and referendums was simpler than dealing with the unique problems of constructing a devolved structure of politics. The question of the site for the National Assembly remained unanswered for almost eight months and caused the Labour Party considerable political discomfort. However, that was more than matched by the acute embarrassment of the 'twinning' process adopted for nominating Labour candidates for the National Assembly. The leadership issue and corruption in Welsh local government compounded the pressures to which the Labour Party was subjected during the twelve months following the referendum. But all four Welsh parties faced difficulties in coming to terms with devolution which for the most part could not be avoided.

## The Conservative dilemma

The Conservative Party's reaction to the narrow 'Yes' majority in the referendum was, at best, confused. In the general election the party had lost all of its remaining Welsh seats and it entered the referendum campaign opposed to Welsh devolution but unwilling to campaign too openly. Instead, the party lent support to the 'No' campaign while keeping a low profile, aware that too strong a Conservative identification with the anti-devolution camp would encourage Labour to run the campaign along partisan anti-Tory lines. While there had been no coherent Conservative campaign, the party had appointed Jonathan Evans, the MP for Brecon and Radnor until the general election, to be the party's official spokesman. In the wake of the referendum result he adopted a trenchant approach, questioning whether the low turnout and narrow majority constituted a clear mandate for constitutional change and suggesting that Parliament might not be satisfied and might throw out the devolution proposals (*Western Mail*, 23 September 1997). Michael Ancram, the Conservative constitutional affairs spokesman in the House of Commons, adopted a similar line, focusing on the inherent weakness of executive devolution; he anticipated the need for a second referendum once the devolution legislation had passed through Parliament. At the Conservative Party's annual conference in Blackpool the following month, William Hague, the newly elected leader, gave notice that the Conservatives were not prepared to accept Welsh devolution without a fight. He declared: 'The Conservative Party has no intention of standing idly by and allowing the Union of the United Kingdom to be torn apart and its historic constitution discarded without the fight of our lives.'[1] The implication was that Labour's devolution proposals would be fought line by line in the Commons and the Lords. The Conservatives were still the Unionist party. However, this posture disregarded two factors: pro-devolution Conservatives who had remained largely silent during the referendum campaign but were now more willing to express their views, and the mass of the Welsh electorate, abstainers or 'No' voters, who now felt the matter was settled.

The first indication of a change in Conservative thinking came immediately after the Scottish referendum and before the Welsh referendum. Sir Wyn Roberts, for sixteen years Minister of State in the Welsh Office and recently elevated to the House of Lords, promised to use his powers in the upper chamber to 'upgrade' the Welsh Assembly. He was unhappy with Labour's proposed committee system (based on local government practice) and instead wanted the Assembly to have 'Cabinet government' like that proposed for the Scottish Parliament. In his judgement, such a change would 'make all the difference between [the Welsh Assembly] being a proper government and a grand regional council'.[2] Sir Wyn stopped short of advising Conservatives to vote 'Yes', but his intervention boosted the 'Yes' campaign. He intervened again after the Welsh referendum on the eve of the Conservative conference. Describing the possible future of Conservatism in Wales, he pulled no punches. His argument was based on two propositions: the referendum result was final and could not be overturned, and the Conservative Party in Wales must begin 'to think the unthinkable'. He noted that in terms of votes the Conservatives were still the second largest party in Wales, but warned that if they refused to have anything to do with the Assembly, or attempted to rely on the blind adherence of its members, then Conservative support could continue to seep away and its traditional base in parliamentary constituencies would crumble.[3] The solution, he argued, was a party with a strong Welsh dimension. In short, Sir Wyn was suggesting that the Conservative Party should accept devolution and establish a more autonomous Welsh party. Before the referendum such views would have been regarded as revolutionary; after the referendum they made good sense to increasing numbers of Welsh Conservatives.

In the closing months of 1997, several Welsh Conservatives came out in support of Sir Wyn's call for change. But the catalyst for change came not from a division on policy but from concern about the organization of the party. To the consternation of Welsh Conservatives, the agenda for the 1997 conference provided no opportunity for debating devolution, a curious decision, given that the Conservatives in the general election had described it as central to the preservation of the United Kingdom. If that was an oversight by Central Office, worse was to come. Party organization had been identified as a factor in the Conservative defeat, and a working party, chaired by Archie Norman MP, produced a 'Blueprint for change' for consideration at a special conference in Harrogate in February 1998. The officers of the Welsh Conservatives discovered in December 1997 that Wales (unlike Scotland) was not to be represented on the proposed Board of Management. Nor was Wales to be represented as an 'English region' because its party membership was not sufficiently large. The proposals incensed Welsh Conservative officers; Audrey Hall, the party's chairwoman, described the proposed structure as an insult to Wales and threatened to resign if Welsh Conservative demands were not met (*Western Mail*, 30 December 1997). The row rumbled on until February 1998, when William Hague, who, because of his experience as Welsh Secretary of State was more sympathetic to Welsh sensibilities, conceded the right for the Welsh Conservative Party to be represented on the Board of Management.

As Hague established his authority over the Conservative Party, its attitude to Welsh devolution underwent a significant change. On 16 January *The Western Mail* carried the story that the Conservatives had decided to drop their opposition to the Government of Wales bill, to be more constructive in tabling amendments and to facilitate the progress of the bill through the Commons. The story was not confirmed, but by March Michael Settle, the paper's political editor, claimed there had been a fundamental shift in Conservative thinking. The party was now ready 'to embrace the Assembly' and Hague was prepared to consider 'radical suggestions' on constitutional reform from which a federalist agenda for the UK might eventually emerge (*Western Mail*, 1 March 1998).

## The continuing devolution debate

In the immediate aftermath of the referendum, it appeared that a final settlement of the Welsh devolution issue was still out of reach. The principle of devolution might have been accepted – albeit by the narrowest of majorities – but its precise form continued to occasion feverish speculation and heated arguments.

A week after the referendum, at the Liberal Democrat conference, Richard Livsey, the party's Welsh leader, advocated a move to give the Assembly the same tax-varying powers as the Scottish Parliament. The Conservative Welsh affairs spokesman, Jonathan Evans, retorted that such a move would require a second referendum and that if there were any attempt to introduce such powers during the passage of the legislation through Parliament, 'then the people of Wales would rightly think they had been conned' (*Western Mail*, 24 September 1997). This revisionist tendency was not confined to the Liberal Democrats and Conservatives. The chairman of the pro-devolution pressure group Welsh Labour Action, Gareth Hughes, wrote to the Prime Minister immediately after the referendum urging that the Welsh Assembly be given law-making powers and that the 'talking shop' be replaced by a 'real Parliament'. On the other side of Labour's devolution debate, Alan Rogers expressed his dissatisfaction with the proposed form of devolution, in particular the proportional element in elections to the Assembly. He promised to introduce amendments to the devolution legislation. The fevered speculation subsided with the onset of winter, but the issue resurfaced in January 1998, when Plaid Cymru's leader Dafydd Wigley intervened during the committee stage of the Government of Wales bill arguing that primary legislative powers were necessary to tackle the problems facing Wales (*Western Mail*, 21 January 1998). This was to be the last flicker of the debate on the Assembly's powers. By early 1998 politicians of all parties were moving on to discuss the organization of the Assembly. The principles underlying Labour's devolution proposals had been accepted, but the details still needed to be resolved.

Undoubtedly the most significant change to the Government of Wales bill was the government's acceptance in March 1998 that the committee structure intended for the Assembly should be replaced by a Cabinet system. Viewed objectively, this was the most significant U-turn by the government during the passage of the devolution legislation. As indicated, much of the initiative for the change came from the Tory peer Lord Roberts, but the National Assembly Advisory Group (NAAG), appointed by Ron Davies, had also come out strongly in favour of a Cabinet system.[4] In the final analysis, the government emerged unscathed and with some kudos; it had shown its willingness to listen to the all-party advisory group and had accepted a Conservative amendment. It could argue that it had displayed its 'inclusivity' credentials while actually improving the legislation. In fact, many of the government's back-benchers were opposed to the local government committee structure for a variety of reasons, not least their determination to ensure that the Assembly would be quite distinct from local government and not susceptible to the accusation that it would be nothing more than a glorified county council.

The committee stage of the devolution legislation also raised a very serious constitutional issue which had implications not just for Wales but the British political system. The problem arose over clause 79, which simply and briefly stated: 'An Assembly member is a Crown servant for the purposes of the Official Secrets Act 1989.' This implied that Assembly members would be subject to unprecedented restrictions on their freedom of speech and would face the prospect of criminal conviction if they revealed any 'damaging' information. On 6 March 1998, *The Western Mail*'s editorial asserted 'Gagging law no way to run an Assembly'. In the *Guardian* (23 March 1998), Richard Norton-Taylor urged Parliament to 'Undo this gag', which could result in the public being ejected from the Assembly 'whenever EU regional grants, European Commission plans to protect the environment, or Brussels proposals designed to promote jobs, are discussed'. The clause had been passed 'on the nod' during the second reading debate and was only spotted by that fierce upholder of parliamentary rights and persistent campaigner against official secrecy, the Conservative MP Richard Shepherd. It soon became clear that the core of the problem was the local-government-style committee system. These were to be executive committees with access to classified information and, logically, the members of such committees would be subject to the Official Secrets Act. If there had been no other reason, this constitutional nonsense marked the death-knell of the local government committee model. On 26 March 1998, the government announced it would drop clause 79 and introduce a Cabinet system. An embarrassing and unnecessary constitutional crisis was defused.

The debate on devolution did not end there, however. In May 1998 the Institute of Welsh Affairs produced a report which argued that the Assembly had insufficient members to run the range of committees envisaged for the Assembly.[5] John Osmond, the institute's director, argued that the Assembly's membership should be raised from sixty to eighty members and reported that he had written to fifty-six Welsh peers to persuade them to table an amendment to the Government of Wales bill during its passage through the House of Lords. But this initiative attracted little support. The reaction of *The Western Mail* (20 April 1998), that the Assembly should be set up according to the terms on which the Welsh electorate had voted in the referendum, probably represented the consensus view. The important thing was to get the Assembly off the ground and then to reform it as and when circumstances and experience indicated.

## Questioning the result

On 9 October, *The Western Mail* carried a report on its front page that James Holloway, a senior Cardiff Conservative, had called for a referendum recount 'because there were so many suspicions surrounding the result'. This reflected continuing Conservative unease with the narrow 'Yes' majority and the hour-long delay in publishing the crucial Carmarthen result. Jonathan Evans, the Tory spokesman, implied that the timing of the results had been manipulated by the Welsh Office for dramatic effect. Predictably Labour's Welsh Office minister Peter Hain vehemently rejected the accusations as 'pathetic, shabby, and disgraceful', and there the issue was set to rest. In the following January, the issue re-emerged in an exclusive report published in the *Scotsman* on Tuesday 6 January. It is not clear how or why the *Scotsman* got the story, but the following day *The Western Mail* took it up and ran it for the next three weeks.

The story was particularly damaging because it was based upon a series of letters, minutes, resolutions and discussion documents prepared by the officers of the Caerphilly Constituency Labour Party which called into question the conduct of the referendum count in Caerphilly. There were two specific concerns raised in the constituency party documents. First, the number of polling agents who were allowed into the count on behalf of the 'Yes' and 'No' campaigns was not high enough to permit proper scrutiny of the ballot papers and, secondly, the election officials did not allow the polling agents to check the final bundles. Subsequently, other procedural discrepancies were listed by *The Western Mail* (7 January 1998): ballot papers were counted haphazardly with some turned face down and others upside down, and counting officers would not allow polling agents to know which were 'Yes' and 'No' allocations.

These procedural deficiencies might have been the product of the novel exercise of counting for a referendum rather than a parliamentary election. There was certainly a considerable concentration of votes in the Caerphilly counting hall, and because the 'Yes' and 'No' campaigns ran alongside party campaigns involving Labour, Conservative, Liberal Democrat and Plaid Cymru, all of which were allowed to nominate scrutineers, there were probably more polling agents present than would normally be the case in a parliamentary election. The *Scotsman*'s story conceded that, following a series of meetings with the returning officer and the consideration of various official documents, the constituency officers had accepted that there had been a misunderstanding. In the opinion of Derek Lamb, the constituency secretary, 'everything had been resolved'.

The whole episode raised a series of perplexing questions. The Caerphilly constituency's initial concerns had been expressed as early as 9 October 1997, and yet the story did not break until January 1998, and then not in a Welsh paper but in one based in Edinburgh. Furthermore, documents received by the *Scotsman* were confidential to the Caerphilly Constituency Labour Party and were probably leaked by a member of that party's executive committee. Finally, there was a strong anti-Ron Davies spin to the stories. It was reported that in Labour's annual conference in Brighton in October, Ron Davies had been overheard boasting that it was his own Caerphilly constituency with its 'Yes' majority of 6,000 which had provided the overall Wales majority for devolution of 6,721. Labour pro-devolutionists who had been active in the 1979 referendum were sceptical, remembering that Caerphilly had been at the heart of the anti-devolution campaign in that referendum. On 8 January, Sir Ray Powell, a veteran MP who had adopted a vigorous anti-devolution line in the referendum, called for an inquiry into the level of expenditure by the government during the Welsh referendum. This demand coincided with warnings from 'No' campaigners that they might present evidence to the police concerning electoral irregularities. A veritable flood of unsubstantiated allegations was now made: that ballot boxes were misplaced en route to the counting centres, that postal votes had been abused, and that some ballot boxes had been stored behind curtains and out of public sight. Research by *Western Mail* reporters indicated that there had been widespread confusion across Wales concerning the determination of invalid votes and that three different methods had been used. Furthermore, guidance from Professor Sunderland, the chief accounting officer, regarding the definition of spoiled ballot papers, had apparently changed between 10.30 p.m. and midnight.

On 12 January 1998, *The Western Mail* spread the story across pages 2 and 3 and ran a raft of quotations: Nick Bourne, the Conservative constitutional spokesman, denounced the referendum as a shambles; Lord Roberts called for a Speaker's Conference; and Jonathan Evans argued that the confusion constituted grounds for a recount. In response the 'Yes' campaigners accused the Tories of 'simply whingeing' and sour grapes.

Throughout, there was an artificial quality to the arguments. The Referendum Act had excluded any recourse to the courts once the votes had been verified by the returning officer. Arguably, the time to raise complaints about procedure was on the night of the count, not three months later. Carwyn Jones, secretary of the 'Yes' campaign in Bridgend, said there was a suspicion at Labour's grass-roots level that the row had been orchestrated with a view to undermining Ron Davies, the Welsh Secretary (*Western Mail*, 9 January 1998). Evidence that Ron Davies and his credibility were the focus of the campaign came with the letter sent by Michael Ancram, the Conservative constitutional affairs spokesman, to Ron Davies. In the letter, Mr Ancram claimed that the Caerphilly party had been 'anxious to keep the matter under wraps to protect Ron Davies's position', that the Secretary of State could not assess the allegations dispassionately, that he could not be judge and jury in his own defence, and that his credibility could only be restored by establishing an independent inquiry headed by a senior judge (*Western Mail*, 14 January 1998). Ron Davies rejected the Conservative demand for an inquiry, insisted that the returning officers had scrupulously followed procedures, and condemned the campaign of 'innuendo and smear'.

By the end of January, the issue had ceased to engage the appetites of the press. Welsh public opinion seemed massively unmoved, and the Conservatives were already moving towards accepting devolution and preparing for the Welsh Assembly. It was a storm in a teacup, a three-week wonder.

## The site saga

Before and during the referendum it was presumed that Cardiff City Hall would house the Assembly. The reorganization of Welsh local government had replaced the two-tier system of South Glamorgan County and Cardiff City with one local authority, Cardiff City and County, which acquired the newly purpose-built County Hall in Cardiff Bay, leaving the old City Hall virtually empty. The previous Conservative government's decision to hold the European Union heads-of-government meeting in the building meant that several million pounds were to be spent on upgrading the building's exterior and interior. Everything pointed to the Welsh Assembly making City Hall its home in Cathays Park – the so called Welsh Whitehall – just a stone's throw away from the Welsh Office. This was not to be. The debate on the site for the Welsh Assembly cast a shadow over Welsh politics, deeply embarrassed the Labour Party and Ron Davies, deepened divisions between Cardiff and the rest of Wales and provided a classic opportunity for the critics of devolution.

On 9 October 1997, *The Western Mail* ran a small news item at the foot of its front page noting that negotiations were to start between the Welsh Office and Cardiff County Council over a lengthy lease of City Hall, described in the official statement as a 'historic building in the heart of the capital'. There was to be detailed survey work, and the district auditor had been asked to set a value. The final announcement was expected early in 1998. In mid-November 1997 there were rumours that negotiations were not going well, and informed observers were talking about a personality clash between Ron Davies, the Welsh Secretary, and Russell Goodway, the leader of the Labour group in Cardiff County Council. However, the root of the problem was finance. Cardiff was seeking £14.2 million to cover the costs of relocating City Hall staff and services, while the Welsh Secretary was unwilling to go above an offer of £3.5 million, the valuation of the building. On 24 November, the Labour group met to consider the matter and unanimously rejected the deal. They were concerned that the district valuer's valuation did not reflect the real value of the building. They also questioned why the government's planned costs for setting up the Assembly were only £17 million, when the Scottish Office had set aside approximately £40 million for the Scottish Parliament. Russell Goodway also questioned the need to spend £13.5 million on upgrading City Hall, while the Welsh Office indicated that the building was in such a poor condition that it was prepared to spend an additional £15 million on refurbishment during the first four years of the Assembly. It was also suggested that Mr Goodway had shaken hands on a deal based on the £3.5 million offer, although this was denied. Thus, what should have been a simple deal between two Welsh Labour politicians descended into an acrimonious dispute. Nigel Evans MP, the Conservative Welsh affairs spokesman, denounced the situation: 'The proposals to site the Assembly have fallen into black farce. The reputation of Wales is going to be tainted by the whole thing.' It was a view not confined to the Conservative Party.[6]

The 'stand-off' between the Welsh Office and Cardiff County Council on the questions of funding removed the certainty that City Hall would be the location for the Assembly. In early December, Ron Davies published a consultative document setting out a shortlist of optional sites. These included a north Wales location (Wrexham), Swansea Guildhall and a site in Cardiff Bay where a new building could be built. The consultation exercise developed into a frenzied debate. Politicians in Swansea and west Wales promoted the virtues of Swansea Guildhall, on the grounds that it would be cheaper, because no refurbishment would be needed, and because of the economic benefits it would bring to south-west Wales. Alan Williams, an anti-devolutionist but a Swansea MP, characterized the decision to locate the National Assembly as 'a piece of inward investment which is absolutely within [the Secretary of State's] personal control' (*Western Mail*, 4 December 1997). In the course of the consultative exercise, other, more exotic sites were suggested. Abercynon emerged in January; the next month a site adjacent to Cardiff Airport was mooted. Neither was a realistic option; it was already apparent that this was a two-horse race between Cardiff and Swansea, despite the fact that twenty-four applications were received by the Welsh Office by the 31 January deadline.

Swansea developed a highly effective and aggressive campaign; Swansea City wanted the Assembly (unlike Cardiff's Council), Swansea had voted for devolution (unlike Cardiff), and Swansea would be the 'all-Wales' option. Cardiff was characterized as greedy and concerned for its own civic interests rather than the needs of Wales. Swansea's campaign developed such a momentum that Cardiff felt obliged to respond. On 18 December 1997, Cardiff's Council produced a glossy brochure extolling the virtues of Cardiff as a home for the National Assembly.[7] Entitled *New Wales, New Future*, it was a response to the Secretary of State's consultative document, but it was also the basis of an expensive public-relations exercise. It emphasized the capital city as 'the established administrative and political heart of Wales', as 'the home to most of Wales's cultural and national institutions as well as academic centres of excellence'. The campaign did not end there. Cardiff's business community, which had been at best neutral on the question of devolution, had always anticipated that economic benefits would flow from the establishment of an Assembly in the capital. These now seemed threatened. The business community in Cardiff suddenly realized that the city had no divine right to house the Assembly. Local Labour councillors in the Valleys and south-west Wales called into question Cardiff's capital status, citing the fact that it had no historical basis and had only been designated as the capital in 1956 (*Western Mail*, 3 February 1998). On 20 January 1998, the Cardiff Chamber of Commerce, Trade and Industry addressed an open letter to the Secretary of State arguing the case for the Assembly to be based in Cardiff – 'the right and natural location'. The letter concluded: 'we wish to restate our commitment to the successful establishment of a National Assembly for Wales, which we believe will best serve our nation by being based in our Capital City' (*Western Mail*, 22 January 1998).

On 15 February 1998, *The Western Mail* reported that the Secretary of State had eliminated bids to house the National Assembly from Wrexham and Flintshire, Powys, Rhondda Cynon Taff, Merthyr Tydfil, Bridgend and Neath Port Talbot. The choice now rested between Cardiff and Swansea, but whereas Swansea was represented only by the Guildhall site, *The Western Mail* reported that Cardiff had the luxury of three sites under consideration: City Hall, the Grosvenor Waterside plan for Cardiff

Bay and the Bute Avenue development (*Western Mail*, 16 February 1998). The Welsh Office indicated that the final decision would be made in early March.

At this stage the situation descended from high drama to low farce. It was intended that the Secretary of State would make the announcement of the site for the Assembly on Wednesday 11 March. Welsh politicians had been booked to give interviews, but these were cancelled late on Tuesday night. A Welsh Office spokesman admitted that Wednesday had been ruled out, but that Ron Davies was 'very keen to make an announcement as soon as he can but he has to make sure he has got all details bolted down before he can make proper comparisons' (*Western Mail*, 12 March 1998). Clearly there were problems in the negotiations but, spurred on by the media, it was announced that the historic decision would be made public on Friday 13 March. In fact, there was no historic decision, only a shorter shortlist which eliminated Swansea Guildhall and Cardiff City Hall and retained the two 'new-build' sites in south Cardiff: Bute Square and Cardiff Bayside. The subsequent week was difficult for Ron Davies. Predictably, Welsh Conservatives rounded on him: Rod Richards who had been a Welsh Office minister in the previous Conservative government, condemned his delays and postponments and called on him to resign. Nick Bourne, a leading member of the 'No' campaign, considered the situation to be 'absurd', while the Conservative Welsh spokesman, Nigel Evans, described it as a total shambles and a pantomime. These attacks on the Secretary of State were predictable and could therefore be discounted to some degree. Criticisms from closer to home were more painful. *The Western Mail*, an enthusiast for devolution for many years, published a bitter editorial, 'The agony goes on for Wales', in which it described 'Ron Davies's dithering over finding a home for the National Assembly [as] farcical'. The paper claimed that Wales was a laughing stock, and that the government's constitutional reform programme had been endangered. The cruellest cut of all came from Rhodri Morgan, a fellow Labour MP who was later to announce his candidature for the leadership of the Labour group in the Assembly. Morgan had always preferred the City Hall option, so he was, in principle, opposed to a new-build site and the consequent architectural competition to design the building. In a memorable phrase he said: 'To call Ron Davies's announcement a dog's dinner would be an insult to the pet food industry' (*Wales on Sunday*, 15 March 1998).

Locked into delicate negotiations, there was little that Ron Davies could say, and it was left to Welsh Office spokesmen to put the best gloss possible on what was clearly a difficult situation. The delays were explained by the need 'to have the most complete assessment possible'; the deal 'had to be watertight' and 'good value for money'. But this did little to stem the tide of dismay and discontent. The final decision to develop the Cardiff Bay option was announced on 28 April 1998, but it was not entirely new-build because it involved using Crickhowell House for the administrative services and the Pierhead building for the Welsh executive (the idea of isolating the executive from the Assembly building was subsequently dropped). Although the announcement attracted publicity, particularly the purchase of the site for the people of Wales for one pound, one could not fully escape the anticlimatic nature of the event.

The site saga occupied the attention of the Welsh public for almost six months. If one accepts the dictum that there is no such thing as bad publicity, then it could be said that the issue kept devolution before the Welsh people. However, there were negative consequences. It generated heated differences and bitterness between Ron Davies and Rhodri Morgan, which percolated the leadership election campaign and reopened divisions between Cardiff and the rest of Wales, which are never far from the surface. Cardiff's political community would have to work hard to re-establish trust and ensure that Cardiff was indeed a real capital for the whole of Wales. There were also suspicions that the whole story had not been told, that there were hidden agendas about the National Assembly's home. Michael Settle, the political editor of *The Western Mail*, reported that the Hampton/Tarmac bid to convert City Hall did not appear to have been taken seriously despite matching the £17 million ceiling laid down by the Welsh Office. A spokesman for the consortium said:

> Since we met the fiscal requirements there has to be a hidden agenda. The requirement by the Welsh Office appears to have been more than was made public. We are very disappointed that the openness that was promised at the beginning did not appear at the end. (*Western Mail*, 17 March 1998)

This was not a new theme. It had been raised two weeks earlier by Michael Settle. He also suggested that there were divisions within the ministerial team as to the respective virtues of Swansea and Cardiff. The article also alleged that Welsh Office civil servants had views and that they had also been involved in the consultation exercise. 'It was even mooted that Ron Davies was isolated' (*Western Mail*, 3 March 1998). These stories were denied, yet they raised sufficient concern for Dafydd Wigley to put down a parliamentary question to the Secretary of State asking: 'What evidence [has the Secretary of State] assessed of the campaigning by senior civil servants for the location of the Assembly?' This implied that Welsh Office civil servants might not be totally impartial in the advice they offered the Secretary of State. As expected this, too, was rejected by a Welsh Office spokesman (*Western Mail*, 7 February 1998).

There might well have been another factor that finally determined the outcome of the site for the Assembly. In an article published in *The Western Mail* on 3 December 1997, 'Why pick outdated City Hall?', Clive Betts suggested that Russell Goodway had overplayed his hand in negotiations about City Hall, that the council's figure of £14.2 million (at one time about £25 million) to quit City Hall was geared to a series of other construction developments in the city. Betts reported: 'To tell Mr Goodway to get lost would be sweetly uttered throughout a country he tried to hold to ransom.' Doubtless such sentiments could also be found in the Welsh Office. What better way to call Russell Goodway's bluff than a new-build Assembly in Cardiff Bay, while at the same time utilizing Crickhowell House which had been a heavy financial burden on the Welsh Office since the Welsh Health Authority had vacated the premises in 1994.

## The National Assembly Advisory Group

Throughout the referendum campaign, Ron Davies had spoken of a new politics being ushered in by devolution, a politics which would be inclusive. The narrow 'Yes' majority and the east/west split in the vote made such an inclusive approach not only desirable but imperative if the full benefits of a devolved National Assembly were to be realized.

The establishment of the National Assembly Advisory Group (NAAG) in December 1997 was consistent with the Secretary of State's approach of developing a consensus on the new devolved institutions which was reflected in NAAG's remit:

> to produce recommendations on which consensus has been developed and which contribute to the establishment of an Assembly which is democratic, effective, efficient and inclusive; learns from experience and develops to meet evolving needs and circumstances; and commands the support of people in Wales and the respect of people outside Wales.[8]

The consensual intent of the exercise was evident in the NAAG's composition, which was carefully balanced to represent the widest set of interests. Of the fourteen members, six were women and eight were men, three were from north Wales and five from west Wales with the remainder from industrial south Wales. The party balance ensured that all four major parties were represented. The vice-chair of the 'Yes' campaign, Mari James, was balanced by the chair of the Just Say No campaign, Nick Bourne, who shortly before joining the NAAG had been designated the Conservatives' Welsh spokesman on constitutional affairs. Five members, including the chairman, John Elfed Jones, were also Welsh-speakers. Trade unions, business, local authority associations and voluntary bodies were also represented. Clearly, great care had been taken to ensure that no significant element in Welsh life was excluded.

The operation of the NAAG was also intended to ensure that the views of ordinary people across Wales would be taken into account. An extensive consultation exercise was undertaken. Between April and May 1998, nine public sessions were held in Llandrindod Wells, Bridgend, Caernarfon, Cwmbran, Wrexham, Swansea, Cardiff, Carmarthen and Aberystwyth, at which twenty-nine organizations and three individuals made oral submissions. However, it is difficult to avoid the conclusion that the exercise made little impact on the general public. In total, around one thousand people attended these meetings, which means that each meeting attracted on average slightly more than a hundred members of the public. Nevertheless, the consultation exercise did attract publicity, in *The Western Mail*, on radio and television as well as in local papers. The fact that the group visited all parts of

Wales reinforced the notion that devolution was relevant to the whole of Wales and not just Cardiff, a misapprehension which had grown during the increasingly heated debates on the site for the Assembly building.

The consultation exercise was extensive. While the general public might have been apathetic, organizations and interest groups of various kinds seized the opportunity to have their say. The NAAG received written submissions from 247 organizations and 101 individuals. The success of the consultation exercise – the group failed to split along party lines and, despite difficulties from time to time, always managed to reach a consensus – resulted in it's not being particularly newsworthy. The only occasion it created a stir amongst the media was with the publication of its consultative document, *The National Assembly: Have your Say on How it Works*, on 17 April 1998. As early as March, it had become clear that the NAAG was intent upon creating the framework of a family-friendly Assembly with crèche facilities and a nine-to-five day (*Western Mail*, 27 March 1998). This was generally welcomed and seen as a desirable departure from the stuffy, anachronistic procedures of the House of Commons. However, the proposals published in April envisaged members of the Assembly having two days a week off to take care of constituency and family matters: two days would be set aside for committee work with only one day – Wednesday – for the National Assembly to meet. These recommendations provoked a storm of protest on two counts: that they failed to take account of the volume of work which the Assembly, with only sixty members, would have to undertake; and that they seriously downgraded the role of the Assembly which, for the general public, would be the symbol of Welsh devolution (*Western Mail*, 6 May 1998).

When the final recommendations were published in August 1998, the NAAG had responded to these criticisms and to others. The consultation exercise was vindicated. In total, the NAAG made seventy-seven recommendations on standing orders for the Assembly's procedures, committee memberships, structures and activities, use of English and Welsh, no-confidence motions, quorums and the records of proceedings. The skeleton outline of the Government of Wales Act was thus fully fleshed, but the final determination of the standing orders would not be made by the National Assembly until after the elections on 6 May 1999.

# Notes

1. W. Hague quoted in *The Western Mail*, 11 October 1997.

2. Wyn Roberts announced his intention to introduce an amendment in the House of Lords to Labour's Government of Wales bill, *Western Mail*, 13 September 1997.

3. Wyn Roberts, 'Tories must face up to the reality of an Assembly', *Western Mail*, 3 October 1997.

4. National Assembly Advisory Group Documentations (August 1998).

5. Institute of Welsh Affairs, Discussion Paper 6, 'The operation of the National Assembly' (Cardiff, May 1998).

6. M. Settle, 'What a way to run a country', *Western Mail*, 26 November 1997.

7. County Council of Cardiff, *New Wales New Future: Response by the City and County of Cardiff to the Secretary of State for Wales' Consultation Document.*

8. All the following details are taken from the NAAG recommendations.

# 12  Labour Pains

J. BARRY JONES

The referendum vote approving devolution, albeit by the narrowest of margins, changed the Welsh political climate. An issue which had dogged Welsh politics for a generation and more could now be regarded as finally resolved. With it, the arid constitutional debate, important thought it was, could be put aside and 'real' politics restored; how to make Wales a better place in which to live, with an integrated transport system, a more balanced economy and improved health and education services. Almost at a stroke the nature of Welsh politics was changed, from being negative and adversarial to positive and consensual. It would have been naïve to expect the mood to last, but despite hiccups along the way – notably the debate on the location of the National Assembly building – the mood remained positive throughout the last quarter of 1997 and into 1998.

There were other indicators which suggested the birth of a new era. Two politicians whose careers had featured prominently in post-war British politics, and who had been fiercely opposed to Welsh devolution, died within a few months of each other. Lord Tonypandy, better known as George Thomas, had been Welsh Secretary of State and Speaker of the House of Commons. His death in September 1997, less than a week after the Welsh referendum, revealed the division in Welsh society. While his memorial service in Llandaff Cathedral was attended by politicians from both sides of the Commons and ordinary people from all over Wales, his passing occasioned as much controversy as his life. A highly critical poem on his life and values was published shortly after his death by Nigel Jenkins in *New Welsh Review*.[1] Two months later, an article by Meic Stephens in *Planet* characterized

George Thomas as 'sanctimonious, vengeful and an inveterate toady'.[2] John Barnie, editor of *Planet*, justified the article and argued that the real significance of Viscount Tonypandy was that 'he represented a strand of Old Labour which geared its politics closely into the British system',[3] implying that such a strand was no longer relevant to the modern, devolved Welsh political system.

Enoch Powell, for many the archytypical Englishman who had gained notoriety and eventual political marginalization because of his controversial views on immigration, died in February 1998. He had fought strenuously against devolution in the 1979 referendum and had subjected the then Labour government's proposals to the full force of his carefully crafted criticisms. On 18 February 1998, *The Western Mail* published an essay originally commissioned in 1978 in which Enoch Powell explained that his opposition to devolution was not based solely on arid constitutional and legal criteria but on a historical, even emotional, sense of Welshness which, he argued, extended far beyond the boundaries of Offa's Dyke. The concept of a 'wider Wales' enabled Powell with his Welsh ancestry to declare: 'I am English, but that is to say, I am Welsh.' Given the continuous historical connection of Saxon and Celt, there was, he argued, no need for devolution. The essay is romantic and almost totally devoid of the acerbic logic of his other political writings. While it might have galvanized opinion in 1979, by 1998 it read like a historical thesis, irrelevant to the needs and demands of modern Wales.

The apparently effortless and relatively painless moves towards political devolution were seriously disrupted at the end of October 1998 by an event on Clapham Common, involving Ron Davies, the Welsh Secretary of State and a 'moment of madness'. That 'moment' was to have a profound impact on the devolution process, and particularly on the Welsh Labour Party, creating doubts where there had been certainty, and divisions where there had been unity. However, it would be a mistake to presume that Welsh Labour was trouble-free prior to the 'moment of madness'. Underlying issues simmered just below the surface of political debate. Although they found expression in many forms, there was a common core: the relative strengths of Old and New Labour in Wales, and their respective impact on the party's organizational structure. Three issues, in particular, emerged as potentially troublesome in the first half of 1998: local government maladministration and corruption, the twinning process of candidate selection for the first National Assembly general election, and the election of the first leader of the Welsh Labour Party.

## Local government matters

Unlike Scotland, local government had always been part of the Welsh devolution debate. It was a central issue in both referendums. The limited form of executive devolution proposed for Wales implied and, in the Government of Wales Act 1998, required a close working relationship with Welsh local authorities. In 1979 that factor had led to all but one Welsh county council opposing devolution, fearful that it might reduce their powers. The local government connection had also been raised by those pro-devolutionists who were fearful that the proposed constitutional reform would produce a National Assembly akin to 'Mid Glamorgan Council writ large'; that is to say, dominated by a Labour Party arrogant and insensitive to minority views. Tony Blair's intervention in promoting a form of proportional representation in the National Assembly elections went some way to alleviate those concerns (see chapter 3). But they were never fully eradicated, and a continuous flow of 'corruption cases' captured the headlines throughout the period between the referendum and the National Assembly election in May 1999.

Welsh local government, particularly the Valley councils with virtual one-party rule, had always been Labour's Achilles heel. The devolved political system, based on consensus and inclusivity, presented the opportunity for local authorities to improve their standing with the Welsh general public. Soon after the referendum, however, a serious breach opened up between Cardiff and Rhondda Cynon Taff local authorities and the Welsh Local Government Association. The two authorities had quit the association over the size of their annual subscription, claiming that they had been obliged to make enforced cuts in the expenditure of their own authorities. While it was embarrassing that the capital city was not a member the Local Government Association, it was politically damaging for Labour. Ron Davies, the Welsh Secretary, warned the two authorities that he would be unwilling to meet their leaders for face-to-face talks if they persisted in their protest.

This spat was hardly the best precursor for establishing the Partnership Council intended to link the National Assembly and local councillors, and raised doubts as to whether the Welsh local authorities had fully embraced the 'New Wales' envisaged in the devolution policy.

More serious were the allegations of corruption in the Isle of Anglesey County Council in late 1997. The district auditor was requested to produce a public-interest report (to be published in April 1998) which was made available to north Wales's fraud squad detectives who were investigating a number of matters relating to the council and its activities. After publication of the report, Gareth Winston Roberts stood down as council leader until the police had completed their investigation. The chair of the council's Complaints Sub-committee, John Owen, also resigned his chairmanship. The issue remained a matter of public concern throughout the remainder of 1998 and into the first quarter of 1999, with more resignations and public protest groups campaigning for change in the organization and ethos of the Anglesey Council.

Successive district auditors' reports on local authority spending were published in April 1998, as the Welsh media indulged in a feeding frenzy. Clive Betts, writing in *The Western Mail* (9 April 1998) listed Welsh local authorities against whom allegations of wrongdoing had been made. The list included Merthyr, Rhondda Cynon Taff, Blaenau Gwent, Bridgend and the Vale of Glamorgan. But it did not stop there. A fraud investigation revealed that ninety Newport County Borough Council employees had cheated the benefit system out of £150,000 with fraudulent claims for housing benefit and council tax benefit. On 16 April, the *South Wales Echo* led with a headline that two Cardiff Council trips to America had cost £10,000 more than had been admitted. It all contributed to a general perception that Welsh local government was rotten.

In both the 1979 and the 1997 referendums those voters sceptical about devolution were apprehensive that Labour-controlled local authorities might provide the model for the National Assembly. In its editorial on 2 April 1998, *The Western Mail* made a similar connection.

One of [the National Assembly's] objectives must surely be to bring its influence to bear on Wales' 22 local authorities to clean up their acts.

The Welsh Local Government Association has expressed a wish to work closely with the new Assembly. Clearly that collaboration is necessary. Its aims must be to ensure the scrutiny, fair play, accountability and to avoid further examples of bad conduct.

The public's association of Welsh local government and the National Assembly would not be clear until the first Welsh general election on 6 May 1999.

## Twinning

The devolution project was part of a wider New Labour political initiative: modernizing the political system. Clearly, decentralization of political decision-making and improved public accountability were central to the exercise, but it was also intended that political institutions should be more representative. In part, this would be facilitated by the use of the additional-member form of proportional representation in elections to the Assembly. High up on the same agenda was the intention to effect a gender balance amongst Labour candidates. As an aspiration, this intention had few, if any, critics. However, the mechanism devised to bring this about had to be forced on Welsh Labour Party activists, many of whom were at best sceptical, with a significant minority openly hostile.

'Twinning' was the term used to describe the process, because it involved twinning constituencies which were similar in terms of occupation (industrial or rural), geographic location (Valleys, central plain or uplands) and electoral majority in the 1997 general election (safe Labour, marginal, or other party). The constituencies so twinned would establish a joint selection conference to select a female candidate for one constituency and a male candidate for another.[4] Even a superficial review reveals the dangers and divisions involved in the process. For example, each constituency is unique, so that any attempt to 'twin' it with another inevitably will involve arbitrary decisions. Furthermore, similar constituencies are not equally vulnerable to the electoral advance of opposing parties. Thus candidate/constituency linking could guarantee victory for one candidate while condemning the other to probable defeat. Even if the Welsh Constituency Labour Parties had been enthusiasts for twinning, it is difficult to avoid the conclusion that problems would have arisen. In fact, many constituency parties, particularly in the industrial south Wales valleys, were fundamentally opposed.

The Labour movement in Wales, based on mining and steel, big industries and a highly unionized workforce, has been traditionally male dominated. However, it would be a gross oversimplification to conclude that the hostility to twinning was the product of a macho political culture. There were at least two other factors. Firstly, Wales is frequently referred to as a 'community of communities', reflecting the strong sense of local identity in people's lives. This is partly the product of geography, the fact that many communities are contained and confined within their respective valleys, and partly of industry, best represented by mining villages clustered around the pithead. The settlement pattern of much of south Wales reflects this somewhat narrow sense of local community, and it was this sense which was outraged by a selection process which enabled one constituency in one community to participate in the selection of a candidate for another constituency. A second factor also played a role: the twinning device was regarded by some Labour activists as a means whereby New Labour could root out Old Labour candidates and enable Millbank (Labour's headquarters in London) to centralize control over not just candidate selection but policy as well. Given this background, it is not surprising that the twinning battle covered a much wider front than gender balance.

During the winter of 1997–8 the twinning debate showed little sign of resolution. Attitudes hardened. The Valleys constituencies generally were unhappy, and Caerphilly, Islwyn and Blaenau Gwent in particular were openly hostile. On 16 March, the Welsh Labour Party executive in effect put the policy on ice until 23 April (*Western Mail*, 17 March 1998). The press reported that twenty of Labour's forty Welsh constituency parties had expressed opposition to twinning and that Labour's executive had therefore decided that more time was needed for consultation in order to gather support for the policy. In early April, Joan Ruddock MP, born and raised in the Valleys, and minister for women, intervened in the debate and accused opponents to twinning of being anti-woman, a charge hotly denied by local Valleys politicians.

The fact that opposition to twinning was not the product of a macho political culture was reflected in *The Western Mail*, which questioned the efficiency of the twinning arrangements proposed by Labour, particularly when it appeared likely that a legal challenge would result.

> Today's indication by the Welsh party executive's John Rodgers that legal action is now an imminent possibility is further evidence that this well-intentioned scheme is a non-starter.
>
> It would be appalling if, after the long struggle for devolution, the democratic process in Wales were to be dragged through the UK and European courts before it starts.
>
> Even if legal redress is avoided, the only criterion for the make-up of Wales's governing body should be that members are chosen on the basis of individual ability regardless of sex and that they adequately reflect the political reality of the nation.
>
> The Wales Labour Party would be better advised to spend its energies on more constructive ways of encouraging Welsh women of high ability to put themselves forward as candidates for the Assembly. (Editorial, *Western Mail*, 9 April 1998)

On 23 April, the date set for the end of the extended consultation process, the pro-twinning campaigners had upped the tempo of their 'Twin to Win' campaign, reminding their opponents that the Scottish Labour Party had overwhelmingly adopted the twinning system in mid-March and reiterating a central point in their argument: that twinning was about 'moving towards a new, forward looking, modern politics, trying to get away from the old-fashioned machine politics to an open, inclusive, family-friendly politics, getting away from the pomp and circumstance of Lord Mayor's ceremonials, Town Hall and smoke-filled committee rooms'.[5]

Despite the counter-attack, the opponents of twinning were not on the defensive. In the first week of April, Welsh members of the Amalgamated Engineering and Electrical Union voted 59 to 1 to oppose twinning and moved to seek a judicial review of the proposed policy. The Welsh Group of Labour MPs was also seriously divided on the issue and *The Western Mail* reported that a majority was probably opposed (8 April 1998). Later in April the group held a private meeting with the Lord Chancellor, Lord Irvine of Lairg. Despite the private nature of the meeting, *The Western Mail* leaked Lord Irvine's considered judgement: 'In my opinion, twinning is unlawful.' A nameless Welsh Labour MP informed *The Western Mail*'s political editor: 'I would be shocked if the government after hearing the advice of Lord Irvine that twinning is illegal would want to put themselves on the side of the law breakers and not the law makers.' By 23 April, the official end of the consultation period, there was a generally held view amongst Welsh opponents to twinning that it was imposed on Wales by London (*Western Mail*, 22 April 1998). After a letter from Ron Davies had been perceived as less than enthusiastic in support of twinning, an editorial in *The Western Mail* concluded: 'twinning is dead in the water' (28 April 1998). However, this view failed to take account of the Labour government's determination to push through the policy as part of its modernization programme. Political heavyweights were deployed at Welsh Labour's annual conference in Swansea on 16 May, including the Deputy Prime Minister and custodian of 'Old Labour values', John Prescott. In his keynote speech he referred to the 'Twin to Win' stickers worn by many delegates and generally expressed support for the twinning policy. This, together with some small concessions and backroom manœuvering, brought the Welsh party into line.

Threats to mount legal action were still expressed by some hardline opponents in a handful of Valley constituencies including Blaenau Gwent and Caerphilly, but the vast majority of the twenty constituency parties initially opposed to twinning accepted the selection arrangement with varying degrees of enthusiasm. In one case, Llanelli, Welsh Labour's executive was obliged to intervene to select and impose the constituency candidate. The matter did not end there. Twinning was merely the first stage of a process that would culminate in the first elections to the National Assembly. On 9 April 1998 *The Western Mail* carried a story on Labour's crisis over twinning which led with the percipient headline: 'Labour fiasco feared in assembly poll.'

## Labour's first leadership election

Even before the election campaign commenced, indeed even before Ron Davies declared his candidacy, there was an element of bad blood between the two leadership candidates. Rhodri Morgan had thrown his hat into the ring at the end of 1997, and in the eyes of some of Ron Davies's supporters was regarded as a divisive candidate. It was no secret that the Welsh Labour Party establishment did not want an election and would have preferred Ron Davies, 'the architect of devolution', to have had a clear run. However, Rhodri Morgan was adamant that an election should take place.

In the early months of 1998, Rhodri Morgan, voicing criticism of Ron Davies's role as Welsh Secretary of State, had been particularly scathing about the Assembly 'site saga'. Rhodri Morgan favoured Cardiff City Hall and had been critical of the 'botched' negotiations involving the Secretary of State, the Welsh Office and Russell Goodway, the Labour leader of the city council. Other issues emerged to divide them. One was the twinning system proposed for nominating Labour candidates for the National Assembly. Rhodri Morgan was a strong supporter, whereas there was a belief in some quarters of the Labour Party that Ron Davies was less than enthusiastic. Furthermore, Rhodri Morgan had from the outset presented himself as the 'unity candidate' to the annoyance of Ron Davies's supporters, who saw this as a clear inference that their candidate would be perceived as divisive.

However, the central problem was not about personality differences or policy disagreements, but the impact of devolution on the structure and organization of the Labour Party. Ron Davies had become *de facto* leader of the Wales Labour Party as a result of his appointment as Welsh Secretary of State. His authority stemmed from the patronage of the Prime Minister, the Cabinet system and the mandate won by Labour in the 1997 general election. No one had seriously considered the implications of an alternative mandate, based upon the vote of Welsh Labour members and affiliated organizations. There were no rules for such a leadership contest and the party displayed an acute lack of urgency in addressing the problem. The issue was not formally considered until late March 1998, when it was decided that a task force would be responsible. However, the 'task force' was not set up until the Welsh Party's annual conference in May, producing an interim report in August and the final report in November. It decided in favour of three electoral colleges, one for the local constituency parties, another for affiliated bodies such as trade unions, and the third for MPs, MEPs and approved Assembly candidates.[6]

In retrospect, one is bound to question the delay. It sustained a protracted and increasingly acrimonious debate on the method of electing the Welsh Labour leader in which Rhodri Morgan and his supporters were increasingly identified with the one-member-one vote (OMOV) system. The decision to go for electoral colleges (with indirect voting) was seen as benefiting Ron Davies who, as Secretary of State, would be able to wield influence on key power-brokers in the party and trade unions. Consequently, the legitimacy of the electoral process itself was called into question. Several local constituency parties were angered by what they saw as a return to 'Old Labour' ways; using the trade-union block vote to stitch up majorities for the party leadership. In late August, the Merthyr Tydfil and Rhymney constituency went so far as to call for a boycott of the leadership election (*Western Mail*, 24 August 1998). The ultimate nightmare scenario was for Ron Davies to win the majority of votes in two colleges but fail to carry the constituency parties, which would have undermined the legitimacy of the result and the authority of the leader. Fortunately for Labour, Ron Davies carried all three electoral colleges.

Table 12.1 Welsh Labour leadership election result 1998

| | Trade union and affiliated bodies % | MPs, MEPs, Assembly candidates % | Local parties % | All % |
|---|---|---|---|---|
| Ron Davies | 91.7 | 60.8 | 52.2 | 68.2 |
| Rhodri Morgan | 8.3 | 39.2 | 47.8 | 31.8 |

But the leadership issue was not fully resolved. Rhodri Morgan had won twenty of the forty constituency parties in Wales, and Ann Clwyd observed that if OMOV had been used he would be the leader. Nevertheless, Ron Davies had a clear majority of the votes cast in the three electoral colleges and could claim a decisive victory. At the end of the count on 19 September 1998, the general mood was that the Secretary of State should 'build bridges' to restore unity to a party badly bruised and divided by the campaign.

## A moment of madness

With the leadership of the Welsh Labour Party apparently decided, politics in Wales slipped off newspaper front pages. On 22 October 1998 *The Western Mail* led with the news that Wales had successfully surmounted the first hurdle to winning 'Objective One' status and carried the slightly 'over-the-top' headline: 'Euro-billions bonanza for Wales'. The following day the newspaper reported that Neil Kinnock, 'student firebrand' and one of the Gang of Six Labour rebels in the 1979 referendum, had been installed as president of Cardiff University, a case of local boy made good. Late October also witnessed the breaking news of another story destined to run and run: the Millennium Stadium builders expected a cost overshoot of millions of pounds. In short, things were returning to normal.

At four o'clock on 28 October 1998, the Press Association broke the news that Ron Davies had resigned as Welsh Secretary of State. Later that afternoon he was interviewed by John Sargeant for the BBC 6 p.m. news. Davies gave as the reason for his resignation, 'an error of judgement on my part, to put myself in a position where I could be a victim of a crime. I have accepted responsibility for that.' The circumstances which led to that error of judgement are still unclear, and possibly will remain so, but the 'facts' presented to the media on that day were brief but confusing. The bare bones of the events were as follows: Ron Davies had met a stranger on Clapham Common on the evening of October 27; he had gone with that stranger to a flat in a housing estate in Brixton where he had been robbed at knife-point by the stranger and two accomplices, a man and a woman; they had stolen his car, his wallet and his private telephone, leaving him standing on the roadside; at 9.30 p.m. that evening Ron Davies had reported the matter to the local police; at 11.00 a.m. the next morning he had tendered his resignation to Tony Blair in 10 Downing Street.

The reaction from his political colleagues in Wales was one of great sadness and shock. Russell Goodway, the Cardiff City Council leader who had clashed with Davies on the vexed question of the site for the Assembly, expressed sentiments shared by many: 'It is tragic for [Ron and his family] and it's tragic for Wales too' (*Western Mail*, 26 October 98).

The news dominated all the newspapers and was the top story of the day. However, the view of the media generally was that the whole story had not been told. The *Independent* contrasted the speed with which Tony Blair had accepted Ron Davies's resignation with the drawn-out departures of Tory ministers. His departure left many questions unanswered. *The Western Mail's* front-page story carried the headline 'What were you up to?' Michael Settle, the paper's political editor, noted that the meeting between Davies and the stranger had taken place on Clapham Common, 'a notorious haunt for homosexuals' (*Western Mail*, 28 October 1998).

All the newspapers, both London based and Welsh, concluded that Ron Davies's political career was 'shattered', 'in tatters' and probably finished. By the next day sympathy for Davies had become qualified with irritation that he had not told the whole truth. Tony Blair's official spokesmen 'hinted that Downing Street was not entirely satisfied with Mr Davies' account of his meeting with stranger on Clapham Common, a well known pickup point for homosexuals' (*Western Mail*, 29 October 1998). Rather belatedly, Welsh politicians realized that, despite his resignation as Secretary of State (and the immediate appointment of Alun Michael as his replacement), Davies still remained leader of the Welsh Labour Party and could be First Secretary of the National Assembly. To the consternation of several party colleagues, it seemed possible that he might 'tough it out'. This was not to be. On the evening of 29 October, after 'forty-eight hours of personal torture', Davies announced he was withdrawing as prospective Labour leader in the National Assembly.

On Friday 30 October, Ron Davies gave an interview on HTV Wales that was both emotional and apologetic. He denied the stories in the London tabloids that the incident on Clapham Common had any connection with 'gay sex or drugs'. The interview, however, did little to assuage the tabloids. All noted that the word 'sorry' was written in red ink on the back of his hand and all interpreted it in the most uncharitable light. *The Western Mail's* headline summed up the dilemma for most people: 'Sorry, says Ron . . . but for what?' It was a question that remained unanswered until after the National Assembly elections.

For the next six months, throughout the difficult and damaging rerun of the Labour leadership election, the disruption and disquiet caused by the twinning system for the nomination of Labour candidates, and the election campaign itself, there was a constant drip-drip of revelations from the tabloids concerning Ron Davies's sexual orientation. This need not have happened. On Monday 2 November, Ron Davies had made his resignation statement to the Commons to set the record straight but declared enigmatically, 'we are what we are'. From this point he began to portray himself as a victim: of his upbringing, of the press campaign to destroy him, and of popular prejudice. His constituency party remained loyal but, for the rest of Wales, the immediate and instinctive sympathy when the news had first broken was increasingly tempered by doubts that his explanations had been full and frank. Despite the changing national mood, Ron Davies did not quit the political scene but remained on the wings, an unspent political force and, for some, the next leader of Wales.[7]

## The Labour leadership election: Mark II

The second leadership campaign was more bitter and divisive than the first, and its impact more profound both for the Labour Party and for Tony Blair's government. The campaign raised questions which had a resonance beyond Wales because they addressed the issue of 'intergovernmentalism' within the United Kingdom and the nature of Tony Blair's leadership.

The Welsh Labour Party executive were dismayed at the prospect of a second election. Their first instinct on 9 November had been to consolidate the party around Alun Michael, with Rhodri Morgan and Wayne David (MEP for South Wales Central) formally recognized as deputies to the new Secretary of State. Given Mr Morgan's strength amongst rank-and-file Labour members, the plan was unrealistic, and it must have come as a surprise to no one when he rejected it as a 'stitch-up'. The party executive, apparently devoid of any alternative policy, decided to see the three candidates later that week, but in the absence of any agreement that meeting failed to materialize. The party and the issue were effectively in suspended animation, a condition subsequently exacerbated by George Wright, the general secretary of the Transport and General Workers' Union in Wales, who rejected OMOV on the grounds that it was too expensive: 'We can't afford it. We have a small political fund in the trade unions. These headstrong MPs full of ambition want to spend that money now.'[8]

Four trade unions in Wales, the TGWU, AEEU (Amalgamated Engineering and Electrical Union), Unison and GMB, dominated the trade-union electoral college. They had delivered 92% of the trade-union vote to Ron Davies in the previous leadership election. To the Rhodri Morgan supporters, this procedure was neither democratic nor consistent with the New Labour approach; it smacked of smoke-filled rooms, block votes and secret deals. From the outset, OMOV was a central issue of the campaign, far more intrusive than it had been in the first leadership election.

Another issue to dominate the campaign was the 'London connection', presented as explicit criticism of Alun Michael. Briefly, the argument ran as follows: Michael was London's man; he would do London's bidding; he was unenthusiastic for devolution and had shown no inclination to seek an Assembly seat before Ron Davies's 'moment of madness'. Alun Michael could – and subsequently did – answer these criticisms but they made a negative impact in the early stages of the campaign and helped set a tone which, despite his vigorous efforts, Michael was unable to erase fully. Rhodri Morgan now presented himself as the advocate for the 'People's Assembly', sleaze-free politics and OMOV. In doing so, he had set the terms of the debate and, in effect, put himself on the side of the saints. Alun Michael was under an additional disadvantage. His late transfer from Westminster brought him to Wales when the process of selecting candidates for single-member seats was well advanced. Two seats with which he was personally associated, Clwyd West and Cardiff South and Penarth, had already chosen their candidates. The idea of pushing him into a constituency and dispossessing a local candidate, or selecting him for a constituency which, under the twinning arrangements, should be represented by a woman, would have been politically damaging and would have rendered him even more vulnerable. The only realistic political option was to go for a regional-list seat. But that also carried a disadvantage. On a regional list, his election would be highly uncertain, dependent on the vagaries of seats won in the constituencies and the distribution of votes in the region. The possibility that he would not be elected to the Assembly was real, and not resolved until the last hour of the count on 7 May. It was to be a serious disadvantage and a potential embarrassment throughout the campaign.

However, one advantage available to Michael but denied to Rhodri Morgan was the Prime Minister's support. During the course of the campaign, Tony Blair visited Wales three times to endorse Alun Michael's candidacy in the hope that his high popularity ratings in Wales would rub off on the Secretary of State. His first visit to Wales on 27 November received extensive coverage in the Welsh press. In an exclusive interview with the *South Wales Echo*, he declared that he was a great fan of Alun and added: 'I would not have appointed him Secretary of State if I did not support him very strongly.' However, aware of the criticisms in some quarters that London was running the show and that he was a 'control freak', Tony Blair made it quite clear that 'the election of a leader is a matter for Welsh Labour Party members and whoever they support I will back. I have always made it clear we will back the outcome, but I make no secret that Alun is the right man to be First Secretary' (*South Wales Echo* 27 November 1998). *The Western Mail*, associated with the view that Alun Michael was not the right man, had made its views clear on 2 November, immediately after his appointment as the new Secretary of State. Its editorial argued the case for a speedy resolution of the leadership issue as the first Assembly elections were only months away. The editorial continued:

> Despite [Alun Michael's] obvious abilities, it may be that his most effective contribution would be in the role of stop-gap Welsh Secretary. There is certainly doubt among some Welsh politicians about whether somebody not already closely familiar with the work that has been done in preparation for the Assembly can catch up in the time now available. Besides if Tony Blair were to parachute anyone into Wales for the job he would be giving damaging ammunition to Labour's main rival in Welsh politics, Plaid Cymru.

To even the casual observer of the Welsh political scene, these comments were seen as damaging to Michael and a barely veiled endorsement of Morgan. Later, in November, commenting on Tony Blair's first visit to Wales in support of Alun Michael, *The Western Mail* (27 November 1998) suggested that 'being a Blair protégé could be a health risk', that Blair was following 'a high risk strategy that could well back-fire and that there was the distinct possibility that Rhodri Morgan could triumph'.

By early December, it was clear that the leadership campaign was no longer confined to the ranks of the Labour Party.

Opposition parties joined in to take advantage of Labour's embarrassment. Dafydd Wigley called on Blair 'to allow Wales to grow up as a nation unfettered by total Whitehall rule', a theme sustained right up to the National Assembly election on 6 May. Other stories critical of Alun Michael also surfaced: according to an unnamed senior Welsh Office source Michael was firmly plugged into Whitehall (*Western Mail*, 27 November 1998), and Martin Caton, Labour MP for the Gower, was reported as having accused Michael of smear tactics (*Western Mail*, 4 December 1998). The decision, announced just before Christmas, that Rachel Lomax was to leave the Welsh Office to take up the post of permanent secretary in the Department of Social Security was generally seen as a blow to the smooth transition to devolution, but it was also interpreted by some as a criticism of Alun Michael's leadership style as Secretary of State.

Throughout January and February, the leadership campaign staggered on, increasingly and obviously doing great harm to Labour's standing in Wales. Criticisms of malpractice, voiced by both sides, only contributed to growing disillusionment within the party. It would be a mistake, however, to condemn the campaign as a purely negative exercise. Important issues were involved. For many of the supporters of both candidates, significant principles were at stake. Kevin Morgan, chair of the 'Yes' campaign, supported Rhodri Morgan because he would be more independent of London: 'Devolution is worthless if it doesn't allow us to make our choice without fear, favour and pressure from London.' Leighton Andrews, one of the founders of the 'Yes' campaign, argued that Alun Michael's Whitehall experience would be crucial in 'building relationships necessary to deliver policies that work for Wales in Whitehall, as well as in the Assembly'.[9] Both points of view were valid, but this hardly seemed important in the overheated atmosphere of the campaign. In the final weeks of the campaign, the evidence of polls, phone-ins and those unions which had balloted their members showed a consistently high level of popular support for Rhodri Morgan. The attempt by the Welsh Labour executive to place Alun Michael at the head of the regional list for Mid and West Wales, also encountered serious difficulties. A heated meeting with local members lasted more than four hours without reaching agreement on Alun Michael's candidature. It was then imposed by the party's executive.

Michael also suffered from the interventions of two Labour politicians no longer in high office. Roy Hattersley, previously deputy leader of the party, described Alun Michael as the Prime Minister's 'poodle', and went on to give his definition of Blairism and devolution:

> Blair dictates that, in principle democracy must be extended at every level. But, in practice, that means only so long as Tony Blair can be guaranteed the result which he wants . . . By its very nature, devolution means that sometimes Cardiff will disagree with London. If the Prime Minister is not prepared to risk the leader of the Welsh Assembly arguing for Wales, he is denying the purpose of the Assembly's existence.[10]

Ron Davies chose the last stages of the campaign to re-enter the political debate. In early February he gave a lecture to a large and enthusiastic Cardiff audience in which he declared his political beliefs, that 'devolution [was] a process not an event', that 'it had an inbuilt dynamic for change' and that 'on devolved matters there could be no policy over-ride by London'.[11] Both interventions were not only damaging to Alun Michael, they also revealed deep divisions within the Labour Party on devolution and internal party democracy. The leadership campaign, which began as a specifically Welsh issue, thus developed into a broad-ranging critique of the nature of Blairism, and a platform for Old Labour.

The result of the second leadership campaign was declared on Saturday 20 February in a new futuristic hotel in Cardiff Bay. The event attracted massive media attention from the London and overseas press and numerous television companies. For some, this was a defining moment in the life of the Labour government. For others, particularly many Welsh Labour supporters, it was the chance to put an end to a long and painful family squabble. The results, however, revealed a party seriously divided within itself.

Table 12.2: Welsh Labour leadership election result 1999

| | Trade union and affiliated bodies % | MPs, MEPs and Assembly candidates % | Local parties % | All % |
|---|---|---|---|---|
| Alun Michael | 64 | 58.4 | 35.6 | 52.7 |
| Rhodri Morgan | 36 | 41.6 | 64.4 | 47.3 |

The party machine had delivered the trade-union block votes and the party's elected representatives and Assembly candidates. The popular vote, however, had gone overwhelmingly to Rhodri Morgan. As *The Western Mail* headline declared, this was 'Labour's worst nightmare' (*Western Mail,* 22 February 1999). All talk of uniting the party, of Alun and Rhodri working together, was sincerely meant, but seasoned observers of the political scene, realizing that the Assembly election campaign would start in three weeks' time, doubted whether the morale of disaffected and disillusioned party activitists could be restored in so short a time.

## Notes

1. Nigel Jenkins, 'An execrably tasteless farewell to Viscount No', *New Welsh Review*, 38 (Autumn 1997).
2. M. Stephens, 'In apotheosis of George Thomas', *Planet* 126 (December 1997).
3. *Western Mail*, 12 December 1997.
4. 'Fair representation for women and men in the National Assembly', Executive Committee Statement, Wales Labour Party, May 1998.
5. Julie Morgan MP, 'The case for twinning', *Western Mail*, 13 April 1998.
6. Interim Report, Wales Labour Party Taskforce, 4 August 1998; Report of the Welsh Executive Taskforce, Wales Labour Party, 19 November 1998.
7. See the Atticus column, *Sunday Times* (7 February 1999). There was also a perception that the Welsh press had been rather more sympathetic to Ron Davies than had the London press. This had nurtured a belief in some quarters that Ron Davies's political career might well be resurrected; see Ian Hargraves, 'Welsh press roots for Comeback Boyo', *New Statesman*, 6 November 1998.
8. M. Settle, 'Unions reject "expensive" OMOV', *Western Mail,* 11 November 1998.
9. K. Morgan and L. Andrews, 'Rival camps champion their candidate', *Western Mail*, 29 January 1999.
10. R. Hattersley, 'Labour back to its bad old ways', *The Times*, 16 February 1999.
11. The speech was subsequently published as R. Davies, *Devolution: A Process not an Event*, The Gregynog Papers, 2, 2 (Cardiff: Institute of Welsh Affairs, 1999).

# 13   The First Welsh General Election

DENIS BALSOM

The elections to the National Assembly for Wales were held on 6 May 1999. Although the election was held concurrently with those for the county councils, it should not diminish the historic significance of the occasion. For the first time, an elected all-Wales representative body was to be formed. Although lacking legislative and tax-varying powers, for the average person in Wales the National Assembly was to be where most decisions concerning their everyday lives would now be taken. The election to select the new Assembly Members and to decide which party was to form the administration, and therefore which party leader was to become First Secretary and *de facto* Prime Minister, was of enormous importance. In the new constitutional framework that now applies to Wales, this was to be the first Welsh general election.

## The campaign

By common consent, the election campaign effectively commenced after the Easter break on Tuesday 6 April. It was only after the formal date for nominations that the exact shape of the election became apparent. In the constituency election, the forty seats were fought by a total of 199 candidates. The four main parties contested every seat, but a large number of fringe candidates also stood, including a number of disaffected Labour or left-wing groupings. The principal parties also all put up lists for the regional election to elect a further twenty Assembly members, as did a number of smaller parties such as the Greens and the Natural Law Party. Individual candidates and a number of fringe groups also put up lists. Forty-four lists were submitted in total, the highest number in one region being nine, carried on the regional ballot form for South Wales Central.

A number of candidates contested both parts of the election, as an individual party nominee for a constituency seat and as a list candidate for a region. In most cases this enabled the party's leading candidates to contest seats, whilst simultaneously increasing their chance of election through the list. Thus, whilst Rod Richards, the then Conservative leader, fought his former seat of Clwyd West and lost to the Labour candidate Alun Pugh, he secured election to the Assembly as the leading Conservative on the North Wales party list. Only Alun Michael and Cynog Dafis were elected as list members without having simultaneously fought a constituency seat. Parties, however, adopted differing tactics concerning list nominations. Primarily seen as a 'second chance' for candidates fighting unpromising constituencies, the list also needed to attract support in its own right and to increase the likelihood of party voters remaining loyal on both ballots. As the candidate names were carried on the ballot, electors could see who was likely to be elected if their party was allocated additional members, even if they could not indicate on the ballot paper which candidate they preferred. Thus the presence of Cynog Dafis, for example, in third place on the Plaid Cymru list for Mid and West Wales was generally thought to be a tactic to enhance the quality of the list by the presence of a heavyweight politician, rather than a conscious ploy to ensure his election. Similarly, the inclusion of Rhodri Morgan and Sue Essex at the head of the Labour list for South Wales Central appeared out of place as both were expected to win their constituency seats outright. Their names, however, may well have boosted the list in an area where Labour was unlikely to be awarded additional members, but where the party wanted members to vote loyally for Labour on both ballots.

## The manifestos

At a conventional general election the competing parties issue manifestos detailing their proposed programmes. These programmes will include proposals for new legislation to tackle the issues that the party has identified as requiring urgent resolution, and proposals for new policy initiatives in certain areas identified as essential to the party's aspirations. If necessary, these new initiatives may require a commitment to raise new money to fund these programmes. In the case of the National Assembly, which has neither legislative nor tax-raising powers, the manifestos published by the principal parties could not make these normal kinds of election commitments and promises. Inevitably, therefore, the campaign lacked substance. The parties could only really offer differing teams to manage Wales, and any promised innovation was largely restricted to cosmetic restructuring of existing programmes within current budgets and resources.

The Plaid Cymru manifesto was perhaps the most substantial, but set out a programme that streched the present powers of the National Assembly. The party's unique selling point, however, was that only Plaid Cymru

> has its policy created in Wales, by the people of Wales, to answer the needs of Wales. Only one party has dedicated its policies and its campaigning to the people of Wales and only one party can make the National Assembly work for the new Wales and for the new Europe.[1]

In the year prior to the Assembly elections, Plaid Cymru had undergone something of a 'make-over' and had adopted an English strap line, 'the Party of Wales', as part of their formal title. This small addition to their logo and identity, however, demonstrated the desire of the party to break out of the Welsh-speaking heartland where its vote had previously been concentrated. It also represented an attempt to alter the mindset of many in Wales who had only ever seen Plaid Cymru as the party for Welsh-speaking Wales.

The Labour Party had little alternative but to fight the election on the record of the Labour government, which had been in power almost exactly two years by polling day. This had the advantage of reminding the electorate that it had been Labour which had delivered the devolution policy, but carried the risk that attention would focus upon the successes or failures of government in London, rather than restricting debate to Welsh issues. In particular, the furore that had accompanied the election of Alun Michael to the leadership of the party in Wales appeared to characterize the fear that the party in Wales was being manipulated by Number Ten and the party headquarters in Millbank Tower.

The Conservative Party, having opposed the establishment of the National Assembly, had, following the referendum, agreed to accept the decision of the people and work within the new institution. However, their leading party spokespersons took the view that they were fighting the election to represent those who had either not voted at the referendum or had voted 'No'. Their manifesto made great use of the cliché 'Fair play' and in particular raised the spectre of language policy being used to discriminate against English monoglots in local authority areas, such as Gwynedd, where Plaid Cymru was in control. Central to the Conservative message was that devolution should go no further and that the preservation of the Union was paramount to the people of Wales. The Liberal Democrats promised to secure greater funding for programmes in Wales through achieving greater efficiency, but their 'big idea' hinged on introducing a form of performance-related pay for politicians. Assembly Secretaries would be denied their salaries if promises made to the electorate were not delivered upon. A poll published by HTV tested the public's reaction to the politicians' manifesto promises, and the performance-pay pledge of the Liberal Democrats generated little enthusiasm.[2]

## The issues

Two issues, perhaps, achieved enough prominence in the campaign to make an impact upon the public. Labour commenced its campaign with a vigorous attack upon Plaid Cymru. Copying the tone of the campaign being fought in Scotland, the nationalists were presented as seeking to establish an independent Wales, and accused of disguising this ambition from the public. Examples were drawn from Plaid Cymru statements and pamphlets, not all of which represented current policy, to show how the nationalists sought to establish a national airline and secure a seat at the United Nations – placing Cymru between Cuba and Cyprus! Plaid Cymru denied any duplicity, stating that its programme was as published in the manifesto and was immediate, rather than setting out long-term goals. Indeed, the nationalists denied that Plaid Cymru had ever stood for 'independence' as such, but the subtle semantic distinction between this and various forms of self-government or freedom was probably lost on most voters. Embarrassingly, however, it was discovered during the campaign that certain phrases that might have suggested an agenda for ultimate independence had been removed from Plaid Cymru's website.

In the period prior to the election campaign, following the Berlin summit of European leaders, it had been confirmed that much of Wales had qualified for Objective One European structural funds. Broadly, the western part of Wales, together with the Valleys, was classified as having a GDP of less than 75 per cent of the EU average and therefore eligible for considerable financial aid. European programmes, however, are dependent upon both matching funds from within member states and assurances that any aid forthcoming is additional to ongoing public spending. Throughout the campaign, the opposition parties pressed Labour to confirm that such funds would be available and would not be drawn from the Welsh block grant at the expense of other programmes. In raising this issue, the parties hoped to demonstrate Welsh Labour's continued dependence upon the Treasury and British economic priorities. There remained a risk, however, that, conveniently close to polling day, Labour would announce that additional funds had been secured and that the expected boost to the Welsh economy was to be guaranteed. Such an announcement was never made, leaving Alun Michael, the Labour leader, to reiterate constantly a statement from the Prime Minister that 'Labour would not let Wales down'. Understandably, this assurance did little to placate the opposition leaders and appeared, once again, to put Labour in Wales, and Alun Michael in particular, in a supplicant position relative to London.

## The electoral system

The new electoral system that had been adopted in the Government of Wales Act retained a link between an individual member and a constituency, but also sought to achieve greater proportionality through the allocation of additional members. Each elector was entitled to cast two votes: the first for an Assembly member in a set of constituencies identical to those used for parliamentary elections, the second for a party list of candidates within one of five electoral regions defined for Wales. The electoral regions adopted the constituency boundaries formerly used for the European Parliament elections and each was to return four Assembly Members. In total, the new system was to elect sixty Assembly Members (AMs).

To achieve greater proportionality, a formula was adopted to elect additional members. The total number of votes cast for a party in the regional list election was divided by the number of constituency members already elected, plus one. The party with the highest average vote per member elected was then awarded an additional member and the process repeated until all four additional seats had been allocated in each region. The regional list election was based on votes for political parties rather than individual candidates, although the names of the candidates making up the party's list were included on the ballot paper. The adoption of this closed-list system of election had been keenly contested, many preferring an open system where an elector could choose which candidate to support from the party list rather than just voting for the party name.

To assist electors, ballot papers were colour-coded – lilac for the constituency contest, peach for the regional list election, and white for the concurrent local election. Party logos were also introduced on to ballot forms for the first time to supplement the usual few words by which candidates are allowed to describe themselves. The combination of these changes raised concerns that the public would not cope very well with the mechanics of the new voting system. Depending upon where people lived, some electors would be casting several votes for their multi-member local government ward, plus two votes for the Assembly election. These concerns, in part, stemmed from the controversy that followed the devolution referendum, when it emerged that returning officers had been issued with potentially conflicting advice during the count and, because of the closeness of the outcome, this undermined still further the legitimacy of the result.

To test the issue of voter comprehension, HTV Wales set up a dummy polling station in Canton in west Cardiff. Over 200 members of the public took part in the trial, but the number of spoilt ballots cast and the level of misunderstanding were negligible. Most electors reported little difficulty with the new system and thought the addition of party logos a very helpful innovation.

Determining the winning candidate in the constituency section of the election, fought on first-past-the post rules, is straightforward.

However, application of a formula to determine which parties would be allocated additional members was new to Britain and difficult to anticipate. There was a widespread anticipation that the electorate would develop complex strategies of tactical voting. In the event, this does not seem to have been the case. Any such tactical approach, however, requires information concerning the likely disposition of voter preferences to be effective. Opinion polls taken during the campaign were on a national, all-Wales basis and therefore unable to forecast with any reliability the exact outcome of the constituency contests. Estimates of the final allocation of additional seats therefore, although formula-based, were, at best, approximate.

## The outcome

The result of the first Welsh general election saw Labour become the largest party in the National Assembly with twenty-eight out of sixty seats, but critically, and surprisingly, Labour was denied a majority. Plaid Cymru achieved the best result of the election, winning nine constituency seats and returning a further eight members from the regional lists. The Labour vote in the constituency contest was 37.6 per cent, a fall of over 17 per cent from its vote at the 1997 general election, whilst support for Plaid Cymru increased 18.5 per cent from its 1997 level to 28.4 per cent.

The national decline in the Labour vote gave an overall swing to Plaid Cymru of about 18 per cent, a level of change that was more or less repeated at the subsequent European elections in June. The Labour Party increased its share of the vote over that achieved in 1997 in only one seat, Cardiff West (where its candidate was the sitting MP, Rhodri Morgan), and lost up to a third of its general election vote in former heartland constituencies such as Merthyr, Rhondda and Islwyn. In contrast, Plaid Cymru increased its share of the vote in all forty seats, ranging from +5.1 per cent in Monmouth to +35.7 per cent in Islwyn. The Conservatives also lost ground in all seats, bar three in Gwent, compared to 1997, which was the party's worst election in Wales for over a century. Throughout Wales, all parties lost support to Plaid Cymru across a range of constituencies, and whilst certain seats attracted the headlines, such changes were not restricted to a particular kind of constituency, such as those in the Valleys, but were widespread.

There is almost an irony at the heart of the National Assembly election results, for whilst the Labour Party polled poorly, when contrasted with the party's past record in Wales, its popularity remained high. Survey evidence shows that when the electorate was asked for which party they would vote if a general election were to be held tomorrow (i.e. an election for a government at Westminster), Labour support remained strong, even exceeding slightly the level achieved by the party in 1997 (see Chart 13.1).

Support for Labour declined only when respondents were asked how they would vote at the Assembly elections. It would appear that two principal factors determined the loss of support for Labour: firstly, the poor level of turnout at the election, and secondly, the number of voters switching from Labour to other parties, particularly to Plaid Cymru.

The key point regarding turnout is that Labour was affected far more than the other parties, and clearly something similar also occurred at the European elections which followed in June.

The data collected by the HTV/NOP surveys show that Plaid Cymru voters were almost 50 per cent more likely to vote in the Assembly elections than supporters of other parties (see Chart 13.2). Furthermore, a breakdown of some of the key demographic variables of age, national identity and linguistic group with intention to vote also favours Plaid Cymru at the expense of Labour.

Electors who switched parties for the National Assembly elections present a rather more interesting issue. As noted above, at the time of the final opinion poll before the Assembly election, the electorate's Westminster general election voting intention appeared to be holding up well for Labour at or about the level achieved in 1997. When asked how they intended to vote in the Assembly election, however, a significant number indicated a change in their party support. The major beneficiary from these transfers was Plaid Cymru. The polls anticipated an increase in support for Plaid Cymru from the 10 per cent polled at the 1997 general election to 29 per cent in the Assembly election for the regional lists. In the event, Plaid Cymru polled 31 per cent in the regional election, suggesting that we can interpret the poll findings with some confidence.

A profile of the source of the Plaid Cymru vote in the Assembly elections shows that a third of those now supporting Plaid were previous supporters at the 1997 election. Sixteen per cent of the

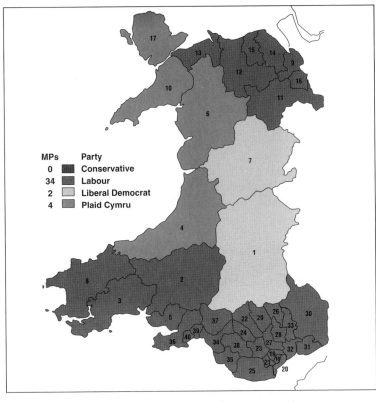

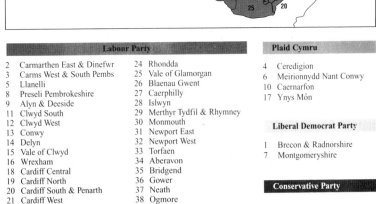

**Labour Party**

2 Carmarthen East & Dinefwr
3 Carms West & South Pembs
5 Llanelli
8 Preseli Pembrokeshire
9 Alyn & Deeside
11 Clwyd South
12 Clwyd West
13 Conwy
14 Delyn
15 Vale of Clwyd
16 Wrexham
18 Cardiff Central
19 Cardiff North
20 Cardiff South & Penarth
21 Cardiff West
22 Cynon Valley
23 Pontypridd

24 Rhondda
25 Vale of Glamorgan
26 Blaenau Gwent
27 Caerphilly
28 Islwyn
29 Merthyr Tydfil & Rhymney
30 Monmouth
31 Newport East
32 Newport West
33 Torfaen
34 Aberavon
35 Bridgend
36 Gower
37 Neath
38 Ogmore
39 Swansea East
40 Swansea West

**Plaid Cymru**

4 Ceredigion
6 Meirionnydd Nant Conwy
10 Caernarfon
17 Ynys Môn

**Liberal Democrat Party**

1 Brecon & Radnorshire
7 Montgomeryshire

**Conservative Party**

Map 13.1: The 1997 general election in Wales

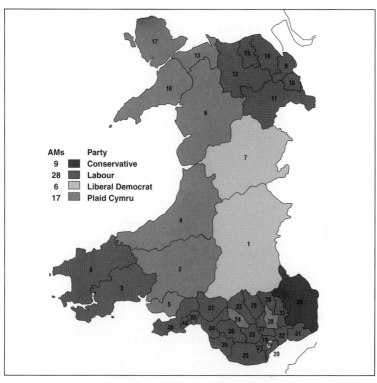

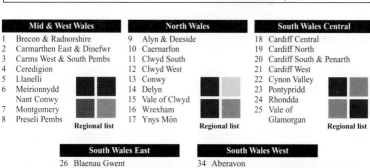

| Mid & West Wales | North Wales | South Wales Central |
|---|---|---|
| 1 Brecon & Radnorshire | 9 Alyn & Deeside | 18 Cardiff Central |
| 2 Carmarthen East & Dinefwr | 10 Caernarfon | 19 Cardiff North |
| 3 Carms West & South Pembs | 11 Clwyd South | 20 Cardiff South & Penarth |
| 4 Ceredigion | 12 Clwyd West | 21 Cardiff West |
| 5 Llanelli | 13 Conwy | 22 Cynon Valley |
| 6 Meirionnydd Nant Conwy | 14 Delyn | 23 Pontypridd |
| 7 Montgomery | 15 Vale of Clwyd | 24 Rhondda |
| 8 Preseli Pembs | 16 Wrexham | 25 Vale of Glamorgan |
| Regional list | 17 Ynys Môn | |
| | Regional list | Regional list |

| South Wales East | South Wales West |
|---|---|
| 26 Blaenau Gwent | 34 Aberavon |
| 27 Caerphilly | 35 Bridgend |
| 28 Islwyn | 36 Gower |
| 29 Merthyr Tydfil | 37 Neath |
| 30 Monmouth | 38 Ogmore |
| 31 Newport East | 39 Swansea East |
| 32 Newport West | 40 Swansea West |
| 33 Torfaen | |
| Regional list | Regional list |

Map 13.2: The 1999 National Assembly election

Table 13.1: Result of the first elections to the National Assembly for Wales May 1999

| Constituencies | Candidates | Number | % of total | Lost deposits | Seats won |
|---|---|---|---|---|---|
| Conservative | 40 | 162,133 | 15.8 | 2 | 1 |
| Labour | 40 | 384,671 | 37.6 | | 27˙ |
| Liberal Democrat | 40 | 137,657 | 13.5 | 2 | 3 |
| Plaid Cymru | 40 | 290,572 | 28.4 | | 9 |
| United Socialist | 9 | 3,967 | 0.4 | 9 | |
| Independent | 17 | 30,544 | 3.0 | 6 | |
| Independent Labour | 2 | 4,134 | 0.4 | 1 | |
| Communist | 2 | 609 | 0.1 | 2 | |
| Green | 1 | 1,002 | 0.1 | 1 | |
| Other | 8 | 7,736 | 0.8 | 6 | |
| Total | 199 | 1,023,025 | 100.0 | 29 | 40 |

| Regional List | Lists | Number | % of total | Lost deposits | Seats won |
|---|---|---|---|---|---|
| Conservative | 5 | 168,206 | 16.5 | 0 | 8 |
| Labour | 5 | 361,657 | 35.5 | 0 | 1 |
| Liberal Democrat | 5 | 128,008 | 12.5 | 0 | 3 |
| Plaid Cymru | 5 | 312,048 | 30.6 | 0 | 8 |
| Green | 5 | 25,858 | 2.5 | 5 | |
| Natural Law Party | 5 | 3,861 | 0.4 | 4 | |
| Socialist Labour | 3 | 10,720 | 1.1 | 3 | |
| United Socialist | 4 | 3,590 | 0.4 | 4 | |
| Communist | 2 | 1,366 | 0.1 | 2 | |
| Others | 5 | 4,673 | 0.5 | 5 | |
| Total | 44 | 1,019,987 | 100.0 | 23 | 20 |

| Total seats won | |
|---|---|
| Conservative | 9 |
| Labour | 28 |
| Liberal Democrat | 6 |
| Plaid Cymru | 17 |
| Total | 60 |

support was from those who had not voted in 1997, and the figure is likely to include many young people who will have entered the electorate since the last general election. Most notable however, are the 38 per cent of current Plaid voters who had formerly supported the Labour Party (see Chart 13.3).

The defectors to Plaid Cymru included 8 per cent of former Liberal Democrat voters, 13 per cent of former Conservatives and 18

## General Election tomorrow

NOP/HTV - May 1999

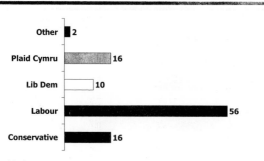

Chart 13.1

## Differential turnout

Percentage certain to vote by 1997 vote
NOP/HTV - May 1999

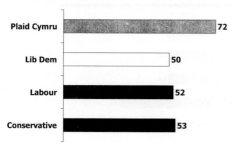

Chart 13.2

## Vote switchers

Profile of Plaid Cymru vote (compared with 97 vote)
NOP/HTV - May 1999

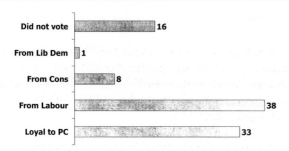

Chart 13.3

## Vote switchers

Defectors to Plaid Cymru (compared with 97 vote)

NOP/HTV - May 1999

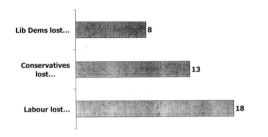

Chart 13.4

## Vote switchers

Why Labour voters switched to Plaid Cymru

NOP/HTV - May 1999

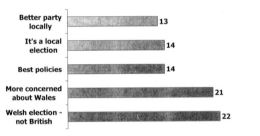

Chart 13.5

## Labour's 1997 vote

By 1999 behaviour

NOP/HTV - May 1999

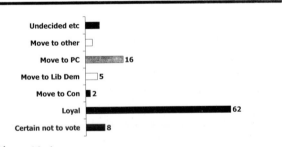

Chart 13.6

per cent of former Labour general election voters (see Chart 13.4). The HTV/NOP poll went on to ask Labour defectors to Plaid Cymru the reasons for their switch. By far the largest group claimed, in an unprompted, spontaneous, response, that the Assembly election was a Welsh rather than a British election and that Plaid Cymru, as a party, were more concerned for Wales (see Chart 13.5).

Plaid Cymru's ability to capitalize upon the Welsh dimension of the election suggests a major shift from the past, allowing it to benefit from the Welsh-identifying section of the electorate as well as from its traditional strength amongst Welsh-speakers. Previous studies of voting behaviour in Wales have demonstrated that self-assigned Welsh national identity is a strong predeterminant of Labour partisanship. Whilst this undoubtedly remains true, in the context of a Welsh-focused election Plaid Cymru have now demonstrated their ability also to tap this strong association.[3]

The final chart (13.6) is based upon voters who had previously voted for Labour in 1997 and shows the distribution of their support at the Assembly elections. Only 62 per cent retained their base loyalty to the Labour Party, even though, had the election been for Westminster, more would have remained loyal. The danger for the Labour Party is that once past habits of political behaviour have been broken, the former absolute attachment and loyalty enjoyed by the party for many years may never be fully regained.

## The double ballot

Prior to the Assembly elections, survey evidence had suggested that there would be a considerable amount of ticket-splitting between the two ballots each elector was able to cast. In aggregate, at least, the final election result suggests that any movements between parties were more or less cancelled out by equivalent movements in the opposite direction. As the electorate becomes more familiar with the electoral system, however, one might expect more sophisticated patterns of voting to emerge. In particular, in areas where the Labour Party retains considerable support, votes for Labour on the regional list will remain largely wasted. Electors wishing to use their votes more effectively will therefore switch to another party for the regional list election. Generally, the political parties would prefer their supporters to vote for them on both ballots. The evidence from the first Welsh general election further suggests the importance of known, named candidates, campaigning for list seats. The danger remains, however, that this may lead to a negative, personalized campaign, as was seen in Mid and West Wales with attacks on Alun Michael. Over time, the new system and the public's use of it will settle down, but parties may not wish to be seen to be exploiting the system. Assembly candidates may have to choose to compete at one level or the other, rather than adopting a 'fail-safe' approach. Comparable evidence from the subsequent European elections suggests that the electorate may prefer to cast a personal vote for an individual, rather than a vote for a party, and this puts a premium on selecting well-known candidates for the list.

## Relative success of fringe candidates

A further notable feature of the Assembly elections was the scale of support achieved by independent and fringe candidates and others standing as individuals. This was remarkably high for a conventional party election. In some cases local factors may have been at work in the candidatures of various renegade Labour, Socialist or Left candidates. Possibly some disaffection with the government was also being expressed through support for un-official candidates. Whilst no fringe candidates actually succeeded in gaining election, it is notable that many AMs, particularly those for the Labour Party in formerly safe seats, have considerably smaller majorities than many of their parliamentary colleagues. The support gained by fringe candidates and the swing to Plaid Cymru both contribute to this effect. In Caerphilly, for example, the sitting MP, Ron Davies, was the Labour candidate for the Assembly and, notwithstanding his personal difficulties, may have expected to be comfortably returned. In Westminster, Mr Davies enjoys a majority of nearly 26,000, but he won the Assembly seat by less than 3,000. In Torfaen, Labour's majority fell from over 24,000 at the general election to only 5,000, with two fringe candidates in second and third place taking nearly 28 per cent of the votes cast. Whilst much of this decline in the number of votes is a product of the low turnout, in these cases the share of the vote secured by the winning candidate also dropped dramatically.

The results of the 1999 election have created a large number of marginal seats in the constituencies. At the next Assembly election, in 2003, this will increase the intensity of party competition, and in doing so is likely to increase turnout and participation in the election. Even though the overall turnout was low in 1999, where a keen party contest was perceived, such as in Carmarthen East and Dinefwr, participation rates were considerably higher than average.

Taking the election as a whole, it is difficult to avoid the conclusion that the electorate saw the first elections to the National Assembly as an extension of the local government contests that were being held simultaneously. As the Assembly has been elected for a fixed four-year term, it seems likely that this concurrence will become the normal pattern of events. The National Assembly and the political parties therefore have a crucial role in demonstrating the importance of the new institution and establishing the election as a 'national' event of the highest significance.

## Conclusion

The evidence of the election to the National Assembly, with low participation and a high level of political volatility, supports the idea that the public did not recognize the event as a first-order, national, election. It is now accepted that the public are able to discern differing levels of election and are likely to adjust their voting habits and political behaviour accordingly. This is not a new finding, and is commonplace in other countries with constitutions providing different levels of government, each seeking a distinct political mandate. In the new Wales, therefore, present evidence suggests that Westminster elections are still first-order events, characterized by high turnout, intense partisan competition and relative stability in party loyalty. Other elections, such as parliamentary by-elections, European elections and local government elections, are of a lower, second-order, significance. At this level, low participation and high volatility are quite common. In 1999, it would appear that the Welsh electorate perceived the Assembly elections as a second-order event and engaged accordingly. The first Welsh administration has four years to demonstrate the importance of the Assembly, to establish its members as 'national' politicians and to deliver a Welsh policy agenda that will engage public attention at the highest level. If successful, future elections to the National Assembly will command the full attention of Wales and become a genuine general election.

## Notes

1. *Working for the New Wales*, The Manifesto of Plaid Cymru – The Party of Wales (1999).

2. HTV/NOP final national poll, 29 April–2 May, N = 1501. Only 22 of those asked believed the Liberal Democrats would implement such a policy.

3. Denis Balsom, P. J. Madgwick and D. Van Mechelen, 'The red and the green', *British Journal of Political Science* 13 (1983).

# 14   The New Welsh Constitution: The Government of Wales Act 1998

KEITH PATCHETT

## Introduction

The National Assembly for Wales[1] is an institution without con-stitutional precedent.[2] The Government of Wales Act 1998[3] creates a unique scheme of executive devolution. Its principal purpose is to transfer to the Assembly most of the central government's respons-ibility for executive action for Wales, such as determining the budget for public expenditure, developing and putting into effect policies within a framework set by Acts of Parliament, setting targets for public bodies and monitoring their performance and the like. The Assembly is not a legislature since it has no general competence to make primary legislation; that function remains with Parliament. Yet the Assembly will have extensive powers to make subordinate legislation, sometimes of wide-ranging effect, within the terms prescribed by Acts of Parliament.

It performs governmental functions in eighteen fields[4] taken over from the Secretary of State for Wales, but it too does so on behalf of the Crown.[5] The functions are vested collectively in the Assembly, as a corporate body,[6] rather than in specific ministerial members, and at law it is the Assembly as a whole that takes responsibility for the policies and decisions made in its name. Yet its entire membership is also expected to contribute to better-informed and focused policies, as well as introducing greater scrutiny, accountability and transparency into its decision-making processes.

In principle, the Assembly has a high degree of freedom in the way that it conducts its activities. But in a number of important respects it will be dependent upon the extent to which its financing, which remains with central government, allows room for manœuvre, and how effectively its relationships with the Secretary of State for Wales and Whitehall departments are established and maintained.

## The bill

The Government's original intention was to refer the bill at the committee stage for consideration by a standing committee of the Commons, leaving a small number of central provisions to be dealt with by the whole House. However, after protests by opposition parties, the convention of dealing with first-class constitutional measures on the floor of the House was in fact followed, although a restricted number of days was allocated to the committee (seven days) and report stages (two days), and the debates programmed.[7] The House of Lords gave five days to the committee stage, two to the report stage and one to the Third Reading.

In most respects the Act that eventually emerged gives effect to the White Paper's proposals.[8] But, in the course of its passage through the two Houses of Parliament, important amendments were made to the bill, almost all moved by government, as is usually the case, some reflecting a rethink of policy by government, others responding to concerns expressed in the parliamentary debates or outside Parliament. The most significant changes related to the role of Assembly Secretaries and committees[9] and the delegation of functions,[10] the application of the Official Secrets Acts,[11] the institution of a Welsh administration ombudsman,[12] the conduct of cross-border functions,[13] furtherance of sustainable development,[14] consultation with business,[15] funding of the Forestry Commissioners,[16] promotion of private bills[17] and the status of Welsh records.[18]

Only two motions for amendment from outside government received affirmative votes, both in the Lords. The first would have disqualified ministers of the Crown from Assembly membership,[19] though it seems to have been designed principally to prevent the posts of Secretary of State for Wales and of First Assembly Secretary being held by the same person.[20] The second would have required the distribution of additional-member seats to be calculated by reference to the votes cast for the forty constituency seats, rather than from a second set of votes.[21] This was designed to prevent participation of splinter parties formed from the main parties deliberately taking advantage of the proportionality system in order to gain a larger number of additional seats than would be allocated to the main party alone.[22] In fact, both amendments were ultimately rejected by the Commons when the bill returned there and were not persisted in by the Lords.[23]

Although the Act is substantial (159 sections and eighteen Schedules),[24] it does not tell the complete story. Many matters of significance are dealt with by supplementary instruments. So, for example, the itemized list of functions within the Assembly's eighteen fields of competence was transferred from the Secretary of State by Order in Council.[25] Other start-up instruments prepared by the Secretary of State made provision for the Assembly elections[26] and specified offices that disqualify from Assembly membership,[27] determined the initial salaries and allowances of members,[28] fixed the first election and meeting dates[29] as well as transferring specific property, rights and liabilities from central government[30] and functions from the Comptroller and Auditor General to the Auditor General for Wales.[31]

Important additional matter appears in the standing orders that govern Assembly proceedings. These determine how the relationships created by its unique structure are expected to work. The first standing orders were made by the Secretary of State, having been developed by a group of commissioners appointed by him and operating on guidance published by him.[32] That guidance took into account the published recommendations of the National Assembly Advisory Group, again appointed by the Secretary of State.[33] Changes to these standing orders require the support of at least two-thirds of the voting members.[34]

Another important source of Assembly practice, and one of the most radical innovations of the devolution scheme, is not mentioned in the Act. Concordats are to set out the ground rules for co-operation between the Assembly and government departments in Whitehall. A series of bilateral concordats are to be entered into with individual departments. Many common matters will be covered, though presumably each will reflect the particular area of policy affected. These are likely to include:

- consultation and advance notification on proposed legislation and policy initiatives;

- exchange of information and access to research and specialist advice;
- joint working and membership of working groups and committees;
- confidentiality;
- financial arrangements, especially the role of the Treasury;
- arrangements with respect to EU (including participation in EU meetings) and to other international matters;
- consultation upon appointments to public bodies and exercise of functions relating to them;
- resolution of disagreements on matters in the concordat.

The concordats, which generally are to be published, will be agreed with the departments by the Assembly, and usually signed by senior officials. They will operate within the context set by a general memorandum of understanding settled at the governmental level. The government resisted efforts in Parliament to lay a legal basis for the concordats in the bill, not wishing the relationships between officials to be governed by enforceable contracts.[35] Arguably, non-compliance could still be the basis of a judicial review on the grounds that they give rise to a legitimate expectation as to how co-operation is to be achieved.[36] But difficulties in application will be expected to be resolved at the official or political level, perhaps with the Secretary of State for Wales playing an arbitral role. As Rawlings has pointed out, these devices enter upon uncharted constitutional territory, in which the parties are not equals.[37] Yet the Act contains no mechanism, for example, facilitating parliamentary scrutiny.

Their importance arises from the changed relationship between the Cardiff and Whitehall officials. Prior to devolution, both sets operated in a common administrative system; although immediately answerable to different ministers, they were fulfilling the aims of the same executive. The arrival of the Assembly means that officials are answerable to different executive institutions with potentially differing objectives or priorities.[38] The likelihood of tensions and differences, with the Assembly cast in a subordinate position, cannot be discounted. The concordats are a mechanism to identify areas in which difficulties may arise between two distinct executive authorities and to make arrangements for their reduction. The true test of their effectiveness is likely to arise when governments of different complexions exist in Wales and Westminster. The aim must be to ensure that the arrangements that they embody become institutionalized, and the procedures for their settlement and alteration well established, before that time. The relationship between the Assembly and central government will be defined by practices grounded in the concordats; in due time the major ones could well strengthen into constitutional conventions.

Assembly practice is also to be governed by a series of codes of practice or guidance which the Assembly has agreed to.[39] Again types of 'soft-law', these are not legally enforceable but they will play an important part in the way in which the statutory rules governing Assembly proceedings and the standing orders are interpreted, applied and enforced within the Assembly. They deal with a wide range of issues: conduct in the chamber, standards of conduct of members and of Assembly Secretaries, members' interests, provision of information to members, public access to information, relations between staff and members, and public appointments.

## Assembly membership

Although equal opportunities in representation, particularly for women, have been frequently emphasized,[40] the Act makes no explicit provisions to bring this about. Attempts to amend the sex-discrimination legislation to allow positive discrimination in favour of women so as to produce gender balance foundered on the advice that these might fall foul of European employment law.[41] Accordingly, the initiative rests with the individual parties to correct the long-standing under-representation of women. The Labour Party sought to meet this by adopting a deliberate policy of twinning constituencies and selecting two men and two women as candidates for pairs of constituencies. In the event, twenty-four of the sixty seats are held by women, nineteen secured by direct election.[42]

The Act does not disqualify MPs from Assembly membership.[43] Indeed, seven were elected. Dual mandates were defended as a valuable device for bringing into the first Assembly persons with national political and executive experience. Their presence at Westminster could help ensure that the Assembly's agenda is not ignored by Parliament or central government. Little public attention has been given to the practical difficulties and possible conflicts, both in time and loyalties, that can arise, and not least for those who take office as Assembly Secretary or as chair of a subject committee,[44] and whose active participation at Westminster could be affected. In practice, it seems probable that dual representation will be confined to the first term of the Assembly or at least during periods when the later stages of the term of one institution overlap with a new term of the other.

Nor is a minister in central government disqualified from election either as an Assembly member or as an Assembly Secretary. Indeed, the Secretary of State for Wales was elected as an AMS member and by the Assembly as its First Secretary. The case for such dual office-holding was largely made on the basis of the possible benefits during the transition in transferring powers and settling concordats.[45] The long-term undesirability of such arrangements both politically and constitutionally has been acknowledged by government,[46] and they are unlikely to continue after the formal transfer of powers to the Assembly. In particular, conflicts of responsibility in the exercise of particular powers conferred by the Act could well disturb the balance between central and devolved governments which the Act intends. For example, it is not obvious how the Secretary of State could 'oversee and maintain good working relationships between the Assembly and the government departments'[47] if he or she is also the political leader of the former. Presumably, the Assembly will look to its First Secretary to represent its position on such issues, especially where there are major differences of judgement between the two sides.

## Electing the Assembly

The number of Assembly members and the type of electoral system were contentious issues. The solutions adopted in the White Paper and the Act appear to be the result of a relatively late compromise within the Labour Party and of the practical convenience of relying on existing constituency arrangements.

The Act does not state the size of the Assembly *expressly* in numbers. Instead it creates a formula: one constituency member for each of the Westminster constituencies (forty), and four additional members for each of the five European Parliament constituencies then existing (twenty).[48] The Act makes clear that the ratio of one additional-member seat to two constituency seats is to be maintained.[49] Accordingly, the size of the Assembly is linked to representation at Westminster, and should increase automatically with any increase in the number of Welsh parliamentary constituencies.[50]

On the other hand, a reduction in Westminster seats would not lead to an automatic reduction of Assembly seats.[51] But if such reduction were under consideration in the future,[52] the size of the Assembly might well become an issue too, even though there is no obvious logic in linking the two. Amendments to the Act would then have to be made to enable the existing number of Assembly members to continue if the number of Westminster seats were to be reduced. In any case, a different statutory formula would be needed if, in the future, the Assembly were to be increased in size without changing the present number of Westminster constituencies.

Constituency seats are to be filled by direct candidate voting; the additional-member seats by a second vote cast for a registered political party,[53] after which seats are allocated by reference to a closed regional party list according to a formula[54] which compensates for party disproportion in the constituency seats. These arrangements are thought likely to favour the larger parties, rather than to ensure true proportionality in relation to the total national vote obtained by each party.[55] Suggestions that the addition of five more AMS seats would radically improve proportionality made no impression on the government. Similarly, criticisms that a closed-list system gives priority to party preferences over elector choice were discounted.[56]

Attempts to prevent the participation of offshoot parties, which under the allocation formula would acquire more additional seats than their parent party, were also defeated. The practice was recognized to be undesirable, but the proposed solutions would have precluded the more desirable objective of direct voting for the regional lists. The major parties have stated their intention not to permit the practice.[57]

The results of the first Assembly elections saw a reduction in the traditional dominance of the Labour Party in elections in Wales to the point that no single party has majority support in the Assembly.[58] In the event, a minority government was formed by

Labour in preference to a coalition. It remains to be seen how effectively the institutional processes and the standing orders will operate in this context. Arguably, as they have been designed to encourage inclusiveness of all members, they should be more readily adaptable to those circumstances.

## Functions

The Assembly has acquired its functions in the main as a result of a formal transfer of functions previously vested in the Secretary of State for Wales, though others are conferred directly by the Act itself, notably for reforming certain quangos.[59] In future, it may be expected that additional functions will be conferred directly upon the Assembly by individual Acts,[60] though the Act does not preclude the possibility of further transfer orders for functions subsequently vested in a minister of the Crown.[61] The transfer orders are marked by the volume and particularity of the entries. The first Order in Council details functions from 300 or so statutes and statutory instruments.[62] In some instances, the transfer extends to all the functions in a particular Act, in others it is confined to some only. Some functions are important, others relatively minor; some are stated in broad terms, while others are very specific. Yet others are made subject to limitations in application or mode of exercise.

The result is an uneven patchwork of provisions lacking underlying coherence, inevitably so as, prior to the Act, the drafting of functions was not premised on devolution. Since every decision and action of the Assembly and its Secretaries must be grounded on statutory authority and is subject to the possibility of judicial review, the Assembly will be heavily dependent upon its legal officials. There are almost certain to be disappointments when policy initiatives in a subject field have to be curbed on legal advice for want of some specific power.

## Structure of the Assembly

The core operating arrangements for the Assembly prescribed in the Act differ from those originally provided for in the White Paper and the bill. Under the latter, the Assembly was required to establish a series of subject committees which, between them, would have had executive responsibilities with respect to the eighteen fields in which the Assembly has competence. The committee members were to be elected by the Assembly so as to reflect the party balance; the committees would each have chosen a subject leader (to be known as an Assembly Secretary). The committees' functions, themselves derived by delegation from the Assembly, could have been further delegated by them to their Secretary as well as to members of the Assembly staff. The Secretaries were collectively to comprise an executive committee to provide political direction of the Assembly, headed by the First Secretary elected by the Assembly. This committee, too, would have derived its functions by delegation from the Assembly, and the First Secretary by delegation from the executive committee.

Technically, then, the First Secretary would have had no direct power to appoint his colleagues or to allocate their portfolios, although no doubt a majority party could have managed the elections to give effect to a distribution of responsibilities previously decided upon by it. More importantly, although the Secretaries would have derived their functions from the subject committees, the scheme was intended to give a central role to the committees themselves in day-to-day decision-making. These arrangements were seen as favouring the practices of local government authorities which have been often criticized as unduly restricting the capacity of the leadership of the Assembly to perform their leadership role and as impairing accountability.

Accordingly, the bill was amended to give greater centrality in decision-making to the First Secretary, the executive committee (now 'Assembly Cabinet')[63] and the Secretaries who comprise it. As Rawlings has pointed out,[64] the need to retain the basis on which the referendum was conducted led to a contrived solution. The changes made allow the Assembly to operate more nearly on cabinet lines, but the legislative framework had to be designed to allow future flexibility. Accordingly, it is open to the Assembly to move in the direction of a committee system by delegating substantial functions directly to the subject committees which could then determine the extent of further delegations to their subject Secretary. But it was made clear that the first standing orders would ensure that responsibility for decision-making would rest principally with the Cabinet and the Secretaries.[65]

As a consequence, the scheme now envisages an extensive delegation of functions in the first instance to the First Secretary by the Assembly (in which the functions are vested by law), and not to the committees.[66] The selection of Assembly Secretaries is made by the First Secretary from among Assembly members;[67] neither the Assembly itself nor its committees have any formal role in that process. The Secretaries acquire their responsibilities for decision-making (or portfolios) by the First Secretary further delegating those of his or her functions that are relevant to them.[68] The Secretaries may delegate their functions to officials who are members of the Assembly's staff.[69] But, as this mechanism does not ensure that the Secretaries are answerable to the Assembly for the fields in which they have functions, the First Secretary must formally allocate accountability for those fields to them.[70] This puts them under a legal duty to answer to members of the Assembly for the performance of the functions delegated to them.[71]

At the same time, the Assembly must establish subject committees equal in number to the Secretaries with subject portfolios; their chairs are to be chosen from a panel of members elected by the Assembly to reflect the party balance; their membership is elected by the Assembly, must reflect the party balance and include the relevant Secretary.[72] Under this scheme, the role of the subject committees is altered from that originally envisaged. They are not engaged in day-to-day decision-making, but have the function of scrutinizing the decisions of their Secretary and reviewing the performance of public bodies in their field. But, in addition, the standing orders put emphasis upon the duty of each to make an informed contribution to the development by its Secretary of policy in its field (for example by drawing upon contacts with outside organizations) and to influence its implementation (for example by examining subordinate legislation).[73] This 'new' approach is seen as creating a more consensual and inclusive approach to policy development by giving a greater role to minority parties and those not holding office than happens under a pure Cabinet system.[74] The remits of the first subject committees are an innovative attempt to avoid departmentalization by assigning responsibility for cross-cutting matters as well as for specific fields.[75]

In some respects the committees' review function and their responsibility in connection with policy development do not sit comfortably together.[76] How easy will they find it to be both co-operative and critical? Is it feasible for the same body of persons to adopt procedures for scrutinizing departmental activities and yet to be a conduit through which external interests are expected to feed into the decision-making process? To what extent will the committees feel able to review activities of a Secretary when that Secretary is a member of the committee and when the committee has become closely associated with the matter on which the Secretary has been acting? Where a party has an inbuilt majority on the committee (of which the Secretary will be part), will it be inclined to give political support to the Secretary and leave the review function to be performed by members from other parties? Can distinctive policy differences between parties be maintained and made publicly transparent in a system which is designed to be inclusive?

The Act also provides wide powers of delegation by the Assembly, its committees and Secretaries to the Assembly staff.[77] These comprise officials transferred from the Welsh Office and new recruits (who also become members of the Home Civil Service). It is for the Permanent Secretary, and not the Assembly, to determine which officials are to perform the functions delegated.[78] It was apparent from early on that those Assembly members not immediately engaged in executive decision-making (both individuals and committees) would need to be supported by their own group of officials, if they were to be perform their functions adequately. Accordingly, those staff who service the Assembly as a whole and its committees have been organized separately in the Presiding Officer's Office.[79] As has been suggested, 'Chinese walls' will have to develop between them and those officials working for the Assembly Cabinet and Secretaries.[80] On the broader front, experience may indicate that the Assembly needs its own civil service in order to pursue distinctive objectives in its dealings with Whitehall.[81]

## Size of the Assembly

The organizational structure of the Assembly created by the Act and the working methods envisaged by the standing orders raise questions as to the capacity of a membership of sixty to carry out its functions. Even given the difference in functions, this seems small in comparison with the Scottish Parliament (129 members) and the Northern Ireland Assembly (108 members).

The Act and the standing orders require the establishment of numerous committees and other representative bodies, and others are envisaged. Provision is made for an Assembly Cabinet of no more than nine,[82] subject committees of between seven and eleven members,[83] a Legislation Committee[84] and an Audit Committee[85] of a similar size, a Business Committee of five members,[86] a Committee on Standards of Conduct,[87] standing programme Committees on Equality of Opportunity[88] and on European Affairs,[89] a Partnership Council with local government,[90] and four Regional Committees, each comprising the members electorally connected with the region.[91] The NAAG foresaw the possibility of other standing programme committees concerned with cross-cutting issues and the use of task and finish working groups.[92] The standing orders merely provide the procedures for establishing additional committees or subcommittees.[93] In addition, some Assembly Members will participate in the proposed British–Irish Council which will be concerned with co-operation on matters of mutual interest within the competence of the Administrations in Ireland and the British Isles.[94]

Although frequency of meeting of some of these bodies is not yet clear,[95] most Members of the Assembly can expect to find themselves members of several,[96] especially since some members are precluded from, or are unlikely to be available for, most committee work by reason of their principal functions in the Assembly (e.g. the nine Assembly Secretaries, the two presiding officers and the leaders of the main party groups). In addition to these duties, members will be expected to take part in the work of the full Assembly (which is likely to meet once or twice a week), as well as to take up constituency matters and, perhaps through subject committee subcommittees, work with organizations and groups whose opinions the Assembly should take into account.

Members, then, will be heavily engaged in the wide range of activities that must compete for their time and fit in an Assembly timetable that aims to be user-friendly.[97] A number of concerns may need to be addressed. Will members be able to develop a satisfactory level of expertise required for subject-committee work, especially for those committees that have composite remits and in the case of those members who must be members of more than one? Will members of minority parties not be particularly hard-pressed in this respect? Will this lead to members becoming too dependent upon the Assembly officials?[98] Will overlap of committee membership present problems of scheduling of meetings? Given the relatively small size of committees and the emphasis on party balance, will committee absences, whether for illness or other commitments, cause difficulties?[99] Will those members holding a dual mandate in Cardiff and Westminster be able to fit in readily with these demands? If the First Secretary wishes to replace an Assembly Secretary or if a subject committee chair resigns, is this not likely to have repercussions throughout the committee system, as there will be no pool of persons without substantial existing Assembly commitments? In short, will the membership be found to be smaller than the Assembly needs for efficient operation?[100]

## Relationship with Whitehall and Westminster

The Act is largely silent upon these issues.[101] On the important matter of Assembly finances, it makes no provision as to how the block grant and other payments to be made to the Assembly are to be calculated. The size of these will depend upon Treasury decisions about public financing. The Act merely provides for payments to be made by the Secretary of State and an annual statement of the sums to be allocated laid before the Assembly.[102] Within the funds provided, the Assembly gives approval to the budget of expenditure developed by the Finance Secretary and the Assembly Cabinet in consultation with each of the subject committees.[103]

Accordingly, expenditure in Wales continues to depend primarily upon the level of expenditure in England; the 'Barnett formula', by which the grant is altered in line with changes in comparable English programmes, continues. Attempts during the debates on the bill to give the Assembly a more direct say with respect to any amendment to that formula (which reflects population size rather than spending needs) or with respect to other payments not covered by it (such as agriculture payments under the common agricultural policy) were not acceded to.[104]

In consequence, negotiations with the Treasury on matters affecting Welsh finances are to be undertaken by the Secretary of State for Wales. The Assembly may make representations on such issues,[105] and can be expected to be consulted if such matters as the Barnett formula come under review and when a public spending survey is under consideration in Whitehall. But advocacy of the Welsh case, and so its effectiveness, rests with the Secretary of State, with no statutory guarantee as to the extent to which, and when, Assembly Secretaries or officials may be involved.[106] Further, there is a distinct possibility that the Assembly's ability to innovate policy will be seriously constrained by the decisions in London on spending on public services, especially as a large part of the block grant is required for local government expenditure.[107]

A second area in which Cardiff–London relations will be important concerns primary legislation.[108] The Assembly derives both its executive powers and subordinate law-making powers from Acts of Parliament.[109] Extension or variation of those powers will come from the same source. Accordingly, the Assembly will need to take an interest in bills that may affect the functions of the Assembly itself or more generally have implications for Wales, both when in preparation in Whitehall and when before Parliament. The Act says very little specifically about this matter, though the Assembly clearly can avail itself of the power to 'consider, and make representations about, any matter affecting Wales' for this purpose.[110]

Circumstances are sure to arise in which the Assembly concludes that it needs legislative authority to act that it does not currently have. It must, therefore, persuade central government to put appropriate provisions in a bill already scheduled for preparation or to include a bill dealing exclusively with a specific Welsh issue in its future programme.[111] The former case is likely to be catered for by concordats between the Assembly and the relevant lead departments. In the latter case, presumably the Assembly will have to look to the Secretary of State, as the department of central government concerned with Welsh affairs, to sponsor the bill and to press the Future Legislation Committee to include it in the legislative programme. The effectiveness of these arrangements may well depend upon how Secretaries of State interpret their role. It cannot be expected that they will see themselves as advocates or mere conduits of the Assembly's case, since they are, after all, members of the central government and have a primary obligation to further its policies. This may be a context in which a constitutional convention develops to limit the extent to which Secretaries of State may interpose their own opinions.

The Assembly will also have an interest in government bills under preparation that touch upon fields that are within its competence. The Act entitles the Assembly to be consulted by the Secretary of State about the bills which form the government's legislative programme for the coming parliamentary session and about bills subsequently introduced.[112] The entitlement, however, is circumscribed by qualifications. The initial consultation is to take place 'as soon as reasonably practicable after the beginning of the session', for subsequent bills when the Secretary of State considers it to be 'appropriate'. The consultation need not take place if the Secretary of State considers that there are 'considerations that make it inappropriate'. The nature of the consultation is such as 'appears to the Secretary of State to be appropriate'. Assurances have been given that these discretions are not intended to devalue the Assembly's role, but to preclude the need to put before the Assembly matters on which there is no Welsh dimension or which are outside its remit.[113] Again, the scheme presumably envisages that the Secretary of State will ensure that the results of the consultation are brought to the attention of the lead departments, when their concordats with the Assembly will determine how the Assembly's position is to be accommodated.

This procedure may not be enough, since these consultations can take place only after the government's legislative programme is announced. By that time, the lead department's work on the legislation is likely to be quite well advanced, thereby limiting the Assembly's ability to influence the fundamentals of the legislation. In cases of this kind, the needs and views of the Welsh administration should be established at a much earlier stage, not least as to the likely resource and financial implications. The Act is silent on these issues too, but again the concordats are expected to require communication between the Assembly and the lead departments and the involvement of Assembly officials in such circumstances. Some restrictions on the involvement of, for example, subject committee members may be called for where confidentiality of the proposals is appropriate.[114]

One issue upon which the Assembly is likely to take a close interest in bills is that of delegation of new powers touching its fields of competence. The extent to which future Acts authorize Assembly action may define its capacity to develop Welsh policies. It is desirable and probable that new functions will usually be conferred directly upon the Assembly,[115] rather than upon a Secretary of State and then devolved by a transfer order. Indeed, this may become conventional practice.

The Assembly will also need to pay close attention to the way that provisions governing new functions are divided between a bill and subordinate legislation to be made under it. It is in the interests of the Assembly that a new primary law affecting Wales confers on the Assembly the power, through subordinate legislation, to devise its own scheme to give effect to the policy objectives of the law, even where for England the equivalent scheme is contained in the bill. The case for such a development is strengthened by the fact that the Assembly's subordinate law-making procedures[116] introduce a far greater representative input than is the case for instruments made in Whitehall, where parliamentary control is notoriously weak.

It follows, too, that the Assembly will wish to express views on the breadth of the functions delegated to it, especially law-making powers. The broader the powers to make subordinate legislation on particular subject matters, the closer the Assembly comes to acquiring the functions of a legislature. Although subordinate legislation must be consistent with the objectives of the parent Act and *intra vires* in terms of the delegated powers, powers generously drafted can make them virtually impervious to legal challenge.

It remains to be seen to what extent government may be prepared to see statutory powers drafted to permit the Assembly to pursue different modes of implementing policy objectives from those to be adopted for England. Lead departments in Whitehall will typically have little operational interest in how their legislation is put into effect in Wales; the most that they may require is that provisions avoid major contradictions which might create implementation problems in England or political difficulties for central government. The extent to which the Assembly is entitled *not* to implement an Act at all might be need to be spelled out expressly, thereby removing an area of legal uncertainty.[117]

On the other hand, there may be reluctance, especially when the governments are of different political colours, to confer powers that would allow the Assembly to pursue contradictory or conflicting policy objectives. The government has made clear that it expects a convention to be adopted whereby Westminster will not normally legislate on devolved matters without the consent of the Assembly,[118] but it is unlikely that any government would allow matters to reach a point where the Assembly appeared to have a veto on the contents of proposed legislation as far as they would apply to Wales. It remains to be seen how the Assembly would proceed if a bill deliberately circumscribed authorizing powers in order to set limits to the Assembly's scope for innovation. The way matters of these kinds are approached in the first terms of the Assembly may lay down a settled practice from which future governments will find it difficult to deviate.

Legislative issues such as these will need to be monitored by the Assembly, in particular by the relevant Assembly Secretary and subject committee, both during the preparation of a bill and its parliamentary stages. Its responses will be channelled through to the lead department and presumably differences resolved by the processes agreed in the relevant concordat. But the final decision on contentious issues is in the hands of the department. The Assembly will have no power, of course, to put its own amendments directly to Parliament, nor would it be appropriate for the Secretary of State to table them.[119] While a sympathetic (Welsh) MP might be primed to take up an issue, he or she cannot do so in the name of the Assembly, even if he or she happens to be a member of it. The proposal would have to take its chance for selection for consideration as any other backbench amendment motion. There is room here for recognition in Parliament's procedures of the special relationship.

## The role of the Secretary of State

As the earlier discussions indicate, the Act is premised on a continuing role for *a* Secretary of State, even if the functions are performed by one with a wider remit than for Wales alone.[120] Whether a separate office can be maintained in the longer term, after the Assembly has settled into an established mode of working, has been questioned.[121] It is the case that many of the powers enjoyed by the Secretary of State are connected with the institution of the Assembly.

However, a Secretary of State is expected to perform important functions in facilitating the working relationship between the Assembly and government departments, as well as in speaking for Wales in Cabinet.[122] In some ways this is anomalous. Although he may be well apprised of Assembly issues by reason of the entitlement to Assembly papers[123] and through liaising with the First Secretary and the Assembly Cabinet,[124] he cannot be expected invariably to endorse their position. Indeed, he is clearly not accountable to the Assembly; he cannot be required to attend,[125] though he may choose to explain his position when he takes part in its plenary proceedings, as is his right.[126] Speaking for Wales may not necessarily mean speaking for the Assembly, in which case the lack of more direct representation may be disadvantageous. As a member of the central government, the Secretary of State cannot be guaranteed to share the views of the Assembly, particularly if it has a coalition or a different party majority. Further, it remains to be seen how influential the office will be in central government when facilitating relationships between the Assembly and Whitehall departments on issues for which it no longer has responsibility and when it has ceased to be a spending department in its own right. The development of procedures to enable the Secretary of State to apply the oil to, and remove the grit from, the machinery of Cardiff–Whitehall relations will be an important task for the office.

## Subordinate law-making

Although it lacks primary law-making powers, legislative activities will constitute an important part of the Assembly's work, though not its principal focus. The provisions of the Act governing this function, and the mode of implementation required by the standing orders,[127] offer the prospects of a process that is more transparent and participatory than is the case for delegated legislation at the moment, perhaps even than for a typical Parliament bill.

The Act is concerned with 'general' subordinate legislation,[128] although most procedural requirements are provided for by the standing orders.[129] Assembly procedures with respect to instruments with localized application, those to be made jointly with a minister of the Crown and subject to parliamentary procedures[130] and those not required to be made in the form of statutory instruments, are governed entirely by the standing orders. Consideration may also need to be given to the procedures for other types of quasi-legislative, or 'soft-law' instruments, such as circulars, directions and guidance; though not strictly subordinate legislation, these can in practice take on greater significance for those required to apply them than the legislation to which they relate.

The Act requires that, except in urgent circumstances, Assembly orders require the approval of the full Assembly by resolution.[131] The Act makes provision for approval or rejection of instruments only, but the standing orders allow for amendment both on the recommendation of the relevant subject committee[132] and by the Assembly.[133] However, approval is permitted only if the Assembly has received and considered a report from the Legislation Committee, and has published and considered any regulatory appraisal carried out on the draft order.[134] Those procedural requirements can be disregarded in a case of urgency,[135] but, in that case, any member may move, within forty working days, for an Assembly resolution disallowing the instrument.[136]

These statutory requirements are a marked improvement on those used by Parliament for Whitehall subordinate legislation, which they displace.[137] For example, consideration by Parliament is the exception rather than the rule, and in most cases then it is on a motion to disallow the instrument rather than to approve it; a scrutiny report is rarely available when Parliament considers such motions; the debates are usually held at awkward times, whereas this matter will be part of standard Assembly business; amendments by Parliament are not possible; the power is to accept or reject.

The Legislation Committee has terms of reference that have much in common with those of the Joint Committee on Statutory Instruments, both, for example, having the duty to draw attention to statutory instruments[138] containing *ultra vires* provisions or technical flaws or involving an unusual exercise of the delegated power.[139] But, in addition, it is likely to be asked to ensure that other processes connected with particular instruments have been properly carried out, such as regulatory appraisals and associated consultations, notably with business, and assessments of an instrument's impact on equal opportunities and sustainable development and consultation with business interests.[140] The Act is innovatory in giving statutory form to the established practice of requiring, where appropriate, an appraisal of likely costs and benefits of complying with particular instruments.[141] The extent to which the other types of impact assessment and business consultation may be required in connection with subordinate legislation will be for the Assembly itself to formulate in pursuing the objectives stated in broad terms in the Act.[142]

The National Assembly Advisory Group sensibly recognized that the Assembly must not be hampered by time-consuming procedures for law-making which could detract from its other functions.[143] The standing orders implement its recommendation that the full set of procedures should apply to 'high-profile' instruments, presumably those making significant policy or legal changes.[144] But the many instruments that are of a routine nature, not involving controversial or substantial issues, are to be dealt with by a fast-track procedure which bypasses consideration by subject committees.[145] The decision as to which procedure to follow in any particular case is for the Deputy Presiding Officer[146] who must set timetables for the subject committee to complete the full procedure, with a sanction of reversion to the fast track if the deadlines are not met.[147]

The subject committees will play an important part in the consideration of the high-profile instruments. They can be expected to have the time to give full consideration to the instruments and to bring to bear their subject expertise. It is they who principally will take account of external concerns about the substantive provisions, through consultation or by taking evidence, and of the findings from the regulatory appraisals and other impact assessments.[148] It will be open to them to recommend amendments to a draft order, as well as its adoption or rejection, before it goes to the full Assembly. But the legislative initiative remains principally with the Assembly Secretary, though a project is likely to be proceeded with only after consultation with the Assembly Cabinet.[149] The case for allowing the committees themselves, and even individual members or groups of members, to initiate legislative projects, rather than by pressing a Secretary to do so, was not accepted.[150]

Subordinate legislation is, of course, one area of Assembly activity where judicial review will occur.[151] Despite the internal procedures for identifying potential cases of *ultra vires*, legal challenges can be expected from those who consider themselves to be adversely affected. In addition, questions as to whether law-making or other action is within the powers of the Assembly, including whether it is compatible with Community law or the European Convention of Human Rights as given effect by the Human Rights Act 1998,[152] are devolution issues for which legal proceedings can be instituted by an appropriate Law Officer or, if they arise in other proceedings, may be channelled through a route that leads to a final appeal before the Judicial Committee of the Privy Council.[153] These could cover new territory in permitting arguments that mandatory standing orders governing the making of instruments have not been complied with.

The Act contains an important new device designed to reduce uncertainty as to the legal consequences of a finding of *ultra vires*. The effect of invalidity of an instrument upon those who may have relied upon it for some substantial time has not been finally established by the courts.[154] Under the Act, a court or tribunal making such a finding is authorized to remove or limit or suspend the retrospective effect of its decision.[155] In this way, courts are able to take account of the interests of others who have governed their affairs in reliance on the instrument as well as those who have been aggrieved by it. Similar provision is made by the Scotland Act[156] and will surely constitute a legislative precedent to be applied to English instruments in due course.

In addition to providing for the control through the courts, the bill at first enabled subordinate legislation incompatible with Community law, European Convention rights, or other international obligations, to be prohibited by direct intervention of the Secretary of State. The Act, however, in its final form, reduced his powers (i.e. to direct that Assembly action be taken or discontinued and to revoke an offending instrument) to the single case of international obligations other than those with respect to Community law[157] and European Convention rights.[158] This further diminution of the governmental override powers[159] in favour of court review makes a welcome contrast with the scheme adopted in the Wales Act 1978.

The early sessions of the Assembly may involve only limited legislative activity. The demands of establishing executive decision-making, budget-allocation and accountability procedures, and making them work effectively, are likely to have priority. Initially, law-making may be concerned primarily with making those instruments that are essential in order to put into operation legislation passed by Parliament since the Act was enacted, such as the Schools Standards and Framework Act 1998. It may be some time before the Assembly initiates substantial policy initiatives that require new instruments or amendments to the large number that have been inherited. But as the 2003 election comes closer, members may feel the need to show achievements, perhaps involving an element of radical divergence from the past, that can only be brought about by changes in law.

## Reform of the Welsh quangos

Reform of appointed non-departmental public bodies in Wales was a major justification for the Assembly made during the campaign for the Assembly. The creation of an elected executive authority is seen as an opportunity to reduce the number and influence of these 'quangos', which have been responsible for spending a third of the Welsh Office budget, and to improve the accountability and the mode of appointment of those that are to continue.[160] Provisions on these matters constitute a substantial part of the Act.

The Act gives effect to the strategy outlined in the White Paper.[161] It recognizes that the substitution of the Assembly itself for all appointed boards, as some had advocated, was neither feasible nor desirable. Many quangos are a valuable source of external advice and expertise or provide a necessary degree of operational independence that the Assembly will not be able to offer.

The Act itself institutes major reforms of some of the principal Welsh quangos. Housing for Wales (Tai Cymru) is abolished and its functions vested in the Secretary of State,[162] from whom the responsibility is transferred to the Assembly. The Welsh Development Agency's functions are broadened to permit it to take action for the social as well as the economic development of Wales,[163] and to absorb the functions of the Land Authority for Wales[164] and the existing rights and liabilities of the Development Board for Rural Wales,[165] both of which are abolished by the Act.

A major plank of the strategy brings the WDA and other specified public bodies within the Assembly's remit. The Assembly will be expected to review their present activities and is authorized to modify their functions or to transfer them to the Assembly itself or to a local government authority or to another public body or in the last analysis to abolish certain of them.[166] More precise powers are accorded with respect to health authorities, whose functions the Assembly may decide to transfer to itself in whole or in part.[167]

In addition to its reforming powers, the Assembly has a continuing responsibility for monitoring the activities of not only these bodies but a list of another forty-four.[168] Appointments to these, as to other public offices in Wales, will in future take place only after consultation with the Assembly[169] and openly and on merit in accordance with the recommendations of the Nolan Committee.[170] The Assembly is to adopt a Code of Practice governing the procedures for making appointments for which it is responsible[171] and it is for the subject committees to oversee compliance for appointments relating to their subject area.[172] The NAAG recommended that the ultimate authority for making appointments should lie with the appropriate Assembly Secretary to ensure clear lines of responsibility and accountability, but that the procedures should be decided in each case by the appropriate subject committee and would involve an advisory panel including two of its members.[173]

The Assembly also has a role in determining the funding of these bodies through the budgetary process, for setting performance targets and objectives and for monitoring performance. It has powers to require attendance of officials or members of these bodies before it or its committees and the production of documents.[174] These functions will be performed principally by the subject committees, which are expected to scrutinize, keep under review and report to the Assembly on the past and proposed activities of the quangos in their fields.[175] But the responsibility for day-to-day decision-making will rest with the appropriate Assembly Secretary, who will ultimately be answerable to the Assembly for the performance of these bodies.[176]

The Act also aims at greater public accountability with respect to the financial activities of public bodies. The Secretary of State may make orders with respect to the preparation of their accounts and their auditing, and to reporting by these bodies.[177] In addition, the Auditor General for Wales is authorized to carry out examinations of the economy, efficiency and effectiveness in the use of their resources by bodies spending public funds, and to report on them to the Assembly.[178] The Assembly's Audit Committee has responsibility for considering and reporting on the Auditor General's plans for performing this function and on the Auditor General's completed reports,[179] and is able to take evidence from the bodies' accounting officers, to call witnesses and to require production of their documents.[180]

## Bilingualism

The Act properly contains important provisions with respect to bilingualism. In addition to a power to do anything appropriate to support the Welsh language,[181] the Assembly is enjoined to conduct its business so far as is 'appropriate in the circumstances and reasonably practicable' to give equal treatment to English and Welsh.[182] As the Advisory Group implied, bilingual functioning will be difficult to implement in every aspect of the Assembly's activities from its inception.[183] The practical difficulties in providing simultaneous translation into both languages for every meeting connected with Assembly business, in enabling officials to work in Welsh if they choose, and in publishing bilingual documentation internally and externally are likely to make prioritizing inevitable. In fact, the standing orders require simultaneous interpretation only for speeches made in Welsh,[184] but verbatim reports and minutes must be published in both languages 'as soon as practicable'.[185] Documents for plenary meetings and committees must be in both languages so far as is 'appropriate in the circumstances and reasonably practicable'.[186]

The position with respect to subordinate legislation is particularly demanding. These instruments must be made in both English and Welsh,[187] unless 'in the particular circumstances it is inappropriate or not reasonably practicable'.[188] The qualifying words suggest that, for example, a general resource problem such as a lack of bilingual law-drafters will not fall within the exception. Indeed, the drafting of these instruments will present linguistic difficulties, not least because Welsh may not have as complete a range of legal terminology as English. The Act attempts to meet this problem by giving the Assembly power to make orders that particular Welsh words or phrases are to have the same meaning as specified English words and phrases.[189] But the process of formulating such equivalences is a gradual one and may not meet the demands of bilingual drafting from the outset.

Ideally, bilingual drafting should not take the form of translation of an instrument that has been first drafted in the other language; this denies the very equality of treatment that is sought.[190] In principle, legislative texts need to be drafted simultaneously as Welsh documents and as English documents, the drafters co-operating to ensure that their work produces identical effects. Such desirable arrangements are not instituted overnight.

The Act also prescribes that both versions of bilingual legislation are to have equal status.[191] In principle, this statutory requirement will open up the possibility of legal challenge on the grounds of language discrepancies, made more likely by problems for Welsh from legal terms and neologisms in English. For that reason, the Legislation Committee is required to report inconsistencies between the two language versions.[192] For the first time, United Kingdom courts could be faced with bilingual versions of domestic instruments of equal status that contain conflicting meanings, almost certainly calling for a new interpretative approach.[193] It remains to be seen whether they will be prepared to consider the argument that an instrument can be invalid by reason of substantial differences in meaning or effect in the two versions.

## The Assembly and the European Union

Despite the importance of the issue,[194] the Act contains no specific provisions on functions of the Assembly with respect to Europe. Attempts to amend the bill to formalize the Assembly's links with central government in connection with meetings of the Council of Ministers, Assembly representation at the EU, the selection of representatives on the Economic and Social Committee and the Committee of Regions and the establishment of a representative office for Wales in Brussels were not successful.[195] The only change enacted allows members of the Assembly to become members of the Committee of Regions.[196]

Instead, the government has expressed the intention[197] that concordats will be used to set out the role of the Assembly in the discussions that settle the United Kingdom approach to coming EU negotiations and to determine Assembly participation in EU meetings. It is intended that the First Secretary, or another appropriate Secretary, will be able to be part of a UK delegation, and to speak to the UK line, on issues in which there is a particular Welsh interest. Such arrangements will be negotiated with the lead minister. The Assembly Secretaries, drawing upon information provided by their subject committees, are seen as the appropriate channel through which EU policy issues can be explored with the Whitehall departments formulating the UK position.

The plenary Assembly will be able to debate EU matters of particular importance to Wales[198] and, more generally, to make representations on EU issues to the appropriate lead department.[199] But the subject committees will be expected to concern themselves with European issues within their fields.[200] As the NAAG pointed out,[201] it will be for the Assembly to determine how to handle its dealings with Europe. Accordingly, the standing orders require the establishment of a Committee on European Affairs to monitor the general impact on Wales of EU policies and to report on proposed EU legislation that cross-cuts the remits of subject committees. It is to keep under review the Assembly's procedures for dealing with EU matters, as well as its relations with the EU and its liaison arrangements with UKREP, Whitehall departments, MPs, MEPs and Welsh representatives on the Committees of the Regions. This committee, which is to be chaired by the First Secretary, is, as far as possible, to have representation from each subject committee and to reflect the party balance.[202]

But what seems clear is that the Assembly will have little room to pursue a policy on such matters as agriculture or fisheries independently of the rest of the United Kingdom. The United Kingdom approach to EU negotiations therefore has to recognize peculiarly Welsh requirements. To that end, the Assembly must be fully engaged in the process, including before and during the negotiations themselves, to safeguard against concessions that may be disproportionately disadvantageous to Wales.

As in other circumstances where concordats are to provide the guarantees for the Assembly's interests, the success of that mechanism may depend upon the respect for, and the effectiveness of, the device in the Assembly's first term and the ease with which a new government might be able to renegotiate existing concordats. The assurances readily given by the present administration about the full involvement of the Assembly in formulating concordats need to be carried into something close to a constitutional convention in the absence of a statutory entitlement.

## Conclusion

Despite its length, the Government of Wales Act, as any other organic instrument, gives an incomplete picture of the National Assembly as a *working* institution. It provides a framework, often detailed, within which further innovation will be needed. The ability to meet (sometimes conflicting) expectations will be determined as much by its operational arrangements and the quality of the first Assembly Members and officials as by the contents of the Act. Some of the concerns expressed, in particular as to how policy is likely to be made and relations between Whitehall and Cardiff conducted, have been represented as based on old-fashioned views.[203] But the success of the scheme will depend upon the way that the elected members and officials respond and adapt to the demands made by hitherto untried arrangements. The separation of the conduct of Welsh affairs from the machinery of central government must not result in their being marginalized.

Given the intention only to devolve executive authority rather than create a quasi-federal institution, as some advocates of devolution sought, the Act provides a workable, though complex, framework. If devolution is a process rather than a one-off event, as the former Secretary of State has often asserted,[204] the Act offers some room for growth in powers. As we have seen, there may be some increase in the Assembly's legislative competence depending upon the ways that Parliament chooses to delegate powers in future legislation. But the scheme contained in the Act cannot easily be restructured to convert the Assembly into a full legislature. However, in the light of the referendum and the first election results, the people of Wales are unlikely to come out in favour of the replacement of the Assembly by a stronger body with primary legislative powers unless the present model has been shown to work. In any case, there seems to be little prospect of major changes until there is a fairly widespread conviction in the United Kingdom generally that devolution has proved itself. It is difficult to envisage government giving priority to further constitutional changes in Wales for a considerable period. There is force in the argument that the Assembly will need time to make this innovatory scheme work to its best effect and for the benefits of this form of devolved government to be proven. But it brings a prospect of political regeneration and energizing self-confidence to Wales.

## Notes

1. The Assembly may be known by its Welsh equivalent – Cynulliad Cenedlaethol Cymru. A much-canvassed alternative term – Senedd Cymru – was presumably not considered appropriate since it implies status as a Parliament.

2. However, it has many features in common with the aborted Welsh Assembly as conceived by the Wales Act 1978. See J. Osmond, *Creative Conflict: The Politics of Welsh Devolution* (Llandysul: Gomer/Routledge Kegan Paul, 1977), ch.4; D. L. Foulkes, 'Wales Act 1978', *Current Law Statutes Annotated 1978*.

3. Government of Wales Act 1998, c.38 (GWA). This chapter is concerned principally with issues connected with the Act that were controversial or problematic before or during its development. For fuller treatment of other aspects, see D. L. Foulkes, 'Government of Wales Act 1998', *Current Law Statutes Annotated 1998*; R. Rawlings, 'The new model Wales', 25 *Journal of Law and Society*, 461–509.

4. GWA, Sched.2.

5. GWA, s.1(3).

6. GWA, s.1(2).

7. This procedure was formulated by the Business Committee based on recommendations made by the Select Committee on the Modernisation of the House of Commons.

8. *A Voice for Wales* (Cm 3718, July 1997 – White Paper), which in most respects built on the broadly expressed objectives contained in the Wales Labour Party reports, *Shaping the Vision* (1995) and *Preparing for a New Wales* (1996).

9. GWA, ss.53, 54, 56, 57.

10. GWA, ss.62, 63.

11. GWA, s.53(4).

12. GWA, s.111 and Sched.9.

13. GWA, s.24 and Sched.3, para.3.

14. GWA, s.121.

15. GWA, s.115.

16. GWA, s.105 and Sched.7.

17. GWA, s.37.

18. GWA, ss.116–18.

19. Amending GWA, s.12(1).

20. See *Hansard*, Lords, vol.591, cols.706–20.

21. Amending GWA, s.4.

22. See *Hansard*, Lords, vol.592, cols.259–76.

23. See *Hansard*, Commons, vol.316, cols.1155–87; Lords, vol.592, cols. 1511–33.

24. The Wales Act 1978 contained eighty-two sections and twelve Schedules, but included far fewer provisions for the reform of public bodies.

25. GWA, ss.22–3; SI (Statutory Instrument) 1999 No.672. The date of transfer is 1 July 1999; the Assembly was formally opened on 26 May 1999. The Assembly also has those functions that have been conferred on it directly by legislation passed or made since the GWA was enacted.

26. GWA, s.11; SI 1999 No.450.

27. GWA, s.12(1)(b); SI 1999 No.449.

28. GWA, ss.16–17. The Secretary of State's determination of salaries and allowances is effective only until the Assembly determines these matters for itself: SO (Standing Order) No.3.

29. GWA, ss.3, 49; SI 1999 Nos.722, 944.

30. GWA, s.25.

31. GWA, ss.96(5), 146; SI 1999 No.672.

32. GWA, ss.50, 51; Standing Orders of the National Assembly of Wales, 8 April 1999 (SO).

33. Recommendations of the National Assembly Advisory Group, August 1998 (NAAG Recommendations). The Group (NAAG) carried out a wide consultation on its initial proposals published in *National Assembly for Wales: Have your Say on how it will Work,* April 1998 (NAAG Consultation Paper).

34. GWA, s.46(6).

35. The basic approach was described in the White Paper, para.3.40, and developed in a written parliamentary answer on 27 February 1998, *Hansard,* Commons, vol.306, col.393. See also Welsh Office, *Concordats,* 1998. As at the end of June 1999, none has been published.

36. See Solicitor-General, *Hansard,* Lords, vol.590, col.277; Rawlings, loc. cit. n.3, 503.

37. Ibid., 502.

38. On this generally, see J. Osmond, *The Civil Service and the National Assembly* (1999).

39. *National Assembly Official Record,* 18 and 19 May 1999.

40. E.g. White Paper, para.4.7; *Preparing for a New Wales,* loc. cit. n.8, s.3.

41. *Hansard,* Commons, vol.307, cols.787–97; Lords, vol.589, cols.909–15.

42. Labour: 15 from 28 (1 by AMS); Plaid Cymru: 6 (4 by AMS) from 17 (8 by AMS) ; Liberal Democrats: 3 (1 by AMS) from 6 (3 by AMS); Conservatives 0 from 9 (8 by AMS).

43. Disqualification by reason of membership of Parliament, as other disqualifications of office-holders, would have to be imposed by Order in Council; GWA, s.12(1)(b). The Act authorizes the Secretary of State to order reduced payments for dual office-holders: s.17: SI 1999 No.1083.

44. Of the seven MPs, two have been elected as members of the Assembly Cabinet and three as subject committee chairs.

45. *Hansard,* Lords, vol.591, cols.706–20.

46. *Hansard,* Commons, vol.316, cols.1181–3; Lords, vol.592, col.1531, where it was stated that it was unlikely that the offices of Secretary of State and First Secretary would be held jointly for longer than twelve months.

47. NAAG Consultation Paper, para.2.7. The Secretary of State also has important functions on behalf of the government to intervene in Assembly actions that he considers to be incompatible with international obligations of the United Kingdom: GWA, s.108.

48. GWA, s.4 and Sched.1. Wales has subsequently become a single constituency for the purposes of European Parliament elections (European Parliamentary Elections Act 1999, c.1), but the earlier five constituencies remain for the purposes of Assembly elections, subject to any boundary changes made in accordance with the rules in the Parliamentary Constituencies Act 1986, c.56.

49. GWA, Sched.1, para.8.

50. Ibid. This contains complicated rules for calculating the consequential numbers of AMS seats.

51. Although the Parliamentary Constituencies Act 1986, Sched.2, para.1(3) only guarantees a minimum of thirty-five constituencies for Wales, the Boundary Commission for Wales in making its recommendations for new constituencies uses the existing number (currently forty) as its base-line figure.

52. On most calculations there are seven or eight more Welsh parliamentary seats than the population size justifies. A reduction might be brought into issue when the matter of Scottish overrepresentation is considered as envisaged by the Scotland Act 1998, s.86. But the White Paper gave the assurances of the present government that the representation at Westminster would not be reduced (para.3.37).

53. The requirements for registration are settled by the Registration of Political Parties Act 1998, c.48. Provision is also made for individual candidates to stand: GWA, s.4(3).

54. The so-called d'Hondt formula: GWA, s.7.

55. Democratic Audit of the UK, *Devolution Votes: PR Elections in Scotland and Wales* (1997), *Making Votes Count* (1997). In the election, Labour won more than 46 per cent of the seats but obtained less than 35 per cent of the total votes.

56. Hansard, Lords, vol.591, cols.681–6.

57. Ibid., cols.687–94.

58. Labour secured 28 seats, Plaid Cymru 17, Conservatives 9 and Liberal Democrats 6.

59. See pp. 250–2 above. The power includes that of amending or repealing the primary legislation governing these bodies (so-called 'Henry VIII clauses'): GWA, ss.27–8 and Sched.4.

60. E.g. Local Government Act 1999, c.27, s.29; Food Standards Act 1999, c.28, s.24(2)(a).

61. GWA, s.22 and Sched.3, para.1.

62. SI 1999 No.672.

63. SO No.2.

64. Loc. cit., n.3, 480.

65. NAAG Recommendations, p.28, implemented by SO No.2.

66. GWA, s.62(1)(b). A proposal to delegate to the First Secretary all the Assembly functions that could be legally delegated was questioned as giving too much power to the executive: *National Assembly Official Journal*, 18 May 1999, pp.20–4.

67. GWA, s.53. SO No.2.5 stipulates a maximum of eight Assembly Secretaries, in addition to the First Secretary.

68. GWA, s.62(5). The First Secretary need not allocate subject portfolios to all the Secretaries: ibid., s.56(4). SO No.2.5 sets the maximum number of those without subject portfolios as two. A Business Secretary and a Finance Secretary have been appointed.

69. GWA, s.63. Similar powers of delegation are given to the Assembly and to committees.

70. GWA, s.56(3).

71. GWA, s.56(5)–(7). Standing orders stipulate the procedures governing oral and written questions and motions, in particular motions of no confidence or censure: SO No.6.3–6.4; 6.26–6.37.

72. GWA, s.57.

73. NAAG Recommendations, para.5.5–5.12; SO No.9.7–9.8.

74. NAAG Recommendations, para.5.12. Non-members are given rights of attendance and limited rights to contribute: SO No.9.12.

75. First Secretary, *National Assembly Official Record*, p.21.

76. On Assembly committees, see J. B. Jones, in *The National Assembly Agenda* (Cardiff: Institute for Welsh Affairs, 1998), ch.5.

77. GWA, s.63(1). In Whitehall, officials are treated as empowered to act in the name of their minister without the necessity of formal delegation: *Carltona Ltd* v. *Works Commissioners* [1943] 2 All ER 560. The relationship created by the Act presumably created doubts whether this doctrine would apply.

78. GWA. s.63(2).

79. NAAG Recommendations, para.4.6.

80. Rawlings, loc. cit., n.3, 481. Generally, see Welsh Office, *Devolution and the Civil Service: Staff Guidance* (1998), reproduced in J. Osmond, *The Civil Service and the National Assembly* (1999), Annex.

81. R. Hazell, *Constitutional Futures* (1999), 138. On the problems facing the Assembly staff generally, see Osmond, loc. cit., n.80.

82. GWA, s.56; SO No.2.

83. SO No.9.1. Six committees have been created, three with nine members, and three with ten members (including the chair and the relevant Assembly Secretary). Complaints as to party balance led to the addition of the tenth member: *National Assembly Official Record*, 23 June 1999.

84. GWA, ss.58, 59; SO No.11.1. An Assembly Secretary cannot be a member. The initial membership is nine.

85. GWA, s.60; SO No.12.1. An Assembly Secretary cannot be a member. The initial membership is nine.

86. SO No.13.2, comprising a member from each political group and a chair.

87. SO No.16.2. The membership is to reflect the party balance. The initial membership is nine.

88. SO No.14.3. The membership is to reflect the party balance and enable representation of each subject committee; it is to be chaired by an Assembly Secretary. The initial membership is eleven.

89. SO No.15.4. The membership is to be based on the same principles as the

Committee on Equality of Opportunity. The First Secretary has been elected to the chair. The initial membership is eleven.

90. GWA, s.113 and Schedule 11. Standing orders for the Council were approved by the Assembly on 8 June 1999. In addition to representatives of local government, the membership is to consist of the First Secretary, not more than six members appointed by the First Secretary and a representative of each political group not represented in the Assembly Cabinet.

91. GWA, s.61; SO No.10.3.

92. NAAG Recommendations, para.5.16–5.21.

93. SO No. 8. See also GWA, ss.54–5.

94. Including the Isle of Man and the Channel Islands. See J. Osmond, *The National Assembly Agenda*, ch.29.

95. An illustrative monthly timetable is contained in NAAG Recommendations, Annex D. Motions proposing outline timetables are to be tabled by the Assembly Business Secretary: SO No.5.1–5.3.

96. Under current arrangements, five members sit on two subject committees.

97. NAAG Consultation Paper, para.7.25; NAAG Recommendations, para.6.3–6.9.

98. J. Osmond, *The Civil Service and the National Assembly* (1999), p.5.

99. Standing orders contain limited provisions allowing alternates: e.g. SO No.9.13 (subject committees); SO No.13.3 (Business Committee). The quorum for committees is inevitably set quite low (two members or one-third of the membership whichever is the higher, though more than one party must be represented): SO No.8.8–8.11.

100. See IWA, *The Operation of the National Assembly* (1998), pp. 2–5.

101. The impact of devolution on Parliament procedures and the role of MPs is also outside the Act. See House of Commons Select Committee on Procedure, Fourth Report, 1998/99, HC 185; Hazell, *Constitutional Futures*, ch.7.

102. GWA, ss.80, 81.

103. GWA, ss.85, 86; SO No.19.

104. *Hansard*, Lords, vol.590, cols.901–47.

105. GWA, s.33.

106. Such matters will be the subject of a concordat between the Assembly and the Treasury.

107. Generally on the financing of devolution, see Hazell, *Constitutional Futures*, ch.11.

108. The Assembly is expressly given powers to promote or oppose private bills before Parliament, though the exercise of the power requires the support of two–thirds of voting members: GWA, s.37; SO No.23.6–23.8.

109. For fuller discussion, see IWA, *The National Assembly Agenda*, ch.6 (P. Silk) and ch.7 (K. Patchett).

110. GWA, s.33.

111. On the procedures for bills exclusive to Wales, see House of Commons Select Committee on Procedure, Fourth Report, 1998/9, HC 185, paras.26–33. The NAAG foresaw that the Welsh Affairs Committee, in liaison with the Assembly, could act as a channel of opinion to Parliament: NAAG Recommendations, para.8.3.

112. GWA, s.31.

113. *Hansard*, Lords, vol.591, cols.783–4.

114. *Hansard*, Commons, vol.309, col.618. Assembly Secretaries and officials, but not other Assembly members, will be bound by the Official Secrets Act 1989 in respect of those matters to which that Act applies, e.g. security, intelligence, defence, international relations, crime and special investigation powers: GWA, s.53(4).

115. This was the method used with respect to the reform of Welsh health authorities and specified quangos: GWA, ss.27, 28. Recovery of powers from the Assembly would be effected by primary legislation too, rather than by cancelling provisions in a Transfer Order: *Hansard*, Lords, vol.590, cols.187ff.

116. GWA, ss.58–9; 65–8. See SO No.22 and pp. 246–50 above.

117. Generally, functions may be exercised differently for Wales from the way they are exercised for England: GWA, s.42.

118. Supported by the House of Commons Select Committee on Procedure: Fourth Report, 1998/9 HC 185, para.26.

119. *Hansard*, Commons, vol.309, cols.600–3. But in cases where the Welsh Affairs Committee debates a Welsh bill at second reading, it could put down amendments in the name of its members: Select Committee on Procedure, loc. cit., n.118, para.21.

120. The Act contains only one explicit reference to a Secretary for State *for Wales*, in connection with participation in Assembly proceedings and access to Assembly documents: GWA, s.76.

121. See, e.g. R. Hazell and B. Morris, in Hazell, *Constitutional Futures* (1999), pp. 137–8.

122. NAAG Consultation Paper, para. 2.5–2.7.

123. GWA, s.76(3); SO No.6.7.

124. NAAG Recommendations, para.8.1.

125. *Hansard*, Lords, vol.590, cols.451–7.

126. GWA, s.76(1).

127. SO No. 22, which gives effect to the recommendations of the NAAG; NAAG Recommendations, para. 7.17.5. See also Silk, loc. cit., n.109.

128. Defined in GWA, s.58(6) and to be known as Assembly Orders.

129. GWA, s.64.

130. Co-ordination between the Assembly's Legislation Committee and the Joint Committee on Statutory Instruments will need to be worked out in these cases: JCSI, Twenty-Seventh Report, 1997/8, HC 33, Appendix I, para.36; Procedure Committee, Fourth Report, 1998/9, HC 185, paras.36–8.

131. GWA, s.66(2). They are formally made when signed by the Presiding Officer; the Deputy Presiding Officer or an Assembly Secretary may sign in the absence of the presiding officer: ibid., s.66(1) and (3); SO No.22.24.

132. SO No.22.7–22.8.

133. SO No.22.14–22.24.

134. GWA, s.66(5); SO No.22.12.

135. GWA, s.67(1); SO No.22.25–22.26. The order must be submitted to the Legislation Committee as soon as possible after it is made: SO No.22.26.

136. GWA, s.67(3); SO No.22.27–22.28.
137. GWA, s.44, except for instruments made jointly with a minister or those concerned with cross-border areas.
138. In the case of the Assembly, Assembly Orders or any other subordinate legislation specifically referred to it: SO No.11.3.
139. GWA, s.58(4); SO No.11.5.
140. SO No.11.5(iv); NAAG Recommendations, Rec.59.
141. GWA, s.65.
142. GWA, ss.115 (consultation with business); 120 (equal opportunities); 121 (sustainable development).
143. NAAG Consultation Paper, para.8.4; NAAG Recommendations, Rec.69.
144. SO No.22, Part One.
145. SO No.22.9. Assembly Secretaries are given greater discretion with respect to instruments not made by statutory instrument: SO No.22, Part Five.
146. The decision is taken after consideration of the advice of the Business Committee: SO No. 22.5, but it may be reversed by the Assembly: SO No.5.7–5.8.
147. SO No.22.9.
148. SO No.22.7.
149. This recommendation of the NAAG appears not to have been included in the Standing Orders: NAAG Recommendations, Rec.69.
150. But individual members selected by ballot may introduce motions calling on an Assembly Secretary to submit a draft on a particular matter to the Assembly: SO No.22, Part Seven.
151. See generally on this issue P. Craig and M. Walters, 'The courts, devolution and judicial review', [1999] *Public Law*, 274–303.
152. The Assembly is expressly prohibited from making subordinate legislation that is incompatible with these obligations: GWA, ss.106(7), 107(1).
153. GWA, s.109 and Sched.8.
154. See e.g. *Boddington v. British Transport Police* [1998] 2 All ER 203 (HL).
155. GWA, s.110. Provision is made for the Assembly and the Attorney-General to take part in the proceedings in so far as they relate to orders for this purpose.
156. Scotland Act 1998, s.102.
157. Existing powers to make subordinate legislation giving effect to Community law in Wales continue to be exercisable by ministers despite being transferred to the Assembly: GWA, Sched.3, para.5.
158. GWA, s.108. The Secretary of State is required to consult the Assembly before using the discontinuance and revocation powers: ibid., s.108(11).
159. The Secretary of State can intervene in cases where water resources or supply are under threat, even though the functions have been transferred to the Assembly; GWA, Sched.3, para.6.
160. E.g. *Preparing for a New Wales*, para.4–4.14; Constitution Unit, *An Assembly for Wales.*, ch.8.
161. Para.3.12–3.32.
162. GWA, ss.140–3; Sched.16, 18, part VI; SI 1999 Nos.61, 781.
163. GWA, ss.126–8; Sched.13, 14, 18, Part III; SI 1998 No.2490.
164. GWA, ss.134–9; Sched.18, Part V; SI 1999 No.372.

165. GWA, ss.129–33; Sched.15, 18, Part IV; SI 1999 No.373.

166. GWA, s.28. The bodies and the functions that are subject to change by the Assembly, some with the particular body's consent, are listed in Sched.4.

167. GWA, ss.27, 148. Other preparatory action is being taken by the Secretary of State under existing powers, such as review and reduction of the number of health trusts: see White Paper, para.3.14; SI 1998 Nos.3314–21.

168. GWA, Sched.5.

169. GWA, s.30. The appointments will be formally made, for the most part, by ministers. The precise consultation requirements are to be provided for by Order in Council.

170. White Paper, para.3.16–3.17. The Commissioner on Public Appointments is to be empowered to monitor these appointments, ibid.

171. SO No.20.1. The Code is to be proposed by the First Secretary in consultation with the Commissioner for Public Appointments.

172. SO No.9.8(iv).

173. NAAG Recommendations, para.7.12–7.16.

174. GWA, s.74.

175. SO No. 9.7(iii).

176. NAAG Recommendations, para.8.2; NAAG Consultation Paper, para.6.8–6.10.

177. GWA, s.144. The range of bodies to which orders may be issued is extended to a number of others which are outside the Assembly's overall supervision: ibid., Sched.17.

178. GWA, s.145; Sched.17.

179. GWA, s.60; SO No.12. The Auditor General and the Audit Committee are, of course, concerned also with expenditure by the Assembly itself: GWA, s.100. See generally, NAAG Recommendations, para.5.32–5.40.

180. GWA, s.74; SO Nos.12.8, 12.9.

181. GWA, s.32. The power applies, too, to other important features of the culture of Wales.

182. GWA, s.47. The Assembly must have regard for the spirit of guidelines relating to schemes for the use of the Welsh language by public bodies made under the Welsh Language Act 1993, s.9: ibid., s.47(2).

183. NAAG Consultation Paper, para.7.31–7.34; see also NAAG Recommendations, Recs.22, 43.

184. SO Nos.7.1 (plenary meetings); 8.23 (committees). Innovatively, those wishing to use e.g. an ethnic-minority language in addressing a committee may do so with the prior agreement of the chair.

185. SO Nos.18.1 (plenary meetings); 18.2 (committees and evidence given to committees in public).

186. SO Nos.6.7 (plenary meetings); 8.19 (committees).

187. SO Nos. 22.1 (Assembly Orders); 22.48 (local statutory instruments); 22.50 (other subordinate legislation). Instruments subject to parliamentary procedures are to be translated into Welsh after they are made: SO No.22.31.

188. GWA, s.66(4). The qualification does not apply in the case of standing orders: ibid., s.47(3).

189. GWA, s.122(2). Construction of instruments is to accord with these orders: ibid., s.122(4).

190. But see D. L. Revell, 'Bilingual legislation: the Ontario experience' (1998) 19 *Statute Law Review*, 32–40.

191. GWA, s.122(1).

192. SO No.11.5(vi).

193. For example, Michael Beaupré, writing about the Canadian experience in *Interpreting Bilingual Legislation*, 2nd edn. (1986), concluded that a distinctive bilingual approach to interpretation was called for, pp.4–5.

194. See generally Sir John Gray and John Osmond, *Wales in Europe* (Cardiff: Institute of Welsh Affairs, 1997).

195. *Hansard*, Commons, vol.305, cols.762–74; Lords, vol.590, cols.305–17.

196. GWA, Sched.12, amending the European Communities (Amendment) Act 1993, s.6.

197. See Secretary of State, *Hansard*, vol.302, col.682. Similar arrangements are to be instituted for Scotland.

198. NAAG Recommendations, Rec.78; SO No.6.5.

199. GWA, s.33.

200. The NAAG recommended that each subject committee should appoint one of its members to be European co-ordinator, who would report monthly to the committee on EU issues affecting its work: NAAG Recommendations, para.8.4.

201. NAAG Recommendations, para.8.4–8.8.

202. SO No.15.4.

203. E.g. Parliamentary Under-Secretary for Wales, *Hansard*, Commons, vol.302, col.889.

204. E.g. R. Davies, *Devolution, A Process not an Event*, Gregynog Papers, 2, 2 (Cardiff: Institute of Welsh Affairs, 1999).

# 15 Aftershock

J. BARRY JONES and DENIS BALSOM

Aftershock: tremors occurring after the main shock of an earthquake, sometimes with an equally profound effect on the landscape.

The road to the Assembly was paved with good intentions: to prevent a 'Thatcher-like' figure imposing alien policies on Wales; to bring politicians closer and more accountable to the Welsh people; to implement policies that would meet the needs of Wales; in short, to make politics in Wales more democratic. However, that same road was criss-crossed by political trip-wires, some predictable but others quite unexpected, an unconvincing referendum victory, a disruptive twinning process for the nomination of Labour candidates, a 'moment of madness', two divisive leadership elections and a minority Labour administration. Given such a background, the vote of no confidence in Labour's First Secretary, Alun Michael, passed by the National Assembly on Wednesday 9 February 2000 should not have been unexpected.

In the first few months of the National Assembly, the greatest challenge for the Labour Party was that of coming to terms with its failure to secure an overall majority. In Scotland, the political arithmetic had always suggested the likelihood of coalition. In Wales no such expectation had existed and consequently none of the parties had made any preparations for such an occurrence. Following the election, Alun Michael assumed the First Secretaryship, appointed his Cabinet and, after brief and non-productive discussion with the Liberal Democrats, launched a minority government. Assuming total loyalty from the Labour group, Alun Michael could reasonably expect that the divisions within the Opposition would sustain him in power. Thus, whilst the rhetoric of the Assembly exalted inclusivity and consensus, the political reality of a fragmented opposition allowed a single-party administration. Periodically, however, events could combine to expose Labour's vulnerability. On several occasions amendments to official motions put down by one of the Opposition parties were carried, causing Labour subsequently to abstain or oppose the revised proposal. Such inconveniences were generally on minor matters; on bigger issues Labour usually attracted the support of one of the smaller parties to ensure a majority. The threat of the Opposition parties acting in concert against Labour could never be totally discounted, however. The potential fragility of Alun Michael's administration first came to attention in the debates concerning beef on the bone and the crisis in the Welsh livestock industry. The Assembly Secretary for Agriculture, Christine Gwyther, worked closely with the Agriculture and Rural Affairs Committee to agree a package of policies to assist farmers. Whilst the rural crisis is an issue that is recognized by all parties, the engagement by the Cabinet of the relevant subject committee ensured that the policies proposed had the support of all parties. When it transpired that the regulations of the European Union prevented implementation of the relief package, however, the 'blame' fell solely upon the Agriculture Secretary's head. A motion of censure against Ms Gwyther was proposed and carried by the Opposition parties uniting against Labour. Alun Michael's subsequent refusal to sack the Agriculture Secretary resulted in his own position coming under scrutiny. The Conservative group put down a motion of no confidence in the First Secretary, citing his contempt for the majority view in the Assembly that Christine Gwyther should be replaced. While the eventual motion of no confidence failed because Plaid Cymru chose to abstain, it demonstrated the potential instability of a minority regime. Unlike the Westminster Parliament, where a successful vote of no confidence would lead to a general election, the Assembly is elected for a fixed term. Should a First Secretary be defeated on a motion of no confidence, standing orders specify an immediate resignation, but require the Assembly to elect a successor. Issues of procedure are thus significant, as, too, are the decisions of the Presiding Officer. The Gwyther episode established a number of precedents and helped to define the evolving operation of the National Assembly. The Cabinet emerged determined not to allow their individual members to be 'picked off' one by one by virtue of being in a minority. The Presiding Officer cautioned the parties to use such motions carefully for fear of bringing the Assembly into disrepute.

Just as there were divisions in the National Assembly, so there were differing, even contradictory, views of the first eight months of devolution. The Welsh Labour Party itself was deeply divided in its assessment of the devolutionary experience. Alun Michael, speaking to the Institute of Welsh Politics in Aberystwyth in November 1999, delivered a broadly upbeat message.[1] He talked about the Welsh 'democratic deficit' having been removed, of 'new politics' at work, of equal opportunities and a more open style of politics and government in which the Assembly committees provided opportunities for the Opposition parties to take 'an active part in policy development'. Reviewing the Labour minority government's record, however, he was more critical, particularly of the Opposition parties 'putting short-term political advantage before consensus-building'. He agreed with Paul Murphy, the Secretary of State for Wales, that the devolution debate had now been settled by the will of the Welsh people. This, he argued, did not mean that devolution was static, that, rather, it retained a dynamic capable of adapting to the changing needs of Wales. In relation to Wales's place in the United Kingdom, he warned that the Welsh Assembly should not be a 'Celtic Dick Turpin, all take and no give'. In his view, the arts of both the diplomat and the statesman were more appropriate. It was a carefully balanced speech which emphasized caution in dealings with the UK government.

A quite different interpretation of the new politics of the National Assembly was given by Ron Davies a month later in a lecture presented to the Welsh Governance Centre in Cardiff University.[2] He was critical of the way Labour was running the Assembly; he said that an inclusive politics style had not developed and that devolution was a process that had 'lost momentum' and 'was prey to the cynical, the pessimists and the critics who never wanted it to succeed in the first place'. He was critical of the role of the Executive which, he argued, all too often offered 'take it or leave it' choices to the committees whose role in the policy process it wished to play down. Despite this, Davies declared, the government was not effective but 'surviving on a day-to-day basis on the basis of one-off agreements with one or other of the minority parties forced on the Assembly by procedural trickery'. Ron Davies's response to the defects was the politically explosive suggestion of 'closer working relationships between the parties or some more formal coalition'. His overall assessment, 'We cannot go on like this', was the headline in *The Western Mail* (20 January 2000). On the same day the Labour-supporting *Welsh Mirror* labelled him 'Judas' across its front page.

The deep divisions within the Labour Party could not have been more transparent. Cutting through the coded phrases, the Ron Davies speech was an attack on Alun Michael's leadership style. It produced a furious reaction from the Labour Party establishment and talk of his Caerphilly constituency Labour Party disowning and even deselecting him. There was a boil of bitterness within the Welsh Labour Party, the product of personality and policy differences, and of disagreements about the style of government. More ominously, Welsh Labour's relations with the Blair government became an issue. Whether the Assembly was the Cardiff headquarters of the Welsh government or the Cardiff branch of the London headquarters was now a defining issue for the future development of the National Assembly. By late January it was clear that the situation would have to be resolved; the boil would have to be lanced.

Objective One status and the vexed question of matched funding was ostensibly the reason for Alun Michael failing to win the vote of confidence tabled by Plaid Cymru. The party regarded Objective One as their issue. It had become a key element of Plaid Cymru's campaign in the first Assembly elections when Alun Michael had made a promise to secure matched funding. At Plaid's annual conference in September 1999, the leadership was subjected to criticisms from rank-and-file members that it had been too accommodating and was obliged to threaten an end to co-operation with the Labour administration and to set a deadline by which a commitment to matched funding must materialize. Many in the Labour Party, including both Ron Davies and Alun Michael, resented Plaid Cymru's hijacking of a policy which was the product of Labour Party action and owed much to Ron Davies's personal initiative – in particular, his decision to redraw the map of Wales and divide it into a relatively impoverished western seaboard and southern valleys and a more affluent eastern border. For many Assembly members, helping the impoverished areas would be the focus of an all-Wales campaign, a classic example of the inclusive politics advocated by enthusiastic devolutionists.

Coincidentally, the map drawn to attract Objective One funding closely approximated to the distribution of the 'Yes' vote in the referendum. It was also largely co-terminous with Plaid Cymru's electoral heartland and those areas of south Wales where their challenge to Labour was most pronounced. Thus electoral interest and the principle of inclusivity neatly coincided with Plaid Cymru's campaign on matched funding. The issue also put Labour under pressure. According to Wayne David, a Labour MEP, Plaid Cymru's campaign provided a strong political incentive for Labour to deliver on the policy.[3] As the pressures mounted, however, the issue became complicated by increasing concerns over Alun Michael's leadership style which increasingly overshadowed Objective One. The debate on the financial aspects of the Objective One issue had an element of unreality. The Opposition parties were pushing for additional Treasury funding for the first year of Objective One projects, when it was clear that this would be met from the financial resources already available to the Assembly.[4] As for the funding of projects in subsequent years, the Treasury proved unwilling to make a firm commitment prior to the completion of the current, three-year, comprehensive spending review. Thus Gordon Brown, the Chancellor, remained unmoved by Alun Michael's appeal. Some conspiracy theorists suggested a personal grudge,[5] but, whatever the reason, a simple form of words indicating a commitment to Wales would probably have sufficed and taken the wind out of Plaid Cymru's sails. It was not forthcoming.

In addition to setting a formidable hurdle for Labour to clear in respect of securing matched funding, Plaid Cymru also called a snap by-election for the parliamentary constituency of Ceredigion. The sitting MP, Cynog Dafis, was one of seven Westminster members with a dual mandate in both Parliament and the National Assembly. Whilst most of these MPs have resolved to stand down at the next general election and commit themselves to their Assembly duties, Cynog Dafis resigned from the House of Commons in January and a by-election date was set for 3 February. Ceredigion is a seat which falls wholly within the area eligible for Objective One funds and the date was carefully chosen. With Edwina Hart, the Assembly Finance Secretary, due to present her Budget on 8 February and the expectation that a no-confidence motion would result, the campaign period provided an ideal opportunity for Labour's management of the Assembly to be put under close scrutiny. There was little risk to Plaid Cymru; they were confident of retaining the seat and sure that, although it was a parliamentary by-election, the major issues of the campaign would focus on Assembly matters. Thus, despite the fact that most domestic concerns are no longer within the remit for Westminster MPs, the campaign revolved around the issues of health, education and, inevitably, Objective One. Indeed, Martin Shipton, political editor of *Wales on Sunday*, stood as an 'Objective One – Matched Funding Now' candidate. Although only polling 55 votes, the *Wales on Sunday* campaign emphasized the importance of the issue. Plaid Cymru's Simon Thomas was duly elected as MP, but the shock result of the election was the Labour Party's slipping to fourth place. Labour had polled second to Plaid Cymru both at the previous general election in 1997 and at the Assembly election of May 1999. Whilst they never expected to win the seat, for Labour to be outvoted by even the Conservative Party proved a deeply humiliating experience. In Wales, but perhaps more importantly in London and in the press, the result was taken to be a damning indictment of both Alun Michael and the Labour Party's management of Wales and the Assembly.

Had the Labour Party secured a pledge from the Treasury, or even a broadly sympathetic hint, it would have been used in the by-election campaign. But by the time the Budget statement was presented for ratification on 8 February, the challenge to Alun Michael's position had become inevitable. Despite lacking additional monies, the Budget was generally welcomed by the Opposition parties in the Assembly. In particular, Edwina Hart was praised for incorporating virtually all of the spending priorities that had been proposed by the individual subject committees. This inclusive approach and Ms Hart's openness and accessibility to the other parties' finance spokespersons won disproportionate, and largely disingenuous, praise. The rather excessive repetition of such remarks was clearly designed to contrast with the growing criticism of Alun Michael's leadership style. As anticipated, the no-confidence motion, in the names of all three Opposition party leaders and their respective business managers, was duly lodged and the debate scheduled for the following day.

The provisions of the Standing Orders of the National Assembly are quite specific concerning the procedures involved concerning a vote of no confidence in the First Secretary. If carried, the First Secretary must tender his resignation, in writing, whilst the Cabinet will meet to elect an acting Chair. The Chair will then assume the duties of the First Secretary until the Assembly is convened to elect a successor. In the lead up to the no-confidence debate on 9 February, considerable attention was paid to the likely judgements to be made by the Presiding Officer. At issue was the expectation that the Labour Party, following the loss of a no-confidence motion, would still re-nominate Alun Michael as their candidate for First Secretary. Such a strategy raised the prospect of successive no-confidence motions being put down and passed, leaving the Assembly in limbo. Lord Elis Thomas, the Presiding Officer, had already given an opinion that those who bring down an administration must assume some responsibility for electing another. Given Labour's minority status, the exact time sequence of these actions was also likely to be of importance if any negotiations were to take place concerning inter-party co-operation or coalition. Thus an expectation arose that the formal re-election of Alun Michael as First Secretary would be followed by an adjournment, and that any subsequent motion of no confidence would be delayed by a few days. It appears, however, that the Presiding Officer reconsidered his position and ruled that a no-confidence motion could be put and voted upon on Thursday morning immediately after a First Secretary had been elected. Alun Michael felt that, by this ruling, the First Secretary, any First Secretary, would be put into an impossible situation. In effect, the no-confidence motion would become a confirmatory vote, a common constitutional device, but one which had been purposefully avoided by the Standing Orders Commission to ensure that the Assembly had to elect a First Secretary and was not able to perpetuate a political vacuum. By changing his mind in this way, the Presiding Officer became liable to the accusation of favouring Plaid Cymru. The Presiding Officer also made several television appearances and faced questioning on his decisions and judgements; he concluded one such interview with the advice to Alun Michael that he should go home and pray. Many felt that the Presiding Officer went further in these public pronouncements than was strictly necessary for the pursuit of open, transparent government.

The debate on the no-confidence motion was taken after questions to the Local Government and Environment Secretary and approval of some Milk Development Council regulations. Ieuan Wyn Jones, acting leader of the Plaid Cymru group, initiated the debate and was followed by Nick Bourne for the Conservatives and Mike German for the Liberal Democrats. When Alun Michael rose to respond there was a noticeable change in his demeanour. His previously combative, urgent stance appeared to be overwhelmed and exhausted. In a well-crafted speech he attacked the opportunism of Plaid Cymru in setting unrealistic goals in respect of Objective One, but was adamant that the Opposition parties were not going to be allowed, *de facto*, to select the leader of the Labour Party in Wales. To ensure this, Mr Michael turned and presented his written resignation from office to the Presiding Officer whilst still speaking from the lectern. Most of those in the Chamber were genuinely shocked and the question was raised as to whether the no-confidence motion could actually be put if the First Secretary was no longer in office. The Presiding Officer invited the proposers to withdraw the motion, but in the absence of a withdrawal, moved to a vote. Amid some confusion, the no-confidence motion was passed by 31 votes to 27 with one abstention and the Assembly was adjourned.

The resignation of Alun Michael had one further element that came to dominate the national news agenda of the day. During Prime Minister's Question time, word of Mr Michael's departure reached the leader of the Opposition, William Hague. Armed with this information, he was able to embarrass the Prime Minister concerning the fall of his own preferred candidate for First Secretary. With these events occurring just a few days before the announcement of the ballot for the Labour candidate for the election for a London Mayor, the many parallels provided ample material for the journalists and broadcasters.

Alun Michael's tactic of a pre-emptive resignation seems to have been predicated on a desire to avoid defeat on the no-confidence motion. It would appear that he anticipated that the Labour group would be more comfortable in re-nominating him as First Secretary if he had not lost the vote of no confidence. The Presiding Officer's insistence on taking the vote seriously prejudiced Alun Michael's position, but he had been more fundamentally undermined earlier that week when an attempt – apparently by Tony Blair – to broker a Labour–Liberal Democrat coalition collapsed in the face of the intransigence of the Liberal Democrat AMs. On Monday 7 February the Labour Group in the Assembly decided that if Alun Michael lost the vote of confidence, the group should meet immediately to discuss and decide its options. On Wednesday morning, 9 February, the group executive, presuming that Alun Michael would lose the vote, decided that the group should meet that afternoon to nominate its candidate for First Secretary by *secret ballot*. This move was interpreted by 'Michael loyalists' as hostile and damaging to his authority. Alun Michael retired to his room to put the finishing touches to his speech and, as is now apparent, to draft his letter of resignation in an attempt to avoid the vote of confidence being put. He failed in that stratagem. The Labour Group meeting that followed the vote revealed just how weak was his position; only a handful of Labour AMs remained loyal. Realizing he had lost the confidence of the Assembly Labour Group, Alun Michael took the next logical step and resigned as leader of the Welsh Labour Party. Thereafter, the nomination later in the afternoon of Rhodri Morgan as caretaker leader, the confirmation by the Wales Labour Party National Executive later that evening and a curious 'presiding' role played by Paul Murphy, the Welsh Secretary of State, invested the events with a spurious sense of continuity.

Rhodri Morgan was finally elected First Secretary on Tuesday 15 February. Although he had been unquestionably loyal to the Alun Michael administration whilst in office, within the grass roots of the party, and on the back-benches of the Assembly, Morgan's supporters had increasingly articulated his case to become First Secretary. The issue was not, in the end, one of Treasury money for Objective One, but one of leadership style. The Michael regime was perceived as overbearing, dominant and incompatible with the minority status of the Labour Party in the Assembly. The smaller Opposition parties all resolved to give Mr Morgan time to assume the full responsibilities of office, whilst the new First Secretary also pledged to consider how the workings of the Assembly might evolve to provide a more open, accessible and consensual approach. The road to the Assembly had not come to an end, but it had come to the end of the beginning. Political highways and byways lay ahead, of uncertain direction, their viability to be determined by the politics of devolution.

## Notes

1. Alun Michael, 'Dynamic devolution in Wales', Institute of Welsh Politics, University of Wales, Aberystwyth, 18 November 1999.

2. Ron Davies, 'New politics in Wales: one year on', Welsh Governance Centre, Cardiff University, 19 January 2000.

3. For a fuller discussion of the development of the Objective One policy strategy, I am indebted to Emma S. Watkins, 'Objective I: a regional input into the policy process: a case study of Wales', unpublished M.Sc. Econ. dissertation, Cardiff University, 1999.

4. Opposition AMs were angry that matching funding for EU moneys earmarked for Wales was not additional to the baseline defined by the Barnett formula but prised out of existing funds. See J. Osmond, 'Devolution: a dynamic, settled process?', Institute of Welsh Affairs, December 1999.

5. Nick Cohen, 'I've seen revolt and it will be Welsh', *New Statesman*, 7 February 2000; see also 'Londoner's Diary', *Evening Standard*, 10 February 2000.

# Conclusion

J. BARRY JONES and DENIS BALSOM

Between 1979 and 1999 Wales experienced a fundamental transformation of its economic and social structures. By 1999, the broad
base of traditional industries, particularly coal and steel, which
had dominated the Welsh economy in 1979 had been radically
reduced; in the case of coal almost to the point of extinction, while
steel became a high-tech operation employing only a fraction of its
previous workforce. In their place, new service industries emerged
along the M4 corridor, bringing a level of affluence which contrasted sharply with the declining Valleys and the rural communities in north and west Wales. The nation which elected the
first members to the National Assembly on 6 May 1999 was quite
different from that which had rejected devolution on 1 March 1979.

Some of the changes were the product of indigenous forces: the
growing sense of a Welsh national community (a development
paralleled in other parts of Europe from Flanders in the north to
Catalonia in the south),[1] and the emerging consensus on the role
and status of the Welsh language. Most changes, however, were a
reaction to external developments. Thatcherism and rolling back
the frontiers of the state had a particularly profound impact on
Wales which, in 1979, was so heavily dependent on state aid and
state industries. Globalization has been even more influential. The
progressive elimination of exchange controls and the growth of a
world money market, with multinational companies seeking
economic advantage regardless of geographic location, reduced the
political and economic options open to national governments and
led to the development of regional economic groupings, like the
European Union. Inevitably, the clout of national governments,
including the British government, was reduced as nation-states

became increasingly porous. These developments presented a unique opportunity to subnational and regional levels of government and administration.[2]

Partly because of the development of a global economy, the British party system also changed. Thatcherism was replaced by New Labour but many of its achievements were left intact. Socialism, as a basis for economic planning, was marginalized and no longer regarded as a panacea bringing modernization and development. Individuals and national communities, like Wales, were now required to take more responsibility in a brave new world. In very large part, therefore, the demand for devolution in Wales should be seen as a political response to changing external economic environments rather than a discrete spontaneous upsurge of national identity.

If the economic restructuring of the state was no longer on the agenda for the new Labour government, constitutional reform was. Devolution to Wales and Scotland, although given priority for party political reasons, was but the first stage of a rolling programme of decentralization to the English regions. The programme had as much to do with New Labour's relations with the Liberal Democrats as its electoral manifesto. Whereas legislative devolution to Scotland was constitutionally straightforward, executive devolution intended for Wales was considerably more complicated. In both cases, however, the Labour government gave the impression that it had not fully thought through the consequences. In Scotland and Wales the devolved arrangements appeared both tentative and temporary. The West Lothian question remained unanswered, the voting rights of Scottish MPs were subject to an ongoing debate, and the Conservative Party alluded intermittently to the need for an English Parliament. The reform of the House of Lords was complicated by the Labour government's lack of clarity as to whether its composition should consist of directly elected or nominated members and whether it should include a 'regional' element. In the view of one eminent academic, 'devolution is unfinished business and any conclusion about its operation must necessarily be tentative'.[3]

As we have argued that Welsh devolution was the product largely of external forces, so its success will depend upon external factors. Wales will continue to depend on Westminster and Whitehall in developing policies specific to Wales. Arrangements will have to be made in the Westminster Parliament to facilitate a Welsh input to the legislative procedure. A special Welsh committee might have to be established, or the powers of the Select Committee on Welsh Affairs extended, to allow it to consider the committee stage of bills which relate to Wales.[4] Question time will need to have the responsibilities of the Welsh Secretary of State clearly defined to prevent overlap with the powers of the National Assembly. The important pre-legislative consultations which precede the introduction of a bill to Parliament will need to take account of the Welsh interest. No doubt concordats clarifying the relationship between Whitehall and National Assembly civil servants will help, provided they are modified regularly in the light of experience. Most important, it would be a serious error to presume that devolution has made the Welsh Secretary of State redundant. His role as a 'Welsh voice' in the British cabinet and in negotiating with the Treasury the annual block grant for the National Assembly will be the linchpin upon which Welsh devolution will develop.[5]

Devolution will not only have an impact upon Parliament. Political parties will have to adapt to the new constitutional environment. Those political parties likely to exercise government functions in Westminster will have to develop a sensitive relationship with their Welsh organizations. In the case of the Labour Party, the need for a changed relationship with the Wales Labour Party is imperative and urgent. In the course of the second leadership contest, between Alun Michael and Rhodri Morgan, many rank-and-file Welsh Labour activists were alienated by what they saw as crass and unnecessary interference by 10 Downing Street. The evidence suggests that this had a sufficiently detrimental impact on Labour's electoral performance in the National Assembly election to deny the party an overall majority. Labour, like the Conservatives when they come into office, will have to understand that devolution of governmental functions must be matched by devolution within the party structure.

Devolution will also have an impact on other areas of public life. Institutions and individuals in Wales will need to develop a bifocal vision of events and occurrences. Cardiff, the Assembly and the affairs of Wales will have a greater salience, but these must be seen in the context of Britain and the traditional centres of power in and around London and Westminster. This issue presents itself most directly in the media coverage of news and current affairs. The advent of devolution gave immediate rise to a debate within the BBC over the extent to which the 'national' news programmes at 6 p.m. or 9 p.m. were genuinely 'national' if, for Wales and Scotland, most domestic political matters were now within the control of their own institutions. The so-called national regions of the BBC in Wales and Scotland both proposed to mount their own early-evening news, but were prevented from doing so by the highest level of intervention within the BBC. Indeed the BBC may now be the last bastion of Britishness and the Union. In the event, the national regions were allocated generous additional funds to cover the greater news and current-affairs output that would arise from the creation of the Assembly and the Scottish Parliament. Although less well financed, the ITV franchise companies covering Wales and Scotland have also allocated additional resources to news and current affairs. HTV used this argument extensively when successfully seeking to have its licence fee reduced in 1999. Furthermore, London-originated programmes, such as *Yesterday in Parliament*, wishing to safeguard their 'national' appeal, have undertaken to include extracts from the proceedings of both the National Assembly and the Scottish Parliament as dictated by 'news values'.

The creation of the National Assembly has also consolidated and given focus to the policy community that has grown in Cardiff since the 1960s. A recent study has shown that at least six professional lobby companies have established offices in Cardiff, whilst an informal association of Assembly liaison officers has been established with over twenty members.[6] Organizations appointing staff to monitor the work of the Assembly include trade unions, voluntary bodies and a range of environmental and other national groups such as the RSPCA, the National Trust and Cytûn, the churches together in Wales. Such organizations are clearly seeking to influence the work of the Assembly and the perception of AMs of their particular interest as well as to access the growing Welsh media and press interest in the affairs of the Assembly.

Implicit in the devolution debate was the idea that the creation of the Assembly would address the democratic deficit in Wales and democratize the growing number of quangos through which Wales has become increasingly governed. The government's White Paper and later legislation contained little specific detail as to how such reforms were to be achieved. Indeed, several of the 'rebel' Labour

MPs who played little part in the referendum campaign justified their reluctance on the grounds that the promised 'bonfire' of the quangos had not been incorporated into the legislation. The most notable change was the amalgamation of the Development Board for Rural Wales and the Land Authority for Wales with the Welsh Development Agency. The only genuine casualty was Health Promotion Wales, a body whose continuation many might have thought justified. Much was made, however, of the new degree of accountability that will apply to the quangos. Now officially classified as Assembly-sponsored public bodies, these organizations, such as the Welsh Development Agency or Wales Tourist Board, report to subject committees of the Assembly. The committees have oversight of strategic plans and budgets, and are also now represented on the appropriate Cabinet Secretary's Panel for all new public appointments. Even prior to the creation of the Assembly, public appointments had largely become the product of public advertisement and competitive interview. The degree to which the Assembly oversees the work of the quangos remains to be seen; it is probably the case, however, that a greater degree of scrutiny will apply and the suspicion of political patronage, that smeared many appointees to quango posts, should also be alleviated.

The passage of the Welsh Language Act in 1993, together with the advent of S4C, the Welsh-language fourth-channel authority, largely depoliticized the issue of language politics within Wales. For over twenty years a high proportion of young people from the relatively small cohort of Welsh-speaking families had confronted the authorities, undertaking various forms of direct action for which a number had received some form of custodial sentence. From the outset it was accepted that the National Assembly would operate in a fully bilingual fashion. The chamber is equipped for simultaneous translation and all publications on the Internet are bilingual. The Presiding Officer, Lord Elis Thomas, the former Plaid Cymru MP, is, of course, bilingual, and whilst the Presiding Officer is not formally required to be a Welsh-speaker, it is difficult to see how this position might be held by an English monoglot, wholly dependent upon simultaneous translation. Assembly members may address the chamber in either language and the translation facilities offered are of an extremely high calibre. It has become apparent, however, that certain members will only address the Assembly in Welsh whilst others do so only in English, even though they may be perfectly competent Welsh-speakers. As First Secretary, Alun Michael tended to mix his contributions, but would always reply to a question in the language in which it was posed. Although language activists, such as Cymdeithas yr Iaith Gymraeg, have continued to attack the Assembly for the lack of spoken Welsh used, it is difficult to define principles of language use. The fundamental question of whether oral English should be translated simultaneously into Welsh was decided in the negative at the outset. Thereafter, individuals must make a decision, but the reality is that pragmatism will generally override ideology. The nature of political debate and intense interpersonal dialogue may also create circumstances where the speaker wishes to relate directly to the audience rather than via a translator. Given that all members of the Assembly are wholly fluent in English, discourse will inevitably gravitate towards English without any conspiracy being suspected. The politics of the language of the National Assembly are thus, perhaps, an exemplar of that elsewhere in modern Wales; Welsh has a recognized status and is used both formally and informally, but the predominant language remains English. The right to use Welsh meets the objections of the activists, but cannot displace their natural wish to maximize the impact of any speech or contribution. Legitimate questions have been raised concerning the concurrent appearance of documents and statements on the Internet, for example, but formal bilingualism is being implemented. Bilingualism, however, is not a language but a construct to allow people to use the language of their choice. Thereafter, the choice made by individual Assembly Members must be respected and accepted.

A slightly different question arises on matters of policy where language is an issue. Whilst past practice has been to entrench the rights of Welsh-speakers in many areas and through the Welsh Language Act, such legislation was enacted in Westminster for Wales. Issues that are now to be resolved within Wales for Wales may be much more vulnerable to arguments to set aside particular language provision. In education, for example, the issue of whether Welsh should remain a compulsory National Curriculum subject until the age of sixteen has become a very salient question in many parts of Wales. In the border areas of Monmouthshire and Flintshire this is especially so, as it also is in traditionally English-speaking parts of Wales such as Pembroke and Milford Haven.

Here, the Conservative Party in particular has been articulating the case for a less stringent language policy. As one of the clear purposes of the National Assembly is to take Welsh decisions for Welsh issues, it might well be the case that the climate of opinion regarding Welsh will become somewhat less benign than that found at Westminster in recent years.

There remains an underlying issue as to whether the present constitutional settlement for Wales, embodying the National Assembly, represents a settled state or is merely the beginning of an evolutionary process towards some new constitutional configuration for the United Kingdom. In Professor Patchett's judgement, the National Assembly is an institution without constitutional precedent which is reflected in the nature of executive devolution to a corporate body rather than to specific ministerial members. The precise relationship between Assembly Secretaries, committee chairs and subject committees remains to be clarified. Tricky procedural questions are likely to be raised. Furthermore, despite the salience of European Union issues in the Welsh devolution debate, the Government of Wales Act conspicuously makes no allowances for formalized links between Wales and the EU. Doubts also remain as to how policy will be made and how relations between Whitehall and Cardiff will be conducted. Professor Patchett argues that the Act provides a 'complex framework' with 'opportunities for innovation'. These 'opportunities for innovation' have led some politicians to regard devolution as a process rather than an event, whilst opponents of devolution present the change as 'the first step on a slippery slope to separatism'. The advent of the National Assembly will undoubtedly reinforce a sense of separate Welsh politics, and with it, perhaps, greater self-confidence in Wales itself. But it appears likely that the relatively modest powers of the National Assembly may be found wanting and unable to address specific Welsh issues. At such a time the demand for further powers will certainly be raised. Similarly, the Assembly's inability to vary tax-raising powers creates a situation where full responsibility for government is not being exercised, and this situation can encourage political and financial demands being made upon the British Exchequer which, otherwise, a more financially independent administration might treat with great caution.

The issue is whether the present asymmetric constitutional settlement is sustainable in the long term. The differing arrangements presently in place for Wales and Scotland are complemented by an elected mayor and a London Assembly, the constitutional settlement in Northern Ireland including some involvement from the Irish Republic; and further, yet more distant devolution to the English regions remains on the agenda. The call for greater standardization within this plethora of constitutional arrangements has already been made with pressure to recognize England as a distinct unit within the United Kingdom.

Labour's hesitant moves towards devolution between 1997 and 1999 might yet require the political establishment to re-evaluate the United Kingdom state. Peter David, the political editor of *The Economist*, has argued that 'the cumulative impact of a dozen constitutional bills published through Parliament by a government with an overwhelming majority [and] with little public controversy, will be revolutionary'. He reinforced his case with survey results indicating that most Scots and Welsh people identified more with their respective nation rather than with Britain. Against this background, he concludes that the devolution settlement is not stable, that the European tide cannot be halted and that the centre cannot hold.[7] A similarly pessimistic view is held by Norman Davies in his scholarly tome, *The Isles: A History*. He expects the break-up of the United Kingdom to be imminent, while conceding that 'devolution might have prolonged the UK's life for an extra season or so'.[8]

However, it is by no means impossible that the constitutional eggs will be unscrambled and that Britain, multinational, multicultural and multi-ethnic, will reinvent itself yet again. We remain unconvinced that a constitutional cataclysm awaits either this or the next generation. Nevertheless, a further development of the present Welsh devolution settlement is not only possible but probable and desirable. This would not presage chaos but a continuing development of a new, modernized constitution in which all our present institutions are redefined. Even the position of the monarchy may change, as much driven by Britain's position in the European Union as by resolving any internal pressures. The presence of the Queen and the style of the official opening of the National Assembly in May 1999 hinted, perhaps, at the emergence of a far less formal relationship. In contrast to the opening of the Scottish Parliament, there was little or no acknowledgement of the old, anachronistic symbols of sovereignty, such as military parades, fly-pasts and flag-raising. The event in Wales and at the Assembly was informal but dignified, respectful, but striving to assert a new confidence. In Wales, as in the rest of Britain, there is developing a new civic culture which must be compatible with our position in Europe rather than with Britain's imperial past. Thus the values of citizenship are assuming greater importance, those of subjects of the Crown increasingly less. Institutional change may well proceed ahead of individual attitudinal change, but a transformation is taking place. The road to the National Assembly for Wales, at the close of the twentieth century, is but part of this broader phenomenon to be realized in the twenty-first.

## Notes

1. J. Barry Jones and M. Keating (eds.), *The European Union and the Regions* (Oxford: Clarendon Press, 1995).

2. M. Keating, 'Regions and international affairs: motives, opportunities and strategies', *Regional and Federal Studies* 9, 1 (1999).

3. V. Bogdanor, *Devolution in the United Kingdom* (Oxford: Oxford University Press, 1998), 287–98.

4. Procedure Committee, 'Fourth report: The procedural consequences of devolution', HC 185 (May 1999).

5. The implications of devolution for the British constitution, fiscal arrangements, Whitchall and Westminster are briefly addressed in Philip Norton (ed.), 'The consequences of devolution', King-Hall Paper No.6, *Hansard Society* 34, 3 (1998).

6. 'The New Lobbyists', *Agenda, The Journal of the Institute of Welsh Affairs* (Summer 1999).

7. 'Undoing Britain: a survey', *Economist*, 6–14 November 1999, 83.

8. N. Davies, *The Isles: A History* (London: Macmillan, 1999), p. 1055.

# Index

Aberavon 'Yes' campaign 64, 65
Abercynon, suggested site for National
    Assembly 186
Abergavenny 'Yes' campaign 64
Aberystwyth 191
Abse, Leo 8, 10, 17, 18, 84
Adams, John 44, 45
AEEU 200, 207
Ainger, Nick 44, 45
Alexander, Ewart 55
Amalgamated Engineering and Electrical
    Union (AEEU) 200, 207
Ancram, Michael 177, 184
Andrews, Leighton 51, 52, 53, 58, 209
Anglesey 6, 9
    allegations of local government
        corruption 197
    referendum results 153
    'Yes' campaign 60, 64, 69
Artists Say Yes 64
Ashdown, Paddy 3, 67
Assembly of Welsh Counties (AWC) 22
Auditor General for Wales 251-2

Balsom, Denis 166, 170
Banks, Tony 67
Barnard, Alan 43-4, 45
Barnie, John 195
BBC
    coverage of referendum campaign
        123-32 passim, 137, 142
    impact of devolution 278
    and referendum vote 173
Beckett, Margaret 11
Benfield, Graham 111
Bennett, Nicholas 9
Best, Keith 9
Betts, Clive 54, 190, 197

Bevan, Alun Wyn 53
Bevan, Aneurin 30-2, 33
bilingualism 12, 24, 252-3, 279-81
Blaenau Gwent
    allegations of local government
        corruption 197, 199
    Labour party twinning 201
    referendum results 153
    'Yes' campaign 60, 64, 68, 69
Blair, Tony 2, 3, 11, 71, 116, 148
    and Labour Party devolution policy 37,
        38, 40-1, 43, 45, 46, 51, 133, 196, 272
    support for Alun Michael 206, 207-9
    'Yes' campaign 55, 62, 67, 94, 111, 114,
        115, 117
Bold, Andrew 38, 44
Bourne, Nick 70, 78, 81-2, 83, 87, 91, 114,
    184, 188, 191, 271
Bowen, Betty 71, 78, 82, 83, 91
Brecon and Radnor 6, 9, 10
    'Yes' campaign 64, 65
Brecon and Radnor Express 105
Brennan, Kevin 51
    on referendum campaign in Cardiff
        140-3
Bridgend 9, 187
    allegations of local authority
        corruption 197
    referendum results 140, 153
    'Yes' campaign 60, 64, 65, 68, 69
Brittain, Mark 105-6
broadcasting see television and radio
Broadcasting Act 1990 124-5
Brookes, Beata 21
Brown, Gordon 66, 269
Bryant, Claire 58
Brynmawr 'Yes' campaign 65
Bushell, John 114

Business Forum on Devolution 53, 54, 66

Caernarfon 191
  'Yes' campaign 60, 66
Caerphilly
  Labour Party 199, 201, 268
  National Assembly elections 227
  referendum results 140, 153, 182–4
Callaghan, James 5, 10
*Cambrian News* 105
Campaign for a Welsh Assembly 50
Campbell, Alastair 37, 45
Cardiff 191
  allegations of local government
    corruption 196, 197
  press and referendum campaign 118
  referendum results 153
  site for National Assembly 185–90, 202
  'Yes' Campaign 55, 60, 62, 63, 64, 65,
    67, 69, 139, 140–3
Cardiff Central 10, 21
Cardiff West 9, 218
Cardigan 8
Carlile, Alex 55
Carmarthen, Carmarthenshire 191
  general election 1979 6
  referendum results 153, 182
  'Yes' campaign 60, 64, 68
Carmarthen East 227
*Carmarthen Journal* 105
Carrog, Eleri 53, 55, 58
Catatonia 55
Caton, Martin 113, 209
CBI Wales 41, 53, 65, 74
Central Welsh Examination Board 20
Ceredigion, Ceredigion and Pembroke
  North
  by-election 2000 269–70
  general election 1992 10
  referendum results 153
  'Yes' campaign 60, 64, 65
Christian Ministers Say Yes 61
Clwyd, Ann 203
Clwyd South West 9
Clwyd West 213
Communist Party 141, 143, 222
Conservative governments 2, 4, 5–11, 12,
  14, 15–27, 46
Conservative Party 19, 281
  Ceredigion by-election 2000 270
  and devolution 4, 128, 276
  European elections 1994 11
  general election 1979 6, 15, 16
  general election 1983 7–8, 18

general election 1987 8–9, 18
general election 1992 9–10, 18
general election 1997 3, 4, 11, 23, 177
National Assembly elections 75–6, 213,
  215, 218, 221 (map), 222–5 *passim*
in National Assembly politics 266, 271
'No' campaign 60, 70, 71–7, 78, 79, 80,
  81, 82, 83, 87, 88–92, 95, 138, 145,
  177
post-referendum politics 176, 177–9,
  181, 182, 184–5, 186, 188
referendum 1979 15
referendum campaign 1997: press and
  115; television and radio 124, 130,
  131, 132
voting patterns in referendum results
  169
and 'Yes' campaign 60, 61, 62, 66, 138,
  141, 143
*see also* Welsh Conservative Party
constitutional change 276–83
Convention of Scottish Local Authorities
  (COSLA) 22
Conwy referendum results 153
Cottey, Tony 55
*County Times and Express* 105, 114
CREST 164
Cwmbran 191
Cymdeithas yr Iaith Gymraeg 64, 280
Cynon Valley 'Yes' campaign 65

Dafis, Cynog 10, 65, 213, 269
*Daily Mail* 109
*Daily Mirror* 62, 67
*Daily Post* 59, 99, 100, 101, 104, 112–13,
  117–18, 120, 137
*Daily Telegraph* 107, 115
David, Peter 282
David, Wayne 38, 39, 139, 206–11, 269
Davies, Mr (of 'No' campaign) 78–9
Davies, Andrew 42, 43, 44, 45, 47, 48, 148
Davies, Denzil 3, 47, 113, 115, 129
Davies, Glyn, on Powys referendum
  campaign 143–6
Davies, Ifor 10
Davies, Norman 282
Davies, Rhydian 54
Davies, Ron 2, 3–4, 11, 116, 180, 196, 201
  Clapham Common affair 195, 204–6
  and Labour devolution policy 35–48, 51,
    79, 87, 102, 151, 180, 190
  and leadership elections 201–3, 207, 210
  National Assembly elections 226
  National Assembly politics 267–8

referendum results query 183, 184
and site for National Assembly 185,
186, 188, 189, 190
and 'Yes' campaign 53, 54, 60, 61, 62,
63, 114, 142
Davies, Sally 141
Deacon, Russell 53
Delyn 10
Democratic Left 64
Denbighshire referendum results 153
Development Board for Rural Wales 250,
279
Dewar, Donald 67, 130, 142
Diana, Princess of Wales, effect of death
on referendum campaign 65–6, 92,
93–4, 109, 142
Dinefwr 227

Ebbw Vale 'Yes' campaign 65
Economic Case for an Assembly, The
('Yes' campaign) 66
economy 4, 6–7, 17, 275–6
Education Act 1984 12
Edwards, Aled 141
Edwards, Huw 113
Edwards, Nicholas 9, 80
Eisteddfod 58, 63
Elis Thomas, Lord 271–2, 279
Essex, Sue 213
European Community, Union 275, 282
influence of the Welsh in 107
influence on devolution campaign 76
National Assembly and 249, 253–5, 266,
281
European Community referendum (1975)
133–4
European Convention rights 249
European elections
1987 21
1994 11
1999 219
Evans, Darren 58
Evans, Fred 10
Evans, Ioan 10
Evans, Jonathan 90, 114, 177, 180, 182,
184
Evans, Nigel 186, 188
Evans, Roger 9
Evans, Stuart 55
Evening Leader 99, 104, 113, 120
Ewing, Winnie 130
Express 109

Falkland Islands war 7

Federation of Small Businesses 64
Feld, Val 53, 58
Financial Times 65
Fishlock, Trevor 98
Fletcher, Robin 102
Flintshire 187, 280
referendum results 152, 153
Flynn, Paul 47
Foot, Michael 5–6, 8, 10
Francis, Hywel 53, 58, 139
Freedland, Jonathan 106–7
Friends of the Earth 64
Fychan, Gwilym 144

Gale, Anita 38, 40, 44, 45
general elections
1979 5, 6, 15, 16
1983 7–8, 18
1987 8–9, 18
1992 9–10, 18, 21, 34–5
1997 2–4, 11, 21, 23, 177, 220 (map)
German, Mike 271
Giggs, Ryan 62
Glamorgan Gazette 105
globalization 275–6
GMB 41, 207
Goldsmith, Sir James 71, 82, 83, 87–8
Goodway, Russell 185, 186, 190, 202, 204
Gould, Philip 28, 46, 148
Government of Wales Act 1998 192, 196,
229–64
Assembly and EU 253–5, 281
Assembly elections 216, 234–6
bilingualism 252–3
bill 179, 180–2, 230–3, 236–7
functions of Assembly 236
membership of Assembly 233–4
reform of quangos 250–2
relationship of Assembly with
Whitehall and Westminster 241–5
role of Secretary of State 245–6
size of Assembly 234–5, 239–41
structure of Assembly 236–9
subordinate law-making 246–50
Greens 143, 212, 222
television and radio coverage of
referendum campaign 130, 131
'Yes' campaign 65
Gregory, Derek 40, 53
Griffiths, James 32–3
Griffiths, Robert 31–2
Grist, Ian 21
Gruffydd, Ioan 65
Guardian 66, 106–7, 181

Gunther-Bushell, Matthew 71, 72
  on 'No' campaign 81–95
Gwent 218
Gwynedd 215
  referendum results 152, 153
  'Yes' campaign 64, 68
Gwyther, Christine 266

Hague, William 3, 19, 25, 89, 111, 114,
  177, 179, 272
Hain, Peter 44, 51–2, 53, 54, 60, 67, 68, 71,
  114, 148, 182
Hall, Audrey 179
Hancock, Jim 44
Hannan, Patrick 97, 99
Hardie, Keir 30
Hart, Edwina 269, 270
Hattersley, Roy 210
Haverfordwest 'Yes' campaign 65
Health Promotion Wales 279
Health Workers Say Yes 64
Hill, Daran 52, 53
Hill, David 43
Hodge, Sir Julian 70–1, 83, 87–8
Hodge, Robert 70, 73, 78, 83, 87, 88,
  89–90, 91, 114
Holloway, James 182
Hopkins, Ken 39, 41, 42
  on Rhondda referendum campaign
  139–40
House of Commons Select Committee see
  Select Committee for Welsh Affairs
Housing for Wales/Tai Cymru 20, 250
Howarth, Alan 113
Howells, Kim 37, 38, 39, 66
Hughes, Gareth 40, 51, 180
Humphreys, Rob 114
Humphries, John 97
Humphries, Jonathan 67
Hunt, David 19, 25

Independent 106, 205
Inkin, Sir Geoffrey 21
independent television
  coverage of referendum campaign
  124–5, 126, 127, 128–32, 137
  effect of devolution on 278
  and referendum vote 1997 173
Independent Television Commission
  124–5, 126
Institute of Welsh Affairs 136, 181
Irish Republic 1, 23
Islwyn 199, 218

James, Mari 52, 53, 58, 66, 139, 191
James, Mike 53
Jenkins, David 61
Jenkins, Nigel 194
Jenkins, Simon 108
Johnson, Boris 107
Jones, Alun 53
Jones, Barry 34
Jones, Carwyn 184
Jones, Elwyn 63, 72, 129
  on 'No' campaign in north Wales 77–81
Jones, Geraint Stanley 53
Jones, Gwilym 55
Jones, Gwyn 21
Jones, Gwyn Hughes 65
Jones, Harry 44, 47
Jones, Ieuan Wyn 9, 271
Jones, John Elfed 62, 191
Jones, Jon Owen 113
Jones, Lyndon 78
Jones, Ron 53
'Just Say No' campaign see 'No' campaign

Kelshaw, Steve, on Neath referendum
  campaign 146–8
Kinnock, Neil 8, 10, 34, 84, 204
Kreppel, Alan 111

Labour government (1965) 19
Labour government (1974–9) 1, 5, 10, 15,
  17, 73, 135, 136
Labour government (1997–)
  adoption of referendum concept 73,
  133, 136–7
  and devolution legislation see
  Government of Wales Act 1998
  devolution proposals 1, 11, 14, 50–1,
  148, 276, 282; see also Voice for
  Wales, A
  involvement in 'Yes' campaign 55, 62–8
  passim, 115
  and leadership of Wales Labour Party
  206–11, 277
  referendum campaign 43–8, 70; in press
  115, 116, 117; television and radio
  coverage 124
  relationship of National Assembly with
  268–73
Labour Party 5–6, 23
  Ceredigion by-election 2000 270
  devolution policy 1–4, 8, 10, 11, 14, 25,
  28–49, 148, 151
  European election 1994 11
  general election 1979 6

general election 1983 8
general election 1987 8–9
general election 1992 9–11, 34–5
general election 1997 11, 14, 140, 220 (map)
impact of devolution on 277
involvement in 'No' campaign 60, 71, 82–3, 84–6, 87, 91
minority government in National Assembly 235–6, 265–74
National Assembly elections 213, 214, 215, 216, 218, 219, 221 (map), 222–6 passim, 227, 234, 235, 236
post-referendum difficulties 194–211
post-referendum politics 176–7, 180, 182–4, 185–6, 187
and provisions of Government of Wales Act 1998 233, 234
and referendum (1979) 8, 17, 33, 74, 84, 128, 151
and referendum (1997) 2, 41, 42–8, 151–2, 278–9; press coverage 101, 107, 115, 116; television and radio coverage 124, 129, 130, 131, 132
and twinning 198–201, 202, 205, 233
and voting patterns in referendum results 168, 169
'Yes' campaign 48, 51–5, 59–69 passim, 140, 141, 142, 143, 147–8
see also Wales Labour Party
Lamb, Derek 183
Land Authority for Wales 250, 279
Lewis, Huw 44
Liberal Democrats
and devolution and constitutional reform 1, 3, 25, 50, 128, 148, 276
general election 1992 10
general election 1997 3, 11, 220 (map)
National Assembly elections 215, 221 (map), 222–5 passim
in National Assembly politics 265, 271, 272
post-referendum politics 176, 180
referendum 1997: press coverage 115; television and radio coverage 124, 130, 131, 132
voting patterns in referendum results 169, 170
'Yes' campaign 51, 53, 60, 62, 64, 65, 67, 69, 141, 143
see also Liberal Party; Liberal Party/SDP Alliance
Liberal Party 15
general election 1979 6

see also Liberal Democrats; Liberal Party/SDP Alliance
Liberal Party/SDP Alliance 8–9
see also Liberal Democrats; Liberal Party
Livsey, Richard 65, 180
Llandrindod Wells 191
'Yes' campaign 62
Llandudno, 'No' campaign 78
Llanelli 201
'Yes' campaign 64, 65
Llanllyfni 'Yes' campaign 66
Llanwern steel production 17
Lloyd, Siân 63, 66
local government 21–3, 46–7, 196–8
Lomax, Rachel 209

Machynlleth referendum campaign 145–6
Mackay, Hughie 98
McMorrin, Anna 58
Madgwick, Peter 166
Madoc, Philip 55
Madoc, Ruth 65
Maesteg 46, 148, 149
Mail 109
Major, John 9, 16, 23, 24, 38, 88, 89, 130
Marek, John 113
media
and Clapham Common affair 204–6
and impact of devolution 277–8
and NAAG 191, 192
'No' campaign 73, 78, 79, 86–7, 91, 97, 111–18 passim, 124–32, 138
and referendum campaign 1997 96, 137–8
'Yes' campaign 55, 58–9, 61, 62, 63, 66, 69, 96–119 passim, 124–32, 138, 141–2
Melding, David 71
on Conservative Party's 'No' campaign 72–7
Merthyr Express 99, 105
Merthyr Tydfil 187
allegations of local authority corruption 197
and Labour leadership election 203
National Assembly elections 218
referendum results 68, 140, 153
Michael, Alun 47, 206–11, 213, 214, 216, 226, 265–73 passim, 277, 280
vote of no confidence in 265, 272–3
miners' strike (1984–5) 6–7
Mirror 108–9
Mitchell, James 24

monarchy 282
Monmouth, Monmouthshire 10, 280
  National Assembly elections 218
  referendum results 153
  'Yes' campaign 60
Montgomery, Montgomeryshire 6, 8
  referendum campaign 144, 145
  'Yes' campaign 65
Morgan, Eluned 40, 53, 55, 65, 114
Morgan, Kevin 53, 54, 55, 58, 60, 61, 68, 209
Morgan, Rhodri 21, 38, 40, 45, 141, 188–9,
    213, 218
  leadership elections 201–3, 206–11, 273,
    277
Morris, David 40
Mungham, Geoff, on referendum
    campaign in Cardiff 140–3
Murphy, Paul 267, 273

National Assembly 3, 4, 176, 178, 180,
    196, 229–30, 255–6, 281
  bilingualism 252–3, 279–80, 281
  elections see National Assembly
    elections
  and EU 253–5, 281
  functions 236
  information deficit challenge 172–3
  membership 233–4
  minority government by Labour Party
    265–74
  opening 282
  policy community 278
  reform of quangos 250–2, 278–9
  relations with Whitehall and
    Westminster 232–3, 241–5, 276–7, 281
  site 176, 185–90, 194, 202
  size 3, 181–2, 234–5, 239–41
  structure 181, 236–9, 281
  subordinate law-making 246–50
  vote of no confidence in Alun Michael
    265, 272–3
National Assembly Advisory Group
    (NAAG) 180, 190–2, 231, 240, 248,
    251, 254
National Assembly elections 75–6, 149,
    201, 212–28, 277
  campaign 212–13
  double ballot 226
  electoral system 39, 40–2, 180, 196,
    216–18, 234–6
  independent and fringe candidates 226–7
  issues 215–16
  manifestos 213–15
  results 218–26

National Eisteddfod 58, 63
national identity 275
  as explanation of referendum results
    1997 156–7
  and voting patterns in referendum 170–2
Natural Law Party 212, 222
Neath, Neath Port Talbot 187
  referendum results 95, 139–40, 153
  'Yes' campaign 58, 60, 64, 65, 69, 144,
    146–8
Neill Committee 57
New Labour 276
  Old Labour versus 71, 83, 93, 195, 199,
    201, 210
  see also Labour government (1997–);
    Labour Party
New Welsh Review 194
Newport
  referendum results 153, 154
  'Yes' campaign 60, 64, 67, 139
Newport Council 47, 64, 197
Newport West 9
Nicholson, Mavis 55
'No' campaign 1997 14, 59, 60, 61, 63, 65,
    68, 70–95, 138, 177
  Conservative Party involvement 60, 70,
    71–7, 78, 79, 80, 81, 82, 83, 87, 88–92,
    95, 138, 145, 177
  Labour Party involvement 60, 71, 82–3,
    84–6, 87, 91, 93
  north Wales campaign 70, 77–81, 91–2
  post-referendum politics 183
  Powys campaign 143–6
  press coverage of referendum 97,
    111–12, 113, 114, 115, 117, 118
  Referendum Party connection 71, 83–4, 87
  television and radio coverage 61,
    124–32, 138
  see also individual places
No Devolution–No Deal 36
north Wales
  'No' campaign 70, 77–81, 91–2
  press coverage of referendum 105–6,
    113, 118; see also Daily Post; Evening
    Leader
  site for National Assembly 186
  'Yes' campaign 58, 60
  see also individual places e.g. Wrexham
North Wales Weekly News 105–6
Northern Irish Border Poll (1973) 133
Norton-Taylor, Richard 181

Objective One funding 204, 216, 268–9,
    270, 272, 273

Ogmore 'Yes' campaign 64
Old Labour *versus* New Labour 71, 83, 93,
  195, 199, 201, 210
O'Leary, Paul 154, 159
O'Neill, Dennis 65
Osmond, J. 35, 100, 102, 181–2
O'Sullivan, Tyrone 55, 63
Owen, John 197

Parliament for Wales Campaign 36, 50, 51,
  52
parties *see* political parties
Patchett, Keith 281
Pearce, Jack 53
Pembroke, Pembrokeshire 9, 10
  referendum results 153, 280
  'Yes' campaign 64
Phillips, Siân 55
Plaid Cymru 25, 26, 30, 36
  and devolution 3, 4, 48, 128
  European elections 1994 11
  general election 1979 6
  general election 1987 9
  general election 1992 9–10
  general election 1997 3, 11, 220 (map)
  National Assembly elections 213, 214,
    215–16, 218, 219, 221 (map), 222–5
    *passim*, 227
  in National Assembly politics 266, 268,
    269–70, 271, 272
  post-referendum politics 176, 180
  and referendum 1979 15, 84
  referendum 1997 50–1; press and 115,
    116; television and radio coverage
    124, 130, 131, 132
  voting patterns in 1997 referendum
    results 168–9
  win in Ceredigion by-election 2000
    269–70
  and 'Yes' campaign 51, 52, 55, 60, 61,
    62, 63, 64–5, 69, 95, 141, 143
*Planet* 194–5
Pliatzky, Sir Leo 20
*Pobol y Cwm* 65
Polish, Peter 53
political parties
  change 176, 276, 277
  identification with, referendum voting
    patterns 168–70
  National Assembly elections 212
  *see also* Communist Party; Conservative
    Party; Labour Party; Liberal
    Democrats; New Labour; Plaid
    Cymru

politics, post referendum 176–93
Pontypool 'Yes' campaign 65
Pontypridd 'Yes' campaign 64, 66, 69
*Pontypridd Observer* 99, 105
Port Talbot
  steel production 17
  'Yes' campaign 60, 69
Porthcawl 'Yes' campaign 65
Powell, Enoch 195
Powell, Ray 130, 183
Powell, Tony 98
Powys 187
  1997 referendum 95, 143–6, 153
  press coverage of referendum 105
  'Yes' campaign 68
*Preparing for a New Wales* 40
Prescott, John 3, 66, 201
press
  Clapham Common affair 204–6
  coverage of 1997 referendum 62, 66,
    96–122, 137, 142; evening press 98–9,
    102–4, 113–15; London press 98,
    106–9, 115, 116, 137; news coverage
    109–16; pressures on 116–18; weekly
    press 98–9, 105–6, 114; Welsh
    national press 98–9, 100–1, 111–13,
    116
  and leadership election 208–9, 211
  and local government spending 197–8
  *see also* media *and individual
    newspapers*
Public Accounts Committee 21
public attitudes to devolution 12–14
Pugh, Alun 213
Pugh, Carys 71, 73, 78, 82, 83, 84, 91, 115,
  130
Pugh, Vernon 55
Pulman, Angela 53

quangos 15–16, 20–1, 64, 250–2, 278–9

radio *see* television and radio
Randerson, Jenny 140
Rawlings, R. 232, 237
Redwood, John 19, 22, 108
Rees-Mogg, William 108
referendum (1979) 14, 15, 16, 17, 29, 128,
  134, 135–7, 140, 153, 159, 195, 196,
  197
  Labour Party and 1, 2, 8, 17, 33, 70, 84,
    128, 151–2
  'No' campaign's neglect of lessons of
    73, 74, 79, 80, 81, 84
  press coverage 97–100, 102, 103, 114

voting patterns 167, 169, 170, 171, 172
referendum (1997) 4, 14, 133–50, 151–2, 196, 197
  Labour Party's devolution policy 2, 41, 42–8, 73, 133, 148
  media coverage *see* media; press; television and radio
  turnout 152, 153, 161, 162, 163 (map), 167, 168, 169–70, 171, 172
  voting patterns 161–75; age 166–8; information deficit 172–3; national identity 170–2; party identification 168–70
  *see also* referendum campaign (1997); referendum results (1997)
referendum campaign (1997) 138–48
  Cardiff campaign 140–3
  Neath campaign 146–8
  Powys campaign 143–6
  Rhondda campaign 139–40
  *see also* 'No' campaign; 'Yes for Wales' campaign *and under individual places*
Referendum Party 71, 83–4, 87, 91
referendum results (1997) 151–60, 161–2, 176
  national identities as explanation 156–7
  'No' campaign and 80–1, 94–5, 144
  questioning 182–5
  social class as explanation 155–6
  three Wales model 157–9
  voting by area 153, 158 (map), 162, 165 (map)
  voting patterns 161–75
  'Yes' campaign and 68, 95, 139–40
Rhondda, Rhondda Cynon Taff 187
  allegations of local authority corruption 196, 197
  National Assembly results 218
  'No' campaign 60, 71
  referendum results 139–40, 153
  'Yes' campaign 60, 139–40
*Rhondda Leader* 99, 105
Rhys, Matthew 65
Richards, Rod 188, 213
Roberts, Gareth Winston 197
Roberts, Huw 44, 45, 53
Roberts, Sir Wyn 129, 178, 180, 184
Robinson, Steve 55
Rogers, Alan 84, 180
Rowlands, Ted 47, 61, 67, 129
Rowntree Trust 51, 52, 56–7
Ruddock, Joan 199

S4C 11, 279
  coverage of referendum campaign 125–7
St David, Viscount 62
Sargeant, John 204
Scotland
  devolution 2, 3, 4, 10, 75, 148, 276
  devolution campaigns 66, 89
  Labour campaign used as model in Wales 215
  London press and Welsh devolution 107
  media coverage of devolution campaign 96, 97, 130–2, 136, 137–8
  *see also* Scottish Parliament
*Scotsman* 182, 183
Scottish Conservative Party 2
Scottish Constitutional Convention 50, 68
Scottish Grand Committee 24
Scottish Labour Party 200
Scottish National Party 30, 124, 130, 131, 132, 136
Scottish Parliament 2, 3, 186
SDP/Liberal Party Alliance 8–9
Secretary of State for Wales 9, 32, 33, 202
  Government of Wales Act 1998 234, 236, 241, 242–3, 245–6, 249, 250, 251, 277
Select Committee for Welsh Affairs 16–18, 21, 24, 277
Settle, Michael 179, 189, 190, 205
*Shaping the Vision* 37, 39, 40
Shepherd, Richard 181
Shipton, Martin 270
Shotton steel production 17
Sloman, Anne 61
Smith, Chris 142
Smith, John 10, 11, 35, 36, 37
Smith, Llew 37–8, 47, 61, 84, 85, 129
Smith, Sir Trevor 51
SNP *see* Scottish National Party
social change 4, 6–7, 18, 275
socialism 276
socio-economic status, and referendum results 149, 155–6
South Glamorgan Health Authority 21
*South Wales Argus* 99, 102, 104, 113, 114, 120
*South Wales Echo* 59, 97, 99, 102–3, 112, 113, 114–15, 120, 142, 197, 208
*South Wales Evening Post* 59, 99, 103–4, 113, 114, 120
south Wales Valleys *see* Valleys
Stephens, Meic 194
Stereophonics 64
Stokes, Kate 58

Students Say Yes 61
*Sun* 98, 109
*Sunday Times* 85
Sunderland, Eric 95, 152, 184
Swansea 191
   press and referendum campaign 118
   referendum results 153
   suggested site for National Assembly
     186–8
   'Yes' campaign 60, 64, 65

television and radio
   coverage of referendum 1997 61, 62,
     86–7, 123–32, 137–8, 141–2
   impact of devolution on 277–8
   impact on referendum results 173
   and NAAG 191
   *see also* media
Terfel, Bryn 65
Terron, Anna 111
TGWU 40, 44, 206, 207
Thatcher, Margaret 5, 7, 9, 16, 19, 20,
   23–4, 66
Thatcherism 5–7, 9, 20, 34, 275, 276
Thomas, George, Viscount Tonypandy 6,
   10, 61, 71, 83, 194–5
Thomas, Marlene 44
Thomas, Peter 9
Thomas, Simon 270
Thomas, Terry 38, 39, 41, 42, 44, 45
*Times, The* 107–8, 115
Tonypandy, George Thomas, Viscount *see*
   Thomas, George
Torfaen
   National Assembly elections 226
   referendum results 153, 154
   'Yes' campaign 60, 64
Torkington, Jill 58
Touhig, Don 47
Transport and General Workers' Union 40,
   44, 206, 207
Trystan, Dafydd 162

unemployment 6, 17–18
   as explanation of referendum results
     155–6
Unison 40, 64, 207
University of Wales Aberystwyth, Department of International Politics 164

Vale of Glamorgan 10,
   allegations of local authority
     corruption 197
   referendum results 153

Valleys 8
   devolution 3, 149
   Labour twinning process 199, 201
   questioning Cardiff as site for National
     Assembly 187
   'Yes' campaign 58, 61, 64, 66, 68,
     139–40
*Voice for Wales, A* White Paper 48, 57, 59,
   62–3, 100, 113, 123, 230, 234, 236,
   250, 278

Wales Act 1978 128, 153, 249
   repeal 17
Wales CBI 41, 53, 65, 74
Wales Labour Action 40, 51
Wales Labour Party
   and boundary revision 1983 8
   Clapham Common affair 204–6
   and devolution 1, 2, 3, 4, 10, 29–48, 51,
     73, 116, 128, 267, 277
   general election campaign 1997 3
   leadership elections 201–3, 205, 206–11,
     273
   local government 196–8
   post-referendum politics 195–211
   and quangos 21
   and twinning 198–201, 202, 205
   'Yes' campaign 55, 64
   *see also* Labour Party
*Wales on Sunday* 54, 55, 59, 65, 99, 100,
   101, 103, 104, 118, 120, 270
Wales TUC 35, 38, 41, 60
Walker, Peter 9, 19, 24
Waterstone, David 53, 54
Watkin, Linda 55
Watkin, Steve 55
Watson, Freddie 111
Welsh Affairs Committee *see* Select
   Committee for Welsh Affairs
*Welsh Assembly: The Way Forward, The*
   (Labour Policy Commission) 36
Welsh Conservative Party 3, 8, 20, 24, 70,
   72, 73, 74, 88, 179
   *see also* Conservative Party
Welsh Consumer Council 21
Welsh Development Agency (WDA) 19, 20,
   21, 250, 279
Welsh Election Survey (WES) 1979 166,
   167, 171
Welsh Grand Committee 24–5
Welsh Greens *see* Greens
Welsh Health Insurance Commission
   20
Welsh Labour Action 180

Welsh Labour Party *see* Wales Labour
    Party
Welsh language 11–12, 275, 279–81
    voting patterns in referendum 171–2
Welsh Language Act 1993 12, 24, 279, 280
Welsh Language Board 12, 24
Welsh Liberal Democrats *see* Liberal
    Democrats
Welsh Local Government Association 41,
    44, 47, 196, 198
*Welsh Mirror* 268
Welsh Office 9, 15, 16, 18, 19, 22, 32, 33,
    60, 182, 185, 186, 188, 189, 190, 202,
    209, 239
Welsh Referendum Survey 1997 164–73
West Lothian Question 148, 276
west Wales 'Yes' campaign 58
*Western Mail* 25, 37, 38, 98, 99, 137, 176,
    195
    Clapham Common affair 204, 205
    and devolution legislation 179, 181, 182
    general election 1997 3
    and Labour twinning 199–201
    and local authority corruption 197–8
    NAAG 191
    and National Assembly politics 268
    news coverage of referendum campaign
        111–12, 116, 118, 120
    'No' campaign 60, 86
    referendum results 182, 183, 184
    and second leadership election 208, 211
    site for Assembly 185, 187, 188, 189–90
    'Yes' campaign 53, 54–5, 56, 59, 61, 65,
        67, 100–1, 103, 104
*Western Telegraph* 105
White Paper *A Voice for Wales see Voice
    for Wales, A*
Wigley, Dafydd 60, 129, 180, 190, 209
Williams, Alan 61, 186
Williams, Alun 44

Williams, Tim 71, 72, 73
    on 'No' campaign 81–95
Women Say Yes 61, 65
Wrexham 46, 191
    referendum 1997 65, 67, 94, 119, 139,
        153
    suggested site for National Assembly
        186, 187
*Wrexham Evening Leader see Evening
    Leader*
Wright, George 40, 206

'Yes for Wales' campaign 14, 26, 50–69,
    76, 79, 91, 92, 95, 138, 178
    communications strategy 58–9
    Conservative involvement 60, 61, 62, 66,
        138, 141, 143
    creation 51–2
    funding 56–7
    Labour government involvement 55,
        62–8 *passim*, 115
    Labour Party 48, 51–5, 59–69 *passim*,
        140, 141, 142, 143, 147–8
    launch 52–6
    lessons 68–9
    Liberal Democrats 51, 53, 60, 62, 64, 65,
        67, 69, 141, 143
    operational strategy 57–8
    organization 56
    Plaid Cymru 51, 52, 55, 60, 61, 62, 63,
        64–5, 69, 95, 141, 143
    post-referendum politics 184
    press coverage of 96–7, 98, 104, 108,
        111–12, 113, 114, 115, 117, 118, 119
    television and radio coverage 124–32,
        138
Ynys Môn *see* Anglesey
Ystradgynlais 'Yes' campaign 64, 65, 144,
    145